THE COMPLETE IDIOT'S GUIDE® TO

Women in Sports

by Randi Druzin

Prentice
Hall
Canada

A Pearson Company
Toronto

alpha
books

Canadian Cataloguing in Publication Data

Druzin, Randi
    The complete idiot's guide to women in sports

Includes index.
ISBN 0-13-089940-2

1. Women athletes—History. 2. Sports for women—History. I. Title

GV709.D78 2001   796'.082   C00-932922-6

ISBN 0-13-089940-2

Editorial Director, Trade Division: Andrea Crozier
Acquisitions Editor: Andrea Crozier
Developmental Editor: Catherine Dorton
Copy Editor: Jodi Lewchuk
Production Editor: Lori McLellan
Art Direction: Mary Opper
Cover Design: Amy Harnden
Cover Image: AFP photo/Hector Mata
Production Manager: Kathrine Pummell
Page Layout: B.J. Weckerle
Illustrations: Paul McCusker

  2 3 4 5 WEB 05 04 03 02 01

Printed and bound in Canada.

ATTENTION: CORPORATIONS
Books are available at quantity discounts with bulk purchase for educational, business, or sales promotional use. For information, please email or write to: Pearson PTR Canada, Special Sales, PTR Division, 26 Prince Andrew Place, Don Mills, Ontario, M3C 2T8. Email ss.corp@pearsoned.com. Please supply: title of book, ISBN, quantity, how the book will be used, date needed.

Visit the Pearson PTR Web site! Send us your comments, browse our catalogues, and more.
www.pearsonptr.ca.

A Pearson Company

Contents at a Glance

Appendices

v

Contents

Foreword

Ten weeks before the Olympic games in 1992, a collision with a German boat almost ended my quest for Olympic gold. The doctors in Germany told me I would never make it to the Olympics. Ten weeks later, I won a bronze medal.

I am only one of many female athletes who have overcome obstacles. Some obstacles aren't as obvious as broken bones and shredded muscle, but they are just as onerous. In ancient Greece, women were not allowed to watch the Olympics let alone participate in them. There were no women's hockey leagues when I was a little girl—and the girls that did play hockey were considered "a little odd." The Montreal Olympics in 1976 marked the first time women competed in the sport of rowing. Eight years later at my first Olympics, I had no idea how hard the women in my sport had fought for the opportunity to play.

The Complete Idiot's Guide® to Women in Sports celebrates the rich history of women in sport and reminds us of the huge debt today's women athletes owe to those who paved the way before them. Trailblazers like Bobbie Rosenfelt, Babe Didrikson and Billie Jean King changed the way we think about women athletes and helped provide the opportunity to play and compete in a wide array of exciting sports.

Today, top female athletes are wonderful role models in a diverse range of sports for girls and women. Manon Rheaume, Catriona Le May Doan and Lori Kane dazzle us with their strength, their fortitude and their confidence. These women will inspire more young women to carry the torch forward and set records of their own.

The future belongs to the girls playing in muddy soccer fields, on barren lakes and in cold arenas all over this country. And we will watch with delight and amazement as they show us how high, how fast, how far they can go.

I hope you will enjoy Randi Druzin's book as much as I did. I certainly learned a thing or two about the rich history of women in sport!

Silken Laumann *is a world champion rower and Olympic medallist. After the greatest comeback in Canadian sports history, she won a bronze medal at the 1992 Olympics in Barcelona, Spain and went on to win silver at Atlanta, GA in 1996. In 1997, she was awarded the Wilma Rudolph Courage Award and in 1998 she was inducted into Canada's Sports Hall of Fame. Silken lives on Vancouver Island with her husband and young family and divides her time between her charitable commitments and her career as a writer and inspirational speaker.*

Introduction

Welcome to *The Complete Idiot's Guide to Women in Sports*!

Don't let the title fool you; this book isn't just for the uninitiated. If you don't know the difference between dressage and dragsters, this book will help you. Even if you know a thing or two about who's who in the wide world of women's sports, there is still enough information in this book to keep you turning the pages.

This book should appeal to those of you interested in sports, in women's accomplishments or just in impressing friends and passersby with your vast knowledge. Most of all, this book should appeal to those of you who like to be entertained.

The Complete Idiot's Guide® to Women in Sports is divided into six parts plus appendices:

➤ Part One, "The History of Us," is a general overview of the history of women in sports from antiquity to the present day, with special emphasis on exceptional athletes and on opposition to women's involvement.

➤ Part Two, "Good Day Sunshine," examines significant developments and personalities throughout history in summer sports such as tennis, golf, track and field, distance running, baseball and softball and soccer.

➤ Part Three, "Cold Feet," outlines major developments and personalities throughout history in winter sports such as skiing, biathlon, figure skating, speed skating, hockey and curling.

➤ Part Four, "The Water's Fine," uncovers important developments and personalities over the years in water sports such as swimming, synchronized swimming, diving and rowing.

➤ Part Five, "Ride Like the Wind," highlights key developments and personalities throughout history in cycling, equestrianism, horse racing and auto racing.

➤ Part Six, "Step Inside," traces major developments and personalities through the years in sports such as gymnastics, basketball, boxing and volleyball. It also discusses volleyball's sexy offshoot—beach volleyball.

The appendices include a bibliography, a list of useful Web sites and a complete list of the Canadian and American governing bodies for major sports in North America. Also look for a list of abbreviations to decode organizational acronyms found throughout the book and a summary of dates and locations for the Summer and Winter Olympic Games.

Extras

Like any *Complete Idiot's Guide®*, this one contains others elements designed to make for a more enjoyable and informative read. Watch for them as they appear:

Sports Shorts

gives you an inside scoop on some great athletes and sporting events throughout history.

Jock Talk

is a collection of quotes from the media, books and the athletes themselves that bring to life the events and sports covered.

Let Me Explain

is a handy guide to the ins and outs of particular sports.

Q & A

tests your trivia knowledge regarding women in sports.

Have fun with the book!

Acknowledgments

First of all, I'd like to thank Malcolm Kelly for recommending me to Prentice Hall. If not for him, I would not have written this book and would never have learned that Bobbie Rosenfeld, one of the best all-around athletes in Canadian history, worked in a chocolate factory, or that British rider Marion Coakes won a silver in show jumping at the 1968 Olympics riding a pony, or that...you get the point.

At Prentice Hall, I must thank Catherine Dorton, whose insight was invaluable and whose patience rivalled that of my Grade 10 math teacher. I also owe much to Jodi Lewchuk; in countless phone conversations, we shared our thoughts on grammar, spelling, punctuation and, of course, bad haircuts.

I'm grateful to Jennifer Fox, who helped me research boxing and curling, and to the many experts I consulted. They provided me with information and checked completed chapters for accuracy. These people are a credit to the newspapers, magazines, governing bodies and halls of fame where they work.

Odds are, I would not have survived writing this book if not for the moral support of family and friends in Canada, the United States and the Czech Republic and of my colleagues at the *National Post*, who put up with my whining eight hours a day, five days a week (I told you I'd get you in here, Lionel!).

I'm also grateful to my roommates, Danny Whelan and Linda Dvali. For the nine months I was absorbed in this project, they pretended not to notice I often left dirty dishes in the sink for days on end. Linda also provided me with caffeine when I needed it most.

Finally, I tip my hat to my brothers, Paul and Bryan, who were actually *nice* to me while I worked on this book. Most of all, I am grateful to my parents, Jack and Bernice, without whose love and support nothing would be possible. This book is dedicated to them and to my late uncles, Jack Gardner and Sol Druzin, whose laughter I miss.

Randi Druzin

Part 1

The History of Us— Historical Overview

Tune in to an all-sports television show or leaf through a sports magazine and what will you find? Women. Female athletes are almost as celebrated as their male counterparts. But this was not always the case. Sportswomen have battled for legitimacy for centuries. From ancient lawmakers who threatened to toss them off cliffs to nineteenth-century doctors who claimed exercise would ruin their reproductive organs, athletic women have encountered as much opposition outside the sports arena as they have inside of it. They have made dramatic gains in recent years thanks in part to the trailblazers who ignored the criticism and pursued their passion.

When Ancient Spirits Battled: Antiquity–1799

Female athletic heroism didn't start with Marion Jones. Long before the American sprinter bolted to stardom at the 2000 Olympics in Sydney, Australia, Greek goddess Atalanta distinguished herself as a supreme hunter, wrestler and runner—quite an accomplishment for someone who was abandoned on a mountainside as an infant and reared by a female bear! Her exploits, and those of females in succeeding centuries, show that women were physically active in the world's earliest civilizations.

Godspeed

Ancient Greek mythology holds that Atalanta, a great beauty, was discovered by a group of men who taught her how to hunt. She topped her first heroic feat—the downing of two centaurs—by participating in the famed hunt of the white-tusked Caledonian boar, which had terrorized the citizens of Caledon. The band of hunters she was with tracked and surrounded the vicious creature. It killed three men before Atalanta wounded it with an arrow, allowing a male contemporary to finish it off.

Atalanta's physical strength was formidable enough to pit her in a wrestling match against Peleus, an Argonaut also present at the Caledonian boar hunt, but who is more famous for fathering Achilles. Some sources credit her with victory in the match, but the outcome is debatable.

More certain is the result of the race of the golden apples. The beautiful Atalanta didn't want to get married, but agreed to accept the first suitor who could outrun her. She defeated several challengers before taking on the crafty Melanion, who ran the race equipped with three golden apples whose appeal was irresistible. Whenever Atalanta began to pull ahead, leaving Melanion in her dust, he would toss one of the alluring apples in her path, causing her to pause. Thanks to these missteps, Atalanta lost the race and her freedom—she ended up Melanion's wife.

Artemis (Zeus's daughter and Apollo's twin sister) was another mythological Greek tower of beauty and strength. She was the gods' chief hunter and the goddess of childbirth, nature and the harvest. She was unwilling to suffer fools gladly, and sometimes turned her weapons on wearisome mortals. Legend holds that she transformed the hunter Actaeon into a stag and he was attacked and eaten by his own hounds.

Atalanta and Artemis captured the imagination of poets and artists, but their feats of physical prowess didn't always reflect the conventional female role in Ancient Greece. Society was, at best, ambivalent about women in sports. While athletic women were often dismissed as unfeminine, they were also celebrated for their role in religious ceremonies and were encouraged for practical reasons—a healthy and active woman could produce offspring and wage war.

The Edge of a Cliff

While Athens soared to its greatest political and cultural heights with the development of democratic government and the building of the Parthenon, Greek women in that city-state were seldom seen outside their homes. Where sport was concerned, females were not only banned from direct participation in the Olympics—which started in 776 BC as a celebration for male athletes—but were also prevented from watching. Wrongdoers were to be thrown off a cliff.

The only woman caught in attendance at these restrictive Olympics was forgiven. She was a widow and her son, a boxer, competed in the 404 BC Olympics. She came disguised as a trainer and when he won, leapt over an enclosure to congratulate him, revealing her gender in the process. Officials forgave her because in addition to her son, her father and brothers were also champions. From that point on, however, Olympic coaches were required to strip before entering the arena.

The non-participation rules excepted young Greek girls, who were allowed to exert themselves at least once every four years. The Heraia, a quadrennial festival in honour of Hera, the wife of Zeus, attracted girls from all walks of Greek society. Participants ran in one of three races that were divided by age. They wore knee-length tunics that exposed the right breast. It's unclear whether these races represented prenuptial or fertility rites or coming-of-age rituals. Whatever the larger significance, winners were rewarded handsomely with a crown of olives and a portion of cow sacrificed to Hera.

Mighty Pretty

Citizens of Sparta (a city-state known for military might and strict discipline) valued overall vigour and endurance for war, so good health and strength was admired in men *and* women. Girls were required to train physically and to compete in athletic contests where they demonstrated their fitness to bear future warriors. While these strapping Spartan girls were regarded as the most attractive in the Greek world, they were also held in low esteem in some quarters for exercising and competing in public.

Times changed, however, and as the Greek language and culture extended eastward with the conquests of Alexander the Great (356–323 BC), women's roles became less restricted. Records show that some affluent women contributed financially to gymnasia (exercise complexes that included bathing pools, wrestling facilities and halls for massage) and sponsored chariots for races at the Olympics and other festivals.

Sports Shorts

A Spartan princess named Kyniska supplied the horses that won the chariot race at the 396 BC Olympics, but she couldn't watch the competition or participate in the winner's ceremony. That slight didn't discourage her, however—she entered the winning horses again four years later.

Jock Talk

"No Spartan girl could ever live clean even if she wanted. They're always out on the street in scanty outfits, making a great display of naked limbs. In those they race and wrestle with the boys, too. Abominable's the word."

—Athenian dramatist Euripides on antiquity's hotties, in *Women's Sports: A History*.

Prime Time Gladiators

Athletic women were not enthusiastically celebrated in the Roman Empire, but nor were they completely shunned. Girls competed in foot races and other events at athletic festivals, and girls' races were even included in the Capitoline Games and in the Augustralia, at Naples.

Likewise, competitive female athleticism was not entirely without recognition in this era. In the first century AD, a wealthy man in Asia Minor named Hermesianax erected statues for his three athletic daughters, all of whom had won foot races. A fourth-century mosaic (known as the "Bikini Mosaic" because its subjects are dressed in two-piece costumes) shows young women throwing the javelin and the discus, doing the long jump, playing ball games and running. We know the activities were competitive because three girls are shown with prizes. How they managed to hang on to their apparel while competing, however, remains a mystery.

Women even managed to make the odd appearance in stadium spectacles. When Romans gathered *en masse* to take in clashes between gladiators, aristocratic women usually watched comfortably from the stands. On one occasion, however, Emperor Nero (37–68 AD) amused himself by ordering the women to descend into the arena and battle each other. Two years before he died, Nero presided over games that featured both male and female gladiators from Ethiopia.

Middle Ground

Thanks to the follies of Nero and his successors—and to the sheer magnitude of their empire—Rome collapsed in fifth century. For the next three hundred years, Germanic tribes swept through Western Europe and North Africa, attacking and destroying towns and no doubt burning some bridges. The mayhem eventually ended and governments emerged. The Middle Ages had arrived.

During this era, women's lots improved; they chose their own husbands and sometimes controlled property. But they weren't more athletic than their predecessors. Why? With more people competing for fewer resources, living conditions were tough and folks had less time for recreation. Furthermore, prevailing Christian doctrine emphasized spirituality over physicality.

But hardships and theologians couldn't stop the fun and games entirely. On Shrove Tuesday, peasant women tussled in games of folk football, a forerunner of soccer, and paid for their pursuits with broken limbs and cracked skulls. Aristocratic women were physically active too, but in ways less likely to leave them face down in the mud with bloody noses. They preferred riding horses and hunting.

Tough Enough

Because lower-class men and women worked together in the field, it was natural for them to play side by side. The Shrove Tuesday folk football matches saw some good-natured pushing and shoving. When these contests were used to settle disputes, however, it was not unusual for competitors to suffer bruises and broken bones. Sometimes the competition went a little too far and players ended up dead. But

Shrovetide football games in England weren't always gender wars. On occasion they became status matches, and pitted married and single women against each other.

Another popular Shrovetide activity for peasant women in England was stoolball. The game, a precursor of cricket and baseball, was devised by milkmaids. One woman tossed the ball at a three-legged milking stool in an attempt to knock it over, and another woman scored points if she successfully defended the stool with a broom. She was out if the pitcher caught a fly ball. When that happened, the women exchanged positions. The game was often played at commercial fairs while drunken men wrestled, lifted barrels and ran races.

Women also ran races, competing for smocks or pieces of cloth. Some of these smock races were viewed as a novelty and all of them had an erotic subtext. Women were encouraged to wear minimal clothing for the sake of male spectators, who grabbed or tripped them as they ran past. These women had it rough all right, but not compared to prostitutes throughout Europe who were all but mauled by male spectators while competing in races for cash prizes.

Smock races became so riotous they were stopped in the late 1500s. However, they were revived in England under Charles II (1630–1685)—known as the "Merry Monarch" for encouraging sports through his fondness for gambling and other pastimes—and continued through the 1700s and 1800s. Women's foot races, which were exported to the American colonies, eventually became more respectable.

Not so, women's boxing. At English fairs, poor and sexually disreputable women delighted male spectators by stripping to the waist and pounding each other senseless. French women were more dignified; they wore bloomers and low-cut chemises in bouts held at music halls and cabarets.

Sports Shorts

In 1744, people gathered in London to take in a race between one woman known as "Black Bess of the Mint" and another promoted as "Little Bit of Blue, the Handsome Broom Girl." Beforehand, a local newspaper promised these "two jolly wenches" would run in their underwear.

Q & A

Q: Who was the lone contestant in the first racewalk in recorded history?

A: It was an 18-month-old girl. Her supporters bet she could walk the half-mile of London's Pall Mall in half an hour. She did it in 23 minutes.

Sports Shorts

Unlike their sisters in the boxing ring, female cricket players were of sound reputation. When the women in the town of Rotherby, England won an away game against another village, their menfolk placed them in a cart decorated with streamers, and serenaded them all the way home.

Q & A

Q: What athletic activity did women in West Africa take part in?

A: Wrestling. Women competed against other women—and sometimes men—at inter-village competitions. Wrestling sometimes became part of marriage rituals, in which a man would have to dominate a woman to marry her or fight other men in mock combat for the privilege of marrying a particular woman.

Bows and Arrows

While the refined woman never knew the joy of landing a solid left hook, she still managed to enjoy herself between social engagements.

Upper crust women rode and hunted with the men, and were expected to breed falcons and release them during the hunt. They became excellent horsewomen—quite an accomplishment considering they wore long, heavy skirts and rode side-saddle, with both legs on one side of the horse.

Archery was also popular among women of means. Anne Boleyn (1501–1536) spent enough money pursuing her passion to upset her husband, Henry VIII. Did her sporting spending spree contribute to his decision to have her executed, or did it have more to do with her failure to produce a male heir? One wonders. Anne's daughter, Elizabeth I (1533–1603), was equally passionate about archery. Not even a war with Spain could distract her from her crossbow.

Some middle-class women also took up archery. In Flanders (a region now divided between Belgium, France and the Netherlands), they were admitted to guilds and annual contests were held for both sexes.

Little is known about women's early involvement with golf, but aristocratic women likely dabbled in the sport, taking their cue from Catherine of Aragon and Mary, Queen of Scots, whose caddies were military aides.

In 1777, a group of wealthy women held a cricket match at a private estate in Surrey, England. The top scorer, Elizabeth Burrell, impressed a duke watching from the sidelines and he later proposed marriage. She accepted.

But that cricket match wasn't the first for women. By the time Burrell and her friends had set up their wickets, middle-class women in England had been playing for decades. In 1747, there was a tournament in which teams represented their villages. In other competitions, married and single women competed against each other. In one such match, the lucky winners were awarded a large plum cake, a barrel of ale and some tea.

And it seems that women dabbled in court tennis, an aristocratic game played with the bare hand. It had caught on with the bourgeoisie in the late Middle Ages. Frenchwoman Margot of Hainault could hit a backhand or forehand as well as any man. In 1427, she visited Paris and beat the men at their favourite game.

The Least You Need to Know

➤ The Greeks worshipped female deities who were superb athletes.

➤ Athenian women got involved on special occasions only.

➤ Spartan women were powerful and sexy.

➤ At least a few Roman women took running seriously.

➤ Women's activities varied dramatically from class to class.

➤ Peasant women were as rough and tumble as the men.

➤ Upper class women didn't need to sweat to have a good time.

Chapter 2

Busy Bees: 1800s

> **In This Chapter**
>
> ➤ Women are introduced to calisthenics
>
> ➤ The women's movement paves the way for women's sports
>
> ➤ Women go crazy for several sports, especially cycling and basketball

When Frenchman Pierre Lallement introduced a wood and metal contraption called the *velocipede* in the 1860s, he could not have predicted the impact it would have on the lives of women. The two-wheeled machine was taxing to ride, and he believed that women were not suited for strenuous pursuits. But what did he know? Two decades later, scores of women had taken up cycling, riding the clunky machines clad in outrageous outfits. They had made great strides since the middle of the 1800s when their physical endeavours were limited to child-bearing.

Get On Your Feet

In the mid-1800s, people started to move from the country to the city, and from the farm to the factory. Health experts wondered what could be done to ensure urban life didn't jeopardize women's well-being. They decided that women needed physical exercise. But how could women exercise without compromising themselves? The Victorian era woman was expected to be gentle and passive.

The solution, suggested European propagandist Phokion Heinrich Clias, was for women to perform "moderate" exercises. European girls were soon doing calisthenics at schools.

Sports Shorts

Catherine Beecher was one of the first educators to advocate formal exercise for women. She promoted routines to enhance grace and good posture. Beecher founded the Hartford Female Seminary in Connecticut in 1824. Students there practised the calisthenics outlined in her book, *Physiology and Calisthenics for Schools and Families*. She suggested performing the exercises to musical accompaniment. (On another historical note, Beecher's sister, Harriet Beecher Stowe, wrote the anti-slavery classic *Uncle Tom's Cabin*.)

Q & A

Q: How did Littie McAlice, age 16, win a gold watch and chain and $2000 in 1870?

A: She beat another teenage girl in a racewalk in Pittsburgh, PA. Pedestrianism, a forerunner of modern racewalking, was popular at the time.

Instructors ensured proceedings didn't get unruly by demanding that students follow regimented drills; German girls, for instance, weren't allowed to lift their legs above their waists or, worse, spread their legs while exercising.

In North America, women's rights leader Elizabeth Cady Stanton (1815–1902) advocated physical education for females as did Catherine Beecher (1800–1878), who wrote *Physiology and Calisthenics for Schools and Families*, a book that provided educators with examples of exercises for girls as well as boys. Female students took gymnastics classes; some classes emphasized aerobics and stretching, and others incorporated militaristic routines using heavy equipment. Strengthening exercises also became popular at schools in the last two decades of the century.

Sports Shorts

Annie Oakley (1860–1926) couldn't do a cartwheel, but she was great with a gun. She won a target shooting contest against a man named Frank Butler. He was a good sport about the loss and married Oakley a year later. He started a touring company with his wife, and later became her manager. She acted and rode a pony in *Buffalo Bill Cody's Wild West Show* in the 1880s. One of her biggest fans was the famous Native American Sitting Bull, who named her "Little Straight Shooter."

It's All The Rage

As the 1800s drew to a close, women forged ahead on all fronts. They lobbied for their right to vote, pursue higher education and work outside the home. And they questioned notions about what kind of physical activities were appropriate for them. Were they entitled to more than calisthenics? The answer was a resounding "Yes!" Upper class women took up tennis, golf, swimming and indulged in a few other crazes:

➤ **Field Hockey.** Eager to provide healthy mothers for their nation's upper crust, the British establishment encouraged women to take up field hockey toward the end of the 1800s. Women's field hockey associations were established across Britain and the pastime soon spread to other continents, including North America. A British educator named Constance Applebee (otherwise known as "The Apple") promoted the sport in the United States by giving demonstrations at new women's colleges throughout the Eastern Seaboard and by establishing a hockey camp in Pennsylvania. Field hockey was a vigourous game, but it didn't offend the arbiters of good taste—women did, after all, play in corsets and high-collared shirts with sweeping skirts.

➤ **Croquet.** A doctor in France developed croquet to provide his infirm patients with outdoor recreation in the early 1800s and within a few decades, the game had become *de rigeur* at picnics and garden parties in Britain. As a quasi-athletic activity, croquet was deemed gentle enough for the "weaker sex."

➤ **Archery.** Archery had been associated with the upper classes in Britain for centuries when it finally caught on with North American women in the late 1800s. The sport was introduced at women's colleges and women were soon competing in national archery competitions. Archery was viewed as an acceptable pastime for women because they didn't have to change into "immodest" attire to participate. Also, it was a quiet activity that proceeded at a leisurely pace.

I Want to Ride My Bicycle

While field hockey, croquet and archery became popular with women who had ample leisure time and money, women of all classes took up cycling for recreation and as a means of transportation.

As the century drew to a close, women were pedalling to places they could not reach on foot and embracing their newfound mobility. Cycling was also a great social outlet for men and women who often went out for a ride together.

Some women competed in races. In France, for instance, a number of women competed in a race at Bordeaux in 1868. The following year, four women competed alongside men in a race from Paris to Rouen.

Jock Talk

"She who succeeds in gaining the mastery of the bicycle will gain the mastery of life."

—Women's rights activist Frances Willard, noting the greater significance of the cycling craze in 1895, in *The Women's Sports Encyclopedia*.

In Full Bloom(ers)

But what could these pedalling pioneers wear on their bicycles? Long skirts tended to get tangled up in the spokes of the wheels. Women addressed the problem by slipping into loose-fitting trousers. These "bloomers" made cycling much easier.

American social reformer Amelia Bloomer (1818–1894) had introduced the new garment in 1851 as an alternative to the giant hooped skirts, long sleeves and corsets that squeezed women's waists and caused them to faint or have trouble breathing. Bloomers were ridiculed in many quarters, but thousands of women in North America and Europe adopted the fashion. Donning bloomers became a political statement for many women, who lobbied for their right to vote and formed Bloomer Clubs to discuss politics and other topical issues.

Thinking 'Bout Basketball

Bloomers were soon spotted in school gymnasiums, where women were introduced to basketball. In 1891, Senda Berenson, an instructor at Smith College in Northampton, MA, introduced her students to the game, which had been invented earlier that year by Canadian Dr. James Naismith at a Young Men's Christian Association (YMCA) training college in nearby Springfield.

Endeavouring to develop a sport to be played indoors during the winter, Naismith had asked a janitor to nail a peach basket to the lower railing at either end of a gym and encouraged participants to toss a soccer ball into the baskets. The janitor used a ladder to retrieve the ball every time it went in. Thankfully for him, that wasn't very often.

Jock Talk

"With the single exception of the improvement of the legal status of women, their entrance into the realm of sports is the most cheering thing that has happened to them in the century just past. The revolution means as much psychologically as it did physically."

—Writer Anne O'Hagen in a 1901 issue of "Munsey's Magazine," in *Nike is a Goddess*. One reason feminists advocated women's basketball and cycling was because they equated sports with liberation.

Berenson changed the rules of the game to lessen physical exertion and contact, and organized intramural games that ended up drawing over a thousand spectators. Quicker than you can say, "full court press," young women were playing the game in schools across the continent. Their dedication to the game was so keen that basketball came to be regarded as a girl's game and was shunned by some boys.

In 1896, the first women's intercollegiate game was played between the University of California, Berkeley and Stanford in San Francisco. The stands were packed with hundreds of cheering women. Stanford won 2–1.

Hail to the Victors

The close of the 1800s was the beginning of the end of an era in which women approached sport solely for fitness or socializing—women had discovered competition. And as the American general Douglas MacArthur later learned, when you discover the thrill of victory, there is no turning back...

The Least You Need to Know

➤ Calisthenics got women active, then bored them senseless.

➤ Cycling changed the way women dressed and thought.

➤ Suffragists advocated women's sports.

➤ Basketball fostered women's need to compete.

WOMEN'S OLYMPIC GAMES 1922

Chapter 3

It's So Serious: 1900s

In This Chapter

➤ Female athletes start the twentieth century with a bang

➤ Women fight for their right to compete in the Olympics

➤ Working women get down and dirty

➤ Schoolgirls climb off the court and into the bleachers

➤ Women everywhere get into the game

➤ Female athletes go where the boys are

➤ Women step out in grand fashion

Suzanne Lenglen competed at Wimbledon in 1919 wearing a knee-length dress that exposed her arms. Some 80 years later, Anna Kournikova appeared on the cover of a popular magazine dressed in white mini shorts and a clingy tube top. Which tennis player was more daring? That question is open to debate, but another one is not: How did female athletes fare in the 1900s? They came a long way, baby.

Golden Years

By the time Babe Ruth was slamming home runs, women were voting in government elections and going to college and to work. They had discarded the corsets that had made breathing a challenge and slipped into something more comfortable—baggy dresses that exposed their arms and legs from the knees down. The media was enamoured with the plucky modern woman, and celebrated her athletic exploits. It was a golden age for women's sports.

Journalists gushed over Frenchwoman Suzanne Lenglen, the grand diva of tennis who sometimes warmed up for matches in a fur coat, and lauded American swimmer Gertrude Ederle, who became the first woman to swim the English Channel, a feat she accomplished in record time in 1926. She was celebrated in New York, NY with a ticker-tape parade attended by two million people.

Jock Talk

"She is beyond all belief until you see her perform. Then you finally understand that you are looking at the most flawless section of muscle harmony, of complete mental and physical coordination the world of sport has ever seen."

—Legendary sports columnist and author Grantland Rice, on Babe Didrikson.

The era also boasted some outstanding all-round female athletes, including American Eleonora Sears (1881–1968). The great-granddaughter of Thomas Jefferson was a socialite who had the time and money to indulge her passion for various sports, from tennis to auto racing, canoeing and shooting. Dubbed "the best all-round athlete in society," Sears once completed a 4.5-mile swim along the shore of Newport, RI, and won four national tennis titles in singles, four in doubles and one in mixed doubles. She took up squash in 1918, and won the first women's national championship 10 years later.

Compatriot Babe Didrikson also excelled in many sports, including basketball, swimming, track and field and golf. At the 1932 Olympics in Los Angeles, CA, she won the javelin throw and the 80m hurdles. She soon took up golf, winning every major women's golf championship. *Sports Illustrated* named her the greatest woman athlete of the twentieth century.

Fanny "Bobbie" Rosenfeld was lionized in the media, too. This Canadian took home two track and field medals from the 1928 Olympics in Amsterdam, Holland. She won tennis titles and excelled in basketball and softball, and was also an excellent hockey player. The Canadian Press named Rosenfeld Canada's outstanding female athlete of the first half of the twentieth century.

In this era, the Amateur Athletic Union (AAU)—an organization that promotes amateur sports and physical fitness in the United States—developed competitions for women and girls in track and field, basketball, gymnastics, handball and swimming. This period also saw the emergence of various women's organizations to examine or oversee women's sports. One of them, the Women's Amateur Athletic Federation (WAAF), was formed by Canadian women to bring a uniform system of administration to seven sports across the country.

Sports Shorts

Amelia Earhart (1897–1937) wasn't an athlete, but her exploits were Herculean. The American aviator became the first woman to cross the Atlantic Ocean by air when she joined two male pilots on a flight. In 1932, she became the first woman to fly across the Atlantic Ocean alone and set a new Atlantic flight record of 13 hours and 30 minutes. In 1935, she was the first woman to fly the Pacific Ocean. Her plane disappeared in the South Pacific two years later during an attempt to fly around the world. Her fate remains a mystery.

Let the Games Begin

Frenchman Pierre de Coubertin revived the Olympic Games in 1896, in part to promote amateur athletics for men. Though he opposed women's participation, the Paris organizing committee included women's tennis and golf at the 1900 Olympics in Paris, France, which were held as part of a World Exhibition.

More women's events were added in subsequent Games thanks in part to Frenchwoman Alice Milliat, who formed the Fédération Sportive Féminine Internationale (FSFI) in 1921. When the International Olympic Committee (IOC) refused to include women's track and field events in the Olympics, the FSFI retaliated and held the Women's Olympics in 1922. Athletes from five countries competed in front of twenty thousand spectators in Paris, France. Eighteen world records were broken at the one-day track and field meet.

Jock Talk

"Alice Milliat deserves to be remembered with honour. She was the first to significantly push the IOC towards gender equity, and her achievements prepared the ground for subsequent advances."

—Canadian sports historian Bruce Kidd, in a 1994 bulletin for the Canadian Association for Advancement of Women in Sport and Physical Activity (CAAWS).

The second Women's Olympics were held in Gothenburg, Sweden, in 1926. Ten nations sent athletes to the event, which opened with a display of pageantry that included the release of three thousand pigeons.

Red-faced IOC officials protested the FSFI's use of the word "Olympics." Milliat agreed to change the name of the event to the Women's World Games as long as the IOC introduced 10 women's track and field events to the Olympics. The IOC agreed but later broke its promise, including just five women's track and field events at the 1928 Amsterdam Games.

Q & A

Q: Which Olympics did British women boycott?

A: The Women's Amateur Athletic Association (WAAA) refused to attend the 1928 Olympics in Amsterdam, Holland, because the organization wanted ten women's track and field events to be included rather than five. The WAAA's is the only feminist boycott in the history of the Games.

Regardless, the door for greater participation by women in the Olympics had been opened. There has since been a steady increase in the number of female athletes at Olympic Games, and in the number of events open to them. In 1900, women represented less than one percent of athletes participating at the Games. One hundred years later, that figure had increased to 38.4 percent.

Women's World Games were held in 1930 (Prague, Czechoslovakia) and in 1934 (London, England).

Working Nine to Five

As more women entered the workforce—especially during World War II, when men left for battlefields on foreign shores—companies began to form teams to boost the morale of female employees and to ensure their continued health and productivity. These women were given the chance to compete, and that development led to a dramatic increase in women's participation in sports in the middle of the twentieth century. Women in the U.S. Midwest joined bowling teams that competed at neighbourhood alleys and basketball competition became so fierce in the South that textile mills started hiring female employees based on their ball-handling skills. In Canada, meanwhile, companies sponsored hockey and softball leagues. In fact, softball became so popular across the continent that it contributed to the development of All-American Girls Professional Baseball League (AAGPBL), which lasted for eleven years starting in 1943.

Women also pursued their athletic interests through the Young Women's Christian Association (YWCA), the Young Women's Hebrew Association (YWHA), churches and youth organizations.

Political Animals

The mid-1900s landscape was very different in certain parts of Europe, where fascist regimes emerged in Germany and Italy. Initially these states advocated woman's return to her traditional role; physical educators prepared men for battle and women for motherhood. Ultimately, however, sports fell subordinate to politics and athletes of both sexes were used for propaganda purposes, to affirm the superiority of a so-called master race.

Soviet Bloc countries also viewed sport as a propaganda tool. Governments devoted much energy to competitive sports, recruiting athletes and pouring funds into their development. Scientists studied methods to enhance athletes' performances, and women were integral to the success of the "big red sports machine."

Sports Shorts

Early in the twentieth century, women's magazines raved about the health benefits of bowling and encouraged readers to take up the sport. But they were advised to be cautious; bowling alleys were often located near halls where men gambled and drank. In 1916, the Women's National Bowling Association was founded in St. Louis, MS. It was the first sports organization in the United States to be run by women for women.

Playing Nice

No sooner had working women in the United States and Canada slipped into gym shorts than women at high schools and colleges discarded theirs for poodle skirts. Following the turbulence of World War II, North Americans yearned for comfort and stability and both sexes were encouraged to return to their traditional roles. Five decades after the first women's intercollegiate basketball game, female students retreated to the sidelines as spectators or cheerleaders.

The National Amateur Athletic Federation (NAAF), which was founded in the United States after World War II, included a women's division to promote a national policy regulating girls' and women's sports. The division discouraged competition, fearing it would lead to the commercialization and exploitation of women. In Canada, some members of the WAAF voiced similar concerns.

As a result, female high school students in the United States and some Canadian cities were encouraged to participate in play days, which stressed social interaction rather than competition. On those days, women from various schools gathered to play volleyball, basketball, field hockey and other sports. They also indulged in hopscotch and took part in folk dances. Scores were not recorded at these events. While the activities kept the students' blood circulating, they didn't address their competitive urges.

Back in Action

In time, educators agreed that intercollegiate competition wouldn't be detrimental to young women. In the United States, the Commission on Intercollegiate Athletics for Women (CIAW) was established in 1967. The organization began offering national championships in golf, tennis, gymnastics and track and field. (The CIAW was succeeded by the Association for Intercollegiate Athletics for Women [AIAW] in 1971. The latter organization folded in 1982.)

In Canada, the Women's Intercollegiate Athletic Union (WIAU), which had been formed some 40 years earlier, was unable to meet the growing demand for expansion of women's sports. The more progressive Canadian Women's Interuniversity Athletic Union (CWIAU) was formed in 1969, and the first national championships in basketball, swimming and volleyball were held a year later. (In 1978, the CWIAU joined the Canadian Interuniversity Athletic Union [CIAU].)

Such efforts were furthered in the early 1970s when activists picked up where suffragists had left off decades earlier. While the civil rights movement challenged segregation and discrimination in the United States through protest marches and boycotts, the women's rights movement used the same tactics in a push for equality.

Thanks to the activists' hard work, the U.S. government passed Title IX of the Higher Education Act, banning discrimination on the basis of sex in educational programs receiving federal funds, including athletic programs. The legislation required schools and universities to offer equal programs, facilities and opportunities for female students.

Statistics provided by the Women's Sports Foundation show that the legislation provided a big boost to women's sports in the United States. In 1971, a year before the law was passed, just 1 in 27 high school girls participated in varsity sports. The figure was 1 in 2.5 in 2000. In addition, according to the National Collegiate Athletic Association (NCAA) in the United States, just 32,000 female college students took part in intercollegiate sports in that country during the 1971–72 school year. That figure doubled within 5 years, and there are now more than 145,000 female athletes playing on teams sanctioned by the NCAA.

Sports Shorts

Billie Jean King, one of the best female tennis players in history, was an outspoken advocate for the equal treatment of women in sports in the 1970s. She helped found the Women's Tennis Association (WTA), the international women's professional tour, and joined some other top female athletes in establishing the Women's Sports Foundation. Perhaps her most memorable achievement was her defeat of former tennis great Bobby Riggs in a "Battle of the Sexes" showdown in 1973. Some 50 million television viewers watched King thump the man who had vowed to "set women's lib back 20 years to get women back in the home, where they belong."

Sports Shorts

Ironically, Title IX hurt female coaches and administrators in the United States; the legislation led the National Collegiate Athletic Association (NCAA) to swallow up the Association for Intercollegiate Athletics for Women (AIAW), which was formerly the Commission on Intercollegiate Athletics for Women (CIAW). Colleges began combining men's and women's programs into one department. The consolidation led to the dismissal of women coaches and administrative staff. Additionally, as more money poured into women's college sports, male coaches became more interested and claimed many of the plum jobs. For example, the percentage of females in charge of women's athletic programs in U.S. colleges fell from 90 percent in 1972 to 17.8 percent in 2000.

Though their lot has improved dramatically, female athletes in the United States still don't play on a level field—they represent 41 percent of intercollegiate athletes, but receive just 26 percent of college sports' operating budgets and less than 28 percent of college recruiting money.

Jock Talk

"You can see the change in women's athletics. Young girls today have more opportunities than I ever had."

—American softball star Dot Richardson, at the 1996 Olympics in Atlanta, GA.

Where the Boys Are

Movie star Grace Kelly made headlines when she married Monaco's Prince Rainier III in 1956, but did she surprise anyone? No. However, a nine-year-old Canadian girl startled the sports world that same year when it was discovered she was playing minor league hockey disguised as a boy. The uproar led Abigail "Ab" Hoffman to hang up her skates, but her saga was a sign of times to come.

Two decades later, people were running naked through public places, growing attached to pet rocks and sporting mood rings. Women got caught up in the zaniness, looked at men suiting up for battle on the playing field and thought, "Why not me?" and then began to tackle sports traditionally associated with men.

Some girls joined boys on school and minor league teams, occasionally causing a commotion. When Canada's Justine Blainey was barred from playing on a local boy's

Sports Shorts

Television has played a key role in the development of women's sports by bringing top female athletes into living rooms. Olympic broadcasts contributed to the continent's love affair with diminutive Russian gymnast Olga Korbut in 1972 and then sent thousands of females running to their hairdressers desperate to look like American figure skater Dorothy Hamill. These winsome women were accomplished athletes, and viewers took notice. Television has been making celebrities of athletic women ever since.

hockey team in 1985, she took her case to the Supreme Court of Canada and won. She laced up with the boys for another three years. Around that same time, American Julie Croteau (b. 1971) was dropped from her high school's men's junior varsity baseball team. She filed a suit and lost, but went on to become the first woman to play on a men's college team.

A few women have even competed with men at the highest levels of sport:

➤ In 1970, American Diane Crump became the first woman to ride in the Kentucky Derby. The year before she had become the first woman to ride at a pari-mutuel track, where bettors backing the first three horses divide the losers' stakes.

➤ American Janet Guthrie became the first woman to compete in a National Association of Stock Car Auto Racing (NASCAR) Winston Cup event in 1976 and switched into high gear the following year when she became the first woman to compete in the Indianapolis 500. She pulled out of the race early due to a breakdown in her car's ignition system, but returned in 1978 and completed the race with a broken wrist.

➤ American Nancy Lieberman became the youngest basketball player in Olympic history to win a medal. The 18-year-old helped the U.S. team clinch silver at the 1976 Olympics in Montréal, QC. Ten years later, she signed with the Springfield Flame of the United States Basketball League (USBL), becoming the first woman to play in a men's professional basketball league.

➤ Canadian Manon Rheaume made history by signing a contract with the Tampa Bay Lightning of the National Hockey League (NHL) in 1992. Before that she had played boys' junior hockey. She joined the women's national team in 1992.

Female athletes have steadily broken new ground at the Olympics, too. At the 2000 Sydney Games, for example, women competed in several events that had previously been reserved for men, including weightlifting, the pole vault, the hammer throw and water polo.

Sports Shorts

Islamic women have been denied opportunities for athletic training. For example, Iranian women can't compete in various sports because it would force them to dress immodestly. "In an attempt to qualify for kayak events [at the 1996 Olympics in Atlanta, GA] Iranian women trained while wearing chodors, hooded robes designed to hide the female form," documents *Sports: An Illustrated History*. "The coach claimed the extra clothing added ten seconds over a 500-metre course."

Algerian runner Hassiba Boulmerka also created controversy when she won a world championship in 1991. She was denounced by clerics in her home country for "running with naked legs in front of thousands of men." Undaunted, she went on to win the 1500m run at the 1992 Olympics in Barcelona, Spain.

Everywhere They'll Be Swingin'

There's no doubt about it: women have made headway throughout the world of sports in recent years.

Professional Sports

While talented women were earning a living playing tennis and golf for decades, professional opportunities in other sports were virtually non-existent for women in North America. For example, the continent's top female basketball players had to move overseas to play professionally. But as the century drew to a close, opportunities opened up in North America, albeit in fits and starts.

The Women's Basketball League (WBL) was launched in 1978 and lasted for three years. The Liberty Basketball Association was launched in 1991 and folded after one exhibition game. Five years later, the American Basketball League (ABL) was launched, followed by the Women's National Basketball Association (WNBA). The ABL folded midway through its third season, but the WNBA, which was founded by the National Basketball Association (NBA) and is collectively owned by the NBA franchises, continues to thrive.

Women have been playing professional beach volleyball on the Fédération Internationale de Volleyball (FIVB) World Tour since 1992. By the end of the century, women were competing in the Women's Professional Softball League (WPSL) and were preparing to launch the Women's United Soccer Association (WUSA). A professional indoor volleyball league for women will be launched in the United States in 2002 and will be called United States Professional Volleyball (USPV).

Endorsements

American skier Suzy Chaffee was a bit of a curiosity when she endorsed Chap Stick lip balm in the late 1960s. But today she would have to compete for billboard space with dozens of top female athletes who have followed the lead of their male counterparts and have cashed in on their fame. How would Chaffee fare against American basketball player Sheryl Swoopes, the first woman to have a pair of basketball shoes named for her, or American tennis ace Venus Williams, who signed an endorsement deal with Reebok in December 2000, estimated at $40 million? (Williams's was the most lucrative endorsement deal ever signed by a female athlete.)

Journalists

When National Football League (NFL) quarterback Terry Bradshaw saw *Boston Globe* reporter Lesley Visser standing outside his dressing room with a pad of paper in 1974, he assumed she was a fan and gave her an autograph. Odds are that wouldn't happen today; the past three decades have seen more women entering the workforce as sportswriters and broadcasters. Indeed, the percentage of women in newspaper sports journalism doubled in the 1980s alone. "Years ago, if I saw another woman in the press box, it was 'There's a buddy, there's another me out there,'" the Associated Press Sports Editor Terry Taylor said in *Girls Rule!* "Now, we are everywhere. We don't stick out and that's when you know you have arrived."

Taylor also noted the emergence of magazines devoted to women's sports. Indeed, two major women's sports magazines were launched in the United States in 1997: *Condé Nast Sports for Women* and *Sports Illustrated for Women*. The Women's Sports Foundation reports that both publications hired predominantly female staff. The organization adds that niche sports magazines such as *Runner's World* are expanding coverage of women in their respective sports and are increasing the number of women writers and editors.

The Least You Need to Know

➤ Female athletes were celebrated at the beginning of the twentieth century.

➤ Women fought an uphill battle to compete in the Olympics.

➤ Industrial leagues boosted women's participation in sports.

➤ Female athletes retreated somewhat in the 1950s.

➤ The turbulent 1960s and 1970s revolutionized women's sports.

➤ Many women have excelled in so-called men's sports.

➤ By the twentieth century's end, women were involved in sports at all levels.

You Can't Do That: Opposition

Serious exercise would make them nervous wrecks and prevent them from becoming mothers. It would turn them into men or, worse, encourage dark, immoral behaviour. Women were continually warned about the perils of sports, but they just didn't listen.

Take it Easy

As women became more active in the late 1800s, they had to battle the perception that they were the weaker sex—too frail emotionally and physically to withstand vigourous exercise. Doctors even warned them that intense physical exertion would lead to nervous disorders. Haunted by visions of female students rocking back and forth in the fetal position in school gymnasiums, many educators opposed serious exercise for women, whether in a recreational or competitive setting. For example, when students from Bryn Mawr College outside Philadelphia, PA challenged their counterparts at Vassar College near New York, NY to a tennis tournament in 1894, faculties of both schools intervened and the competition never took place.

This conceptualization of the emotionally fragile woman lingered for years. The *Encyclopedia of Women and Sports* cites a 1928 article in "Hygeia" magazine noting

Jock Talk

"Athletic competition for women harms the nervous system, encourages rowdiness and leads to injury and exploitation."

—National Amateur Athletic Federation (NAAF), Women's Division, circa 1924.

that "girls are nervously more unstable than men" and that competitive sports would distract them from their studies and lead them to lose sleep and acquire "nervous injuries." Ethel Perrin, head of the women's division of NAAF in the United States, weighed in by commenting that "the fact a girl's nervous resistance cannot hold out under intensive physical strain is nature's warning."

Perrin must have felt vindicated when women's track and field made its Olympic debut at the 1928 Amsterdam Games; it was reported that several competitors collapsed after the 800m run, which sparked a protracted debate about women's participation in sports. Some doctors argued women were incapable of such strenuous activity. This view was echoed by the Pope and the president of

Let Me Explain

Queen Victoria ruled Britain from 1837 until her death in 1901. Her reign was the longest of any monarch in British history, and the time period came to be known as the Victorian era. *Encarta Online Encyclopedia* describes the era as one "represented by such 19th-century ideals as devotion to family life, public and private responsibility, and obedience to the law."

Source: "United Kingdom," *Microsoft® Encarta® Online Encyclopedia 2000.* Available at: **www.encarta.msn.com** © 1997–2000 Microsoft Corporation.

the IOC, Comte de Baillet-Latour, who proposed eliminating all women's sports from the Olympic Games. Instead, the IOC banned only the 800m run until 1960.

When these kinds of warnings about the general mental and physical repercussions of strenuous exercise failed to convince the Victorian woman to remain docile, doctors and educators warned her that sports could damage her reproductive organs—a compelling argument given that her sole purpose, apparently, was to bear and raise children.

Doctors posited elaborate theories about how sports were dangerous, insisting that when a woman exercised, her blood was drained from certain body parts—including her reproductive organs—in order to support the parts being exerted. They also speculated that running and jumping could jar or displace organs in a woman's pelvic region and added that cycling was dangerous for women because bicycle seats could collapse the uterus or induce spinal shock. Field hockey was also not advised under the assumption it could hinder a woman's ability to breast-feed.

Sports Shorts

Where did the Victorian perception of women as weaklings originate? Some historians charge the male-dominated establishment (i.e., doctors and educators) fabricated the so-called "frailty myth" in an attempt to keep women subdued as they started to press for more rights and freedoms. Other historians have a less cynical view; they suggest these men truly believed women were feeble, and recommended submissive roles only because they wanted the best for them.

She's (Supposed to Be) a Lady

Doctors stopped sounding alarm bells over time as an increasing number of women became active and not only survived, but also bore children. However, opposition to women in sports persisted based on the notion that athletic competition was appropriate for men but not women, and that female athletes were unfeminine. All that sweating and aggression—why, it was about as ladylike as *belching*. Of course, sports in which the female participants' competitive zeal was masked by grace and beauty were acceptable. Thus, figure skaters were deemed charming while runners or soccer players were considered beastly.

Baron Pierre de Coubertin established the modern Olympic Games in 1896, an era in which women were expected to be pious, pure, domestic and most of all, submissive. Not surprisingly, the Frenchman

Jock Talk

"[The Olympic Games should be] a solemn and periodic exaltation of male athleticism with internationalism as a base, loyalty as a means, arts for its setting, and female applause as reward."

—Pierre de Coubertin, founder of the modern Olympic Games.

ruled out women as competitors. "Let women practise all the sports if they wish," he said. "But let them not show off." It seems immodesty was not much of a female virtue, either.

Gender War

Critics soon charged that female athletes were downright masculine. Even as women took big steps forward in the sports world in the first half of the 1900s, the criticism was ever-present.

The same year women's swimming made its Olympic debut at the 1912 Olympics in Stockholm, Sweden, the *Ladies Home Journal* ran an article under the headline "Are Athletics Making Girls Masculine?"

In that same year, American socialite Eleonora Sears caused a stir when she attempted to join a men's polo practice. She rode on to the field riding astride—ladies were supposed to ride side-saddle—and wearing jodhpurs. The polo team refused her request to participate in the practice and she was roundly criticized. According to *Getting into the Game*, a women's club passed a resolution urging Sears to wear "normal" feminine attire (she responded by wearing trousers all the time).

Reporters who covered the incredible exploits of Babe Didrikson—best remembered for her accomplishments on the track at the 1932 Los Angeles Games and on the golf links—disparaged her cockiness and brashness as unfeminine and described her as a

Sports Shorts

There was, of course, a homophobic element to complaints about the so-called masculinity of Babe Didrikson and other female athletes of her time. Sports were generally considered a male domain and the popular perception of a lesbian at the time was one of a masculine woman interested in male activities. Since then, women have made dramatic gains in the sports world and, in the process, have expanded the boundaries of acceptable female activities. There are now fewer sports in which female participants are automatically suspected of being homosexual. Furthermore, the public's perception of lesbians is not as parochial as it once was. Nonetheless, female athletes—both homosexual and heterosexual—still suffer from the public's entrenched homophobia. As a result, women are often shunned by companies looking for athletes to endorse their products, and are still disparaged in the media, though perhaps not to the same extent as they once were, and not as blatantly.

"Muscle Moll." Didrikson responded by toning down her demeanour and appearing publicly in dresses.

Since then, social and political changes have altered concepts of femininity and have narrowed the gap between what is accepted male and female behaviour. It's now easier for women to be strong and aggressive without being perceived as unfeminine. In September 2000, *Sports Illustrated* noted that Swedish swimmer Therese Alshammer (b. 1977) had "a physique sculpted for power and speed." Did those attributes make the muscular athlete unfeminine? Not according to a popular men's magazine in her homeland—it named her that country's sexiest woman in 1998.

Let's Talk About Sex

Alshammer's popularity shows that femininity and muscular athleticism are no longer mutually exclusive terms. But not all women's sports advocates are exchanging high-fives about the appreciation of female athletes' physicality. Some contend the swimmer's popularity also shows how far women have left to go in the sports world. They feel too many magazines celebrate female athletes based on their *appearance* rather than their *accomplishments*. Would Alshammer have been featured in *Sports Illustrated* if she didn't have "cover girl" looks?

The answer is unclear, but one thing is certain: there has been an erotic undercurrent in women's sports for as long as female athletes have been sweating and breathing heavily. For example, men were not allowed to watch the first women's intercollegiate basketball game between the University of California, Berkeley and Stanford in 1896, lest they become aroused and lunge at the competitors. For the same reason, men were prevented from watching women's swimming races in Germany. According to *The Women's Sports*

Jock Talk

"They come with signs, like 'Anna, you're so hot' and frequently yell during her matches, like the man who shouted, 'Anna, will you have my baby?' The people who cater to these fans are no less vigilant: Giving in to what one of the local tabloids likes to call 'Annamania,' the newspapers of Fleet Street have virtually turned into pages of Kournikova wallpaper."

—*The Washington Post*, on the appearance of popular Russian tennis player Anna Kournikova at Wimbledon in 2000.

Encyclopedia, organizers softened up after a few years and allowed the lascivious creatures to attend—as long as they sat at least 30 yards from the contestants.

In the United States in the 1920s, Lou Henry Hoover, the head of a national committee investigating mixed gender sports events, deemed the concept unsavoury and decided that men should not even be spectators at female sporting events. It's enough to make one wonder how the Victorian man would respond to modern ad campaigns and magazine photo spreads featuring female athletes without their bloomers—or much else. Odds are he'd all but spontaneously combust leafing through the August 2000 issue of *Sports Illustrated*, in which American swimmer Jenny Thompson stands on a beach wearing just a bikini bottom—with a stars and stripes pattern, of course, since she was about to represent her country at the Sydney Games—with her hands placed strategically over her breasts. Would he have preferred Thompson to her compatriot soccer star Brandi Chastain, who posed in *Gear* magazine covered only by a soccer ball? How would Chastain have stacked up against members of the Australian women's soccer team, who posed topless in a fundraising calendar?

Sports Shorts

It wasn't just men who had to be protected from themselves in the Victorian era; women were also considered vulnerable to their own sexuality. Arbiters of decency worried that female cyclists might use the upward tilt of the seat to masturbate and that cycling might lead to promiscuity. Manufacturers rode to the rescue (no pun intended) and introduced a bicycle with a wider seat.

Certainly there would be much flesh for feasting eyes; sexuality in women's sports has moved from backstage to centre stage. Modern female athletes are standing proud—with their hands covering their breasts, of course.

Jock Talk

"When you've spent half your life looking down at the line at the bottom of the pool—and you've given up everything—it's incongruent to take the body you worked so hard to build and use it for sex."

—Women's Sports Foundation executive director Donna Lopiano, in the *Orlando Sentinel*, responding to a *Sports Illustrated* photo in which U.S. swimmer Jenny Thompson appears in just a bikini bottom.

The Least You Need to Know

➤ Doctors were among the most outspoken critics of women's participation in sports.

➤ Women couldn't be simultaneously athletic and feminine until recently.

➤ There was a sexual undercurrent to women's sports long before athletes like Jenny Thompson and Brandi Chastain arrived on the scene.

Part 2

Good Day Sunshine—
Summer Sports

It's a pleasure to run, toss a ball or swing a club or racquet in the summer sun. It's even more of a rush to do so with the roar of the crowd spurring you on. Just ask soccer player Mia Hamm, runner Marion Jones, golfer Karrie Webb and a host of other top female athletes. Of course, these modern girls of summer are not the first to have captured headlines. More than two decades before reigning tennis ace Venus Williams cranked up her serve to a blistering 127 miles per hour, Billie Jean King emerged victorious from a highly publicized Battle of the Sexes. Half a century earlier, officials increased the seating capacity at Wimbledon to accommodate fans who flocked to see Suzanne Lenglen. The list of women who have made their mark in the hot summer sun goes on and on...

Chapter 5

Anyone For Tennis?: Tennis

In This Chapter

➤ Women swat balls around with their bare hands

➤ Tennis becomes all the rage on both sides of the Atlantic Ocean

➤ France produces Suzanne Lenglen, the game's the first superstar

➤ Althea Gibson wins titles and breaks down barriers

➤ Billie Jean King gives women's tennis a shake, rattle and roll

➤ Martina Navratilova introduces muscle and controversy to the game

➤ Steffi Graf steals the show

➤ New stars' power and panache raise the profile of women's tennis

---

Anna Kournikova has caused a stir with her award-winning looks but she certainly isn't the first female tennis player to have made an impression. Decades before the Russian's sex appeal was tapped to sell sports bras, Frenchwoman Suzanne Lenglen was sucking brandy-soaked sugar cubes between sets and cavorting like a rock star off-court. From Renaissance woman Margot of Hainault, who beat the men at their own game, to current powerhouse Venus Williams, top female tennis players have made people sit up and take notice.

Palms of Victory

On the eve of the Renaissance, noble people gathered in England's castle courtyards to play court tennis or "royal tennis," a game first played by French monks, who batted a leather ball stuffed with hair over a net. They hit the balls with their bare hands, but by the 1400s many enthusiasts were using a racquet strung with strips of sheep intestines. The balls and racquets were heavy so women, already weighted down with elaborate headdresses and massive skirts looped up around their hips, watched rather than participated.

The French upper classes were less keen on racquets; they preferred *jeu de paume*, an indoor game where players used their palms to hit the ball. The game had at least one female enthusiast. At the age of 28, Margot of Hainault arrived in Paris and outplayed all her male challengers in 1427.

New Beginning

England's Walter Clopton Wingfield is credited with inventing the sport as we know it today. He codified the outdoor game in 1873 and then sold it commercially. Soon, tennis was being played in North America. In 1874, Dr. James Dwight brought an imported set of equipment to an estate in Massachusetts; Ella Wilkens Bailey reportedly introduced the sport to an army outpost in Tucson, AZ, where her husband was stationed; and Mary Ewing Outerbridge of Staten Island, NY reportedly brought tennis equipment back with her from Bermuda, where she had seen British officers playing the game.

The sport spread quickly through country clubs. The United States Lawn Tennis Association (USLTA) was formed in 1881, and the organization held its first men's national championship that year. The first such competition for women was added six years later. Tennis also became popular at schools. American women played at several colleges including Vassar and the Boston School of Gymnastics, while Englishwomen got active at Oxford and Cambridge.

Early Exploits

The first national championship for women was played at the facility now known as the All England Lawn Tennis and Croquet Club in the London suburb of Wimbledon in 1884. That final pitted two sisters against each other. Maud Watson, 19, defeated her older sibling, Lilian. But the sister-slayer was soon eclipsed by Blanche Bingley, who married the club's general secretary and then competed as Mrs. G.W. Hillyard. She captured six Wimbledon titles before 1900.

That was the same year tennis was added to the Olympics. It was removed after the 1924 Olympics in Paris, France, due to a dispute over the distinction between amateurs and professionals, and didn't return until 1988.

In the meantime, while suffragettes closed in on the vote in the early 1900s, a few individuals made their mark on the tennis court. Born in England, May Sutton (1887–1975) moved to California with her family when she was six years old. She and her sisters honed their skills on a clay court built on the family ranch. Disdainful of the spins, slices and strategic drop shots that characterized women's tennis at the time, Sutton relied on a powerful forehand delivered with topspin. She won the U.S. championship in 1904, but dismissed the event as uninspiring. She turned down invitations to compete there for the next 17 years and focused instead on Wimbledon. In 1905, she became the first foreign woman to capture a title there.

Let Me Explain

Some tennis basics:

➤ A groundstroke is any stroke used to hit a ball after it has bounced.

➤ Topspin is achieved when the player makes contact and brushes the racquet up and over the ball, causing it to arc downward and bounce high when it lands.

➤ Slice, or underspin, is achieved when the player cuts underneath the ball with the racquet, causing it to curve in the air and bounce to the left or right when it lands.

Compatriot Alice Marble (1913–1990) was passionate about baseball as a young girl and performed so well with a men's minor league team—the other players initially mistook her for a boy—she was asked to be the team's mascot and bat girl. Her horror-stricken brother bought her a tennis racquet, insisting she take up a "ladylike" game. Marble became one of the best players in tennis, sweeping U.S. singles, doubles and mixed doubles titles three years running. She relied on a serve-and-volley game that only men played at the time (she lacked confidence in her groundstrokes and compensated by rushing to the net). Her career was sidetracked in 1934 when she was diagnosed with tuberculosis and advised to give up tennis. But she returned to the court two years later.

Femme Fatale

Despite their skill, Sutton and Marble couldn't hold a candle to Frenchwoman Suzanne Lenglen (1899–1938), the grand diva of tennis and one of the first female athletes to attain true superstardom.

Lenglen was born to a wealthy family and was introduced to the game by her father when she was 11 years old. He recognized her talent and groomed her for top-level competition. In 1919, Lenglen made her Wimbledon debut, defeating six-time champion Dorothy Lambert Chambers in the final. For the next six years, Lenglen dominated headlines.

She was stocky with a big nose, bad teeth and dark circles under her eyes. But what she lacked in classic beauty, Lenglen made up for in style. She tantalized crowds by wearing short skirts or silk gowns that revealed the contours of her body in the sunlight, and sleeveless blouses or sweaters and brightly coloured silk chiffon scarves around her head. She also competed in full make-up. In rejecting the hoop skirts and bodices that had confined her predecessors, Lenglen strengthened the comfort case being made by female cyclists who were donning loose-fitting trousers (i.e., bloomers) and riding into a brave new corset-less world.

Jock Talk

"I am the great Lenglen."

—Tennis legend Suzanne Lenglen to an usher who asked to see her ticket at the 1920 Olympics in Antwerp, Belgium.

Lenglen's dramatic dress was matched by her temperament. She was emotional on the court and dissolved into tears more than once. On one occasion, she defaulted a match in which she was behind claiming ill health; within a few hours she was out on the town doing the foxtrot. Arrogance? The famously volatile John McEnroe had nothing on Lenglen, who sometimes demanded wine before her matches and routinely sucked on sugar cubes laced with brandy during breaks between sets.

But there was no denying her talent. Between 1919 and 1926, she won 269 of her 270 matches, 21 of which were major titles. Among those were eight singles titles, including two at the French championships and six at Wimbledon. She also picked up two gold medals at the 1920 Olympics in Antwerp, Belgium—one in singles and one in mixed doubles.

Lenglen was so popular that the most famous male player of era, Bill Tilden, admitted she was a bigger draw than he was. In 1922, Wimbledon expanded its seating to accommodate fans who flocked to the competition to see her.

The Rivalry

A 1926 match against Helen Wills (1905–1998) was the highlight of Lenglen's career. Four thousand spectators crammed the rickety bleachers of the Carlton Club in Cannes, France to watch the showdown between the hometown *femme fatale* and the American known as "Little Miss Poker Face" for her steely demeanour. Lenglen won the contest, and was mobbed by fans.

One young man, however, approached Wills and complimented her performance. It turned out to be the smoothest of moves—Wills married him three years later and became known as Helen Wills Moody. The athlete—whose dark hair and beautiful face was celebrated by artists and poets of her time and elicited thousands of fan letters—won 38 major titles. Among them were 19 singles titles, including 8 at Wimbledon, 7 at the U.S. championships and 4 at the French championships. She also won two gold medals at the 1924 Paris Games—one in singles and one in doubles.

When the Going Gets Tough

A few decades later, Althea Gibson (b. 1927) was the main attraction in tennis. She was black, and her presence raised eyebrows in the white, upper crust tennis world. Nonetheless, she overcame race and class obstacles to become the first black player to win a major event, which effectively ended segregation in American tennis.

Gibson was born on a cotton farm in South Carolina but soon moved with her family to Harlem, a poverty-stricken neighbourhood in New York City, NY. She grew up playing basketball and stickball and started hitting tennis balls against a wall when she was 14 years old. Before long, she was asked to join New York's interracial Cosmopolitan Club. The club sent her to tournaments sponsored by the All-Black American Tennis Association (ATA), which had been established in response to the segregationist policies of the USLTA. Her success in those competitions won her a benefactor with whom she lived while attending school and honing her skills in North Carolina.

Under the guidance of a top coach, she zipped to the top of the black tennis world. In 1949, she reached the quarterfinals of an indoor tournament sponsored by the USLTA. She won the event the following year, too, but was excluded from more prestigious outdoor events because they were held at exclusive all-white country clubs. But when Alice Marble wrote an open letter to the USLTA in 1950 urging the organization to give Gibson more opportunity, doors began to open.

Later that year she became the first black to play at the West Side Tennis Club in Forest Hills, NY, competing in the U.S. championships. She then started her climb to the top of the tennis world, putting her speed, height (5-foot-10) and incredible reach to good use. In three seasons starting in 1956, Gibson won 18 major titles. Among those were five single titles, including two at Wimbledon, two at the U.S. championships and one at the French championships. Gibson made history by becoming the first black champion at Wimbledon and the U.S. championships, but her exploits weren't limited to the tennis court. She appeared on the *Ed Sullivan Show*, popped up in a few movies, wrote an autobiography and recorded an album. When she failed to topple Elvis in the charts, she decided to give another sport a try and joined the women's pro golf tour in the 1960s.

Open Season

Later that decade, competitive tennis went through dramatic change. In the sport's formative years, governing associations had decided that competition would be open to amateurs alone and players wouldn't win money for participating. But over time players had become more and more unhappy with that arrangement. So, in 1968, governing associations like the USLTA opened up their competitions and began offering prize money.

This marked the beginning of the Open era. The U.S. championships became the U.S. Open, the French championships became the French Open and the Australian championships became the Australian Open. These majors, along with Wimbledon, came to be known as grand slam events.

The Legend of Billie Jean

Billie Jean Moffitt King (b. 1943) not only dominated the court for over a decade, she also made unparalleled contributions to women's tennis, and to the women's movement in general.

Growing up in California, King was an excellent softball shortstop but, like Alice Marble decades before, she was urged to take up a more "ladylike" sport and turned to tennis. The near-sighted girl had earned eight dollars doing odd jobs around the neighbour-hood and purchased her first tennis racquet. She set out to be the world's best tennis player, and by the mid-1960s, she was.

Between 1961 and 1980 King won 39 major titles. Among those were 12 singles titles, including 6 at Wimbledon, 4 at the U.S. Open and 1 each at the French and Australian Opens (During King's career, the names of three major tournaments changed due to the start of the Open era).

Power Politics

Though she was winning accolades in the late 1960s, she wasn't winning much money—at least not compared to her male counterparts. At the time, there was a great disparity between prize money offered to men and women. In 1970, King convinced eight other female players to join her in a boycott of a tournament that offered $12,500 to the winner of the men's competition and just $1500 to the female victor. Instead, the women played in an event organized by Gladys Heldman, publisher of *World Tennis* magazine, and financed by tobacco giant Philip Morris, eager to promote Virginia Slims, a new brand of cigarettes designed for women.

The "rebels" were suspended by the USLTA, making them ineligible for grand slam events and the Federation Cup. But the women stood their ground. A year later, the Virginia Slims tournament had grown into a 19-event tour and its marketing slogan had become a catchphrase: "You've Come A Long Way, Baby." Indeed. King became the first female athlete to earn more than $100,000 in annual prize money.

Sports Shorts

In 1923, American player Hazel Hotchkiss Wightman donated a silver vase to be used as the prize in a team tournament she established and named The Wightman Cup. The Federation Cup (nicknamed "The Fed Cup") is an international team competition for women tennis players. Established in 1963, The Fed Cup usurped The Wightman Cup as the premier team event in women's tennis.

In 1973, the USLTA lifted the sanctions against King and her fellow athletes, and when King threatened to stage a boycott of the U.S. Open, agreed to give equal prize money to men and women at the event. That year, both champions received $25,000.

Also that year, King convinced her colleagues to form a players' union, the Women's Tennis Association (WTA). Today, the organization has its own tour and controls all women's professional tournaments except the four grand slam events, which fall under the jurisdiction of the International Tennis Federation (ITF) and its member organizations.

The Battle of Evermore

Bobby Riggs (1918–1995), a former champion on the men's tour and a gifted self-promoter, said women didn't deserve equal prize money and he was willing to prove it. He challenged King to a match. She balked at the aging showman, so he took on another top women player, Margaret Court (b. 1942), and trounced her in front of a national television audience. He challenged King again. This time she accepted.

Sports Shorts

Australian Margaret Court was one of the top female players of the 1960s. She won 66 major titles, including 26 singles titles. She won 92 titles overall. In 1970 she became the first woman since Maureen Connolly (1934–1969) in 1953 to win all four majors in a single season. She had done the same in mixed doubles seven years earlier. Despite her success, Court was often criticized for collapsing under pressure, and is best remembered for her 1973 loss to Bobby Riggs, the self-declared male chauvinist pig who later lost to Billie Jean King.

Thanks to the women's rights movement, Riggs's bravado and media hype, the match, for which the winner would take the full $100,000 purse, took on larger than life dimensions and was promoted as the ultimate "Battle of the Sexes." The contest was held at the Astrodome in Houston, TX, in September 1973. King was so nervous before the match that she vomited in the locker room, but she cleaned up her act in time for the main event. Some thirty thousand spectators and fifty million television viewers saw her enter the stadium like Cleopatra, on a litter carried by four bare-chested men. Riggs arrived in a rickshaw pulled by scantily clad women.

Jock Talk

"This absurd match became for women's tennis the drop shot and volley heard round the world."

—"London Sunday Times" on the King-Riggs showdown, in *Women's Sports: A History.*

King defeated Riggs in three straight sets. It may not have been much of an athletic achievement—Riggs was 55 years old, while King was just 29—but the victory for women's tennis was undeniable. It was also a big boost to the women's movement. "[The victory] helped validate the idea that women could hang in there, not just on the tennis court, but on the job or in the home. It was proof not so much of physical prowess but of mental toughness," said Grace Lichtenstein, former executive editor of "World Tennis" magazine in *The Sports 100: The One Hundred Most Important People in American Sports History.* "Feminists had not yet reached out to the masses. Billie Jean reached out, grabbed them by the hair, and made them take notice."

King capitalized on the fanfare by founding a women's sports magazine and the Women's Sports Foundation, a non-profit organization dedicated to promoting and enhancing athletic opportunities for girls and women.

Jock Talk

"Almost every day for the last four years someone comes up to me and says, 'Hey, when are you going to have children?' I say, 'I'm not ready yet.' They say, 'Why aren't you at home?' I say, 'Why don't you go ask Rod Laver why he isn't at home?'"

—Billie Jean King in *Sports: An Illustrated History*.

Reign Czech

While King's career was winding down another star was on the rise. Martina Navratilova (b. 1956) battled to the top of the tennis world with powerful, aggressive play and dominated women's tennis in the late 1970s and into the 1980s. Like King, she was active in the women's rights movement. Navratilova was also openly homosexual and a proponent of gay rights.

Born in Prague, Czechoslovakia (now the Czech Republic), Navratilova was named after Martinovka, a ski lodge where her parents had lived (her father was a professional skier and her mother was an instructor on the slopes). Her parents divorced when she was three years old, and her mother soon remarried a tennis instructor. The family's life revolved around the court sport. By the time she was five, Martina was hitting balls against a brick wall.

She played in her first tournament when she was eight and eventually became the best female player in the country. She drew international attention by leading her team to victory in the 1975 Federation Cup. Later that year, Navratilova defected to the United States.

She went on to win 55 grand slam titles. Among those were 18 singles titles, including 9 at Wimbledon, 4 at the U.S. Open, 3 at the Australian Open and 2 at the French Open. She won 167 singles championships overall, the women's all-time record. Some 17,000 fans gathered at New York's Madison Square Garden for her final singles match in 1994. At the end of the competition, they gave her a two-minute standing ovation. Navratilova dabbled in doubles the following year, but then faded from view. She reappeared in 2000 to play doubles in seven tournaments including the French Open, Wimbledon and the U.S. Open.

Sports Shorts

Martina Navratilova battled weight problems early in her career. Thanks to her passion for milkshakes and hamburgers, she gained a whopping 25 pounds in one extended trip outside her native Czechoslovakia. She once referred to herself as "the great wide hope." Eventually she hired a personal trainer who designed a rigorous weightlifting program for her, and she adopted a regimented diet. These measures made her into the lean, mean tennis machine her opponents feared.

Q & A

Q: What famous tennis player also penned mystery books?

A: Martina Navratilova, who co-wrote a series centered on a fictional character named Jordan Myles, a former tennis champion turned sleuth.

Navratilova's on-court accomplishments endeared her to sports fans, but she was also well respected in the gay community and beyond. She responded to rumours about her sexual orientation by acknowledging that she was homosexual. She lived openly with a woman (who later filed a palimony suit against her) and advocated lesbian and civil rights, though it cost her millions of dollars in endorsement money. Navratilova also contributed her prize money and her time during the 1980s to a youth foundation she established to help economically disadvantaged kids learn to play tennis.

Sweet, Sweet Smile

Despite her accomplishments and activism, Navratilova may be best remembered for her fierce rivalry with American Chris Evert (b. 1954). The women were polar opposites; while Navratilova's muscular frame and homosexuality rankled some observers, Evert's wholesome good looks and conservative demeanour endeared her to all but a few misanthropes. Who could help but love "Chrissy," the fabulous girl next door?

The athletes' games were different, too. Evert hovered near the baseline, beating her rivals with well-placed hits, whereas Navratilova unnerved her opponents by attacking the ball at the net. They were well matched despite these differences, with Navratilova winning just over half (43) of their 80 matches.

When she retired in 1989, Evert had won 21 grand slam titles. Among them were 18 singles titles—the same number as Navratilova—including 3 at Wimbledon, 6 at the U.S.

Open, 7 at the French Open and 2 at the Australian Open. She won 157 singles titles overall, just 10 less than her Czech rival. "I think we both realized that we pushed each other and, in the end, made the other one a much better player," Evert later told *Sports Illustrated*.

Wunderbar

In time, both Navratilova and Evert would lose to a young German whose intensity, speed and powerful forehand would catapult her to the top of the tennis world. Stefani Graf's cool disposition didn't win sports fans' hearts, but she earned their respect by thumping opponents left, right and centre in the late 1980s and 1990s.

"Fraulein Forehand," as she came to be known for her trademark shot, was born in Mannheim, Germany, in 1969. Thanks to her tennis-loving parents, Graf was swinging a racquet before she was old enough to tie her shoes. She became the star pupil at her father's tennis school and turned professional when she was just 13 years old, in 1982.

Sports Shorts

Steffi Graf was reserved and shy, and provided little grist for the gossip mill. That role was reserved for her father, who was described as "a walking tabloid headline." The media devoted much coverage to his extramarital affair with a German model, his bouts with alcoholism and, last but not least, his prison sentence. Peter Graf served 15 months in jail for tax evasion on his daughter's earnings.

She hit her stride five years later, winning her first grand slam title—she defeated Navratilova in the French Open—and then becoming the top-ranked woman in the world. In 1988, Graf became the third woman to win all four grand slam events in a single year and also won a gold medal at the 1988 Olympics in Seoul, South Korea, the first Olympics since 1924 to include tennis.

Graf held that winning momentum for over a decade despite a rash of injuries, and retired in 1999, having captured 23 grand slam titles. Among those were 22 singles titles, including 7 at Wimbledon, 5 at the U.S. Open, 6 at the French Open and 4 at the Australian Open. She won 107 singles titles overall and spent a total of 377 weeks as the top-ranked player, more than anyone else in history.

Stab in the Back

At one point, it seemed Graf had met her match. Between 1990 and 1993 she lost three grand slam finals to a Yugoslav-born rival with an unusual two-handed forehand and backhand; Monica Seles (b. 1973) replaced Graf as the top-ranked female player.

The status quo didn't sit well with a German fan named Guenther Parche, who stabbed Seles in the back while she rested between sets during a match in Hamburg, Germany, in April 1993. Police arrested the unemployed lathe operator, whose motive was to help Graf regain her top ranking. In the end, he achieved his goal. Seles's physical wounds soon healed, but the psychological scars lasted much longer. She stayed away from competitive tennis for two years while Graf reclaimed the top spot. And what became of Seles's assailant? He was given a two-year suspended sentence. The lenient ruling angered many players and fans but no one stabbed *him* in the back. Instead, Seles pushed for a retrial. The court upheld the initial ruling.

Seles returned to tennis in 1995 and in the next five years hovered near the top of the tennis rankings, but she was no longer the dominant force she had once been. A new crop of young stars were proving too hot to handle.

Kids Wanna Rock

When Navratilova described the women's tennis circuit in 1994 as "Steffi and the seven dwarfs," few disagreed. Women's tennis had become a one-woman show. That changed later in the decade with the arrival of several excellent players. "A crop of teenage prospects have burst on to the professional tour around the same time," *The Washington Post* reported in 2000. "Women's tennis is flushed with so much youth, depth and talent that players are recognizable by their first names."

Jock Talk

"There might be someone who comes bigger than me and taller and who has better form, but I don't think it's going to happen."

—Top-ranked tennis star Venus Williams.

One of the names had a familiar ring to it. Martina Hingis (b. 1980) was born in Czechoslovakia, and named after her famous compatriot, Martina Navratilova. Hingis's mother, a former top tennis player in Czechoslovakia, and her father, a tennis coach, introduced their daughter to tennis when she was three years old and started entering her in tournaments two years later. Her parents soon divorced and Hingis moved to Switzerland with her mother, who became her coach.

Hingis rose through the ranks and turned professional in 1994, when she was 14 years old. Thanks to her exceptional court sense, Hingis became one of the top players in the world. By the end of the 2000, she had won 13 grand slam titles, including 5 singles titles. Of those, one was at Wimbledon, one at the U.S. Open and three at the Australian Open. She had won 35 singles titles overall.

One of Hingis's major rivals was a 6-foot-3 American whose father had played on the American men's volleyball team at the 1968 Olympics in Mexico City, Mexico. Lindsay Davenport (b. 1976) turned pro in February 1993 and made an impact the same year, reaching the fourth round of her first U.S. Open. She also won a gold medal in singles competition at the 1996 Olympics in Atlanta, GA. By the end of 2000, Davenport had won six grand slam titles, including three singles; she captured one each at Wimbledon, the U.S. Open and the Australian Open. She had won 30 singles titles overall.

Davenport towered over most opponents, but compatriot Venus Williams (b. 1980) could look her in the eye without craning her neck. Just two inches shorter than Davenport and a tad stronger, Williams appeared on the scene in 1994 boasting beaded hair and a saucy, in-your-face attitude. Williams improved steadily over the next few years, raising her serve to a blistering 127 miles per hour. In 2000, Williams became the first black woman to win the singles title at Wimbledon since Althea Gibson in 1958, and she won gold in the singles competition at the Sydney Games.

Sports Shorts

While power and personality electrified women's tennis in the late 1990s, the antics of "tennis dads from hell" captured headlines. A handful of men were caught behaving badly while their daughters competed on the WTA Tour. Mary Pierce's father, Jim, was banned from the Tour from 1993–1998 for behaviour deemed abusive by Tour officials. He was later readmitted with "severe restrictions." Croatian Mirjana Lucic fled her father by moving to the United States. In 2000, fans were treated to tales of naughtiness from the father of promising young Australian Jelena Dokic. Prone to describing tennis officials as "fascists," Damir Dokic was ejected from Wimbledon after breaking a reporter's cell phone while stumbling around the grounds yelling and waving an English flag. A few months later, he erupted over the price of fish in the players' dining area at the U.S. Open. He was apprehended by police in the parking lot screaming at the top of his lungs. Later, in an interview with the *Daily Telegraph*, Dokic hinted that alcohol might have played a role in his outburst. "If you touch me ... anytime ... I will not touch you," he said. "If I drink one or two wines and you touch, who knows."

Williams also won gold in the doubles competition, playing alongside her talented younger sister, Serena (b. 1981). Their victory didn't surprise tennis fans; by the time the dynamic duo touched down in Australia, they had already won three grand slam doubles titles. Serena had also established herself as a threat in singles competition, becoming the first black woman since Gibson to win the U.S. Open.

By the end of 2000, Venus had won seven grand slam titles, including two singles, one each at Wimbledon and the U.S. Open. She had won 15 singles titles overall. Serena was close on her heels, having won six grand slam titles, including one in singles, at the U.S. Open. She had won eight singles titles overall.

From Russia with Love

These players' power and precision were awe-inspiring, but their popularity was eclipsed by a lower-ranked Russian whose image made admirers quiver with desire. Anna Kournikova (b. 1981) turned professional in 1995 and became the most popular women's player in the world without winning even one singles title. Her blonde good looks won her countless devotees. Some of them waved signs begging her to bear their children. Others plastered her photograph across the pages of newspapers and magazines. They were all swept away by "Annamania."

"[Kournikova] has never won a tennis tournament, yet she's currently being billed as the most famous female

Jock Talk

"If she obtains results to match her beauty, Anna [Kournikova] will be the most adored player in history."

—Professional tennis player Nathalie Tauziat.

Jock Talk

"Kournikova, the most downloaded female athlete on the Internet, has graced the covers of *Vogue* and *Esquire* and, most recently, *Sports Illustrated*. She's comfortable on *Late Night With David Letterman*, appearing in Jim Carrey's *Me Myself & Irene*, or dating hockey superstars."

—*The Toronto Star*, on Anna Kournikova, whose romance with (much older) professional hockey player Sergei Fedorov titillated fans and non-fans alike.

athlete on the planet," reported *USA Today*. "The reason for this is simple: She's blond, she's flirtatious and she's pretty. Never, ever, underestimate the power of a male sports editor smitten." The furor pleased some in women's tennis circles—it brought attention and, of course, money to the game. But others claimed it undermined the accomplishments of female athletes. Critics argued that sportswomen should be respected for their athleticism, not their looks.

Causing a Commotion

That being said, Kournikova's sex appeal, the Williams sisters' power and panache and the pitched battle for top spot made women's tennis a bigger draw in 2000 than ever before. In fact, women's events are currently drawing higher television ratings than men's events. The WTA Tour has become a multi-million dollar venture and is spawning some very wealthy women. "Women's tennis is awesome right now," player Mary Pierce (b. 1975) told the *St. Louis Post-Dispatch* in 2000. "We're getting quicker and faster. A lot of girls are hitting harder. Everybody's got different looks. Everybody's got different personalities. And everybody that you talk to says, 'Man, I love watching women play more than men.'"

Table 5.1: Initiation of Major Worldwide Competitions

Event	Men	Women
U.S. Open (singles)	1881	1887
U.S. Open (doubles)	1881	1889
Wimbledon (singles)	1877	1884
Wimbledon (doubles)	1884	1913
French Open (singles)	1891	1897
French Open (doubles)	1925	1925
Australian Open (singles)	1905	1922
Australian Open (doubles)	1905	1922

The Least You Need to Know

➤ Margot of Hainault trounced her male competitors in *jeu de paume*.

➤ Modern tennis started in England in the 1800s.

➤ Suzanne Lenglen was the first female athlete to attain superstar status.

➤ Althea Gibson was a trailblazer for black tennis players.

➤ Billie Jean King left her mark as the most influential women in tennis history.

➤ Martina Navratilova introduced raw power to the women's game.

➤ Steffi Graf had no problem dominating women's tennis, after Monica Seles was stabbed in the back.

➤ Women's tennis is more popular today than ever before.

Join the Club: Golf

Since the Ladies' Golf Club was established at St. Andrews in 1867, talented individuals have transformed the women's game from a hobby into a competitive pursuit. American Babe Didrikson, an athletic marvel who scooped up a few gold medals on the Olympic track before heading for the putting green, put women's golf on the map in the 1940s. Compatriot Nancy Lopez later pushed the game to new heights, paving the way for the big money earners who now come to play on the Ladies' Professional Golf Association Tour from all over the world. But now we're getting ahead of ourselves; women's devotion to golf goes back a long way...

A Queen in Love

Scottish soldiers learned golf from their Flemish counterparts in the early 1400s and became so devoted to the game that it distracted them from their military duties, and Scottish parliament banned them from playing. The ban was lifted in 1502, four years after Scotland signed a peace treaty with England, and sooner than you can say "Fore!," James IV (1473–1513) ordered a set of clubs.

The Scottish king wasn't the only royal who loved the game, however. Catherine of Aragon (1485–1536), the first wife of Henry VIII, was an enthusiast. So was Mary, Queen of Scots (1542–1587), who is believed to have introduced the caddy to the game. Legend holds that Mary travelled with a group of cadets, who carried her clubs when she golfed. The French word "*cadet*" then morphed into the English word, "caddy."

Mary invited scorn when she took to the links shortly after the death of her husband; this behaviour was deemed unacceptable. Many people suspected Mary was responsible for his demise and their suspicions were heightened by her decision to play golf rather than mourn his passing. In the end, she was convicted of treason and executed.

Here, There and Everywhere

Mary's unfortunate fate didn't deter other women from taking up golf. In fact, the game became so popular that many of the nation's women were teeing off by the end of the 1700s.

The Royal Musselburgh Golf Club of Scotland offered prizes to women as early as 1810, and the first golf club known to include women, the North Berwick, was established in 1832. Momentum increased and the Ladies' Golf Club, the first just for women, was founded at St. Andrews in 1867. By the end of the century, one-third of Scotland's golfers were women.

Not to be outdone, a handful of English women founded the Ladies' Golf Union (LGU) in 1893 and were determined to promote and fund an annual championship tournament. The first women's British amateur championship, then called the Ladies' Championship, was held in 1893. Lady Margaret Scott defeated 37 participants from England, Ireland and France to win the competition, which was played over 9 holes.

In 1901, the LGU lobbied for permission to hold a tournament at St. Andrews and was turned down. But there was no denying these iron maidens, and they were granted permission seven years later—on the condition that competitors stay out of the locker room and the lounge. Thus, the British Women's Open was born.

Golf was also popular in other parts of the world. In Australia, the first national championship for women was held in 1894, a year before the men's. Meanwhile, North American women were embracing golf, too. At a time when it was odd for a woman to watch a baseball game let alone participate in one, the wives and daughters of wealthy men were swinging their clubs with abandon—in the privacy of their own country clubs, of course. One can only marvel at these women for surviving hot and sunny days on the links dressed in long skirts, shirtwaists buttoned tightly around their necks and wrists, long scarves and girdles.

The first U.S. women's amateur championship was held at the Meadowbrook Country Club in Westbury, NY in 1895 under the auspices of the United States Golf Association (USGA). Mrs. Charles S. Brown was first among 13 competitors with a score of 132 for an 18-hole course.

By the early 1900s, many Americans were travelling to England for competitions. Two of these women, Margaret and Harriet Curtis, came from an affluent family in Boston. The sisters' effort to organize a match between Great Britain and the United States resulted in the inaugural Curtis Cup match in 1932. This event is still one of the most prestigious amateur women's competitions in the world.

Sports Shorts

In 1926, an enterprising American woman named Frieda Carter, who was part owner of a resort, invented miniature golf. Her idea was an instant hit and over twenty-five thousand courses were built in the following four years.

Talent Show

It was only a matter of time before some big golfing talents emerged. Connecticut-born Glenna Collett (1903–1989) loved to play baseball, but was encouraged by her parents to take up pursuits more befitting a girl. Rather than knit sweaters and bake cookies, she dabbled in tennis and then golf. She wasn't half bad with her clubs, winning six U.S. amateur championships, along with the Canadian Ladies' Open in 1923 and 1924 and the French Ladies' Open in 1925. Collett was one of the longest hitters in the game— she once topped the 300-yard mark—and drew large crowds when she played.

Businesses closed shop and workers were given time off to watch matches between Collett and her archrival, Joyce Wethered (1901–1977). The English golfer was a powerhouse in the 1920s, winning four British Opens and five English Ladies' Championships.

Wethered took up the game as a youngster, and turned out to be unflappable on the links—she once sunk the winning putt oblivious to a freight train rumbling by the course—but she was fazed by public attention. She was so well known that she was mobbed whenever she appeared on the links, and the reserved golfer found life in the limelight unbearable. She retired in 1926.

But three years later, when it was announced the British Open Amateur Championship would be held at hallowed St. Andrews, Wethered couldn't resist. She returned for the match, and edged out Collett in a dramatic finish. Both women were swarmed by spectators and had to be escorted off the links by police.

Let Me Explain

What does a golfer do when her ball is inches from the hole? She pulls out her putter, of course, because it is perfectly designed for precision shots.

Today's Vare Trophy—given each year to the player with the lowest scoring average—is named in honour of Collett, who married Edward H. Vare. Wethered married Sir John Heathcoat-Armory and, as a horticulturist, became almost as skilled with a spade as she was with a putter.

The limelight was never a problem for Margaret Abbott (1878–1955)—she was never in it. While studying art in Paris in 1900, the American socialite entered a nine-hole golf tournament for fun, and won. None of the participants knew it was an Olympic event, and only recent research indicates that it was indeed just that. Abbott was awarded the gold medal posthumously. It was the first and last time women's golf was included in the Olympics. (Male golfers competed in the 1900 Games and the 1904 Games.)

Like a Pro

Soon amateur competition wasn't enough for female golf enthusiasts. With financial help from her father, Hope Seignious founded the Women's Professional Golf Association along with a handful of women in 1944. But the Tour suffered from internal discord and was replaced by the Ladies' Professional Golf Association (LPGA) in 1950.

The LPGA's early days were difficult. Only nine tournaments were included on the Tour and there were limited, if any, financial rewards for those events. The association's founders not only competed on the Tour, but also assumed administrative duties. Most of the women lived on modest incomes. Dressed in sweaters and pleated pants or tweed skirts, they played in tournaments with entire purses smaller than first place prizes on the men's Tour. But their talent and personalities eventually brought credibility to the association.

First Family

Even now Patty Berg (b. 1918) is one of the biggest names in women's golf thanks to her success on the links and her efforts promoting the game. The Minnesota native took up the game at the insistence of her parents, who were unhappy that their 14-year-old daughter was quarterback of the local boy's football team (she also played sandlot baseball and ran and skated competitively, but who's keeping track?). Berg won 29 amateur titles before she turned pro in 1940, earning money on the side by giving clinics. She also worked for a sporting goods company promoting a line of golf clubs bearing her name, and competed in the few women's pro tournaments of the era. She was in a serious car accident a year later, but returned to the game in 1943. Then, lest anyone doubt her restored health, Berg joined the marine corps during World War II.

She was back on the links before long, and was elected the first president of the newly formed LPGA. In a career that spanned almost 4 decades, Berg amassed 60 pro wins, including 15 majors. She also won three Vare Trophies and was the first woman to reach $100,000 in career earnings. Berg also wrote three instructional books for women and conducted classes and playing exhibitions across the United States. The organization now gives the Patty Berg Award to women who make outstanding contributions to the game.

Tall and blonde, Betty Jameson (b. 1919) of Oklahoma was also instrumental in the formation of the LPGA. She was considered one of the game's first glamour girls, but she was more than just a pretty face. Her winning score of 295 in the 1947 U.S. Women's Open made her the first woman ever to shoot under 300 in a 72-hole tournament. Jameson had 13 pro career wins, including 3 majors. She retired in 1956.

Fellow founding member Louise Suggs (b. 1923) was less glamorous, but no less talented. Though she was quiet, her performance spoke volumes. She hit the ball so powerfully, comedian Bob Hope once referred to her as "Miss Sluggs." In 1961, she outplayed 10 male golfers in a par-3 invitational tournament in Palm Beach, FL. She shot 156 for 54 holes, beating the legendary Sam Snead by 2 strokes. The Georgia native, who served three terms as LPGA president, notched 58 pro wins, including 11 majors. She won the Vare Trophy once before retiring from the Tour in 1984.

Newborn Babe

Of all the pioneers in women's golf, none compares to the incredible Babe Didrikson (1913–1956). Perhaps the best all-round athlete in history, Didrikson excelled in many sports. She won the most accolades in track and field and women's golf, which she single-handedly put on the map.

Born in Texas as Mildred Didriksen (she later changed the spelling of her surname), she was nicknamed "Babe" either by her parents or by neighbourhood boys who marvelled at her ability to hit home runs like Babe Ruth.

Didrikson was a big-boned woman. In her formative years she looked like a boy and, in the opinion of many people, acted like one. She played poker and boasted about her athletic exploits. She was regarded as self-centered, and was known to blow on her harmonica to interrupt conversations that didn't revolve around her.

Jock Talk

"Before I was even out of grade school, I knew what I wanted to be when I grew up. My goal was to be the greatest athlete that ever lived."

—Babe Didrikson.

Q & A

Q: What female golfer was so athletic as a youngster that she washed floors by putting scrub brushes on the bottom of her feet and skated in circles to spread the soapsuds?

A: It was Babe Didrikson, who also tried to outrun streetcars and leapt over hedges, pretending they were hurdles.

Early on, Didrikson's brash behaviour led reporters and fans to side with her rivals, few of whom had a chance against the marvel known as the "Muscle Moll." But their attitudes changed when her exploits reached epic proportions (Didrikson also conceded to some of the social pressures placed on her and started wearing dresses, which helped her public profile).

In high school, Didrikson excelled in a handful of sports, including basketball and golf. She dropped out of school to play basketball for the Casualty Insurance Company, and led the team to an AAU title in 1931. She then turned her attention to track and field, and in the next year won six AAU events and three Olympic medals—two gold and a silver. Soon after, she was barred from amateur track and field competition for appearing in a car advertisement. No problem. Didrikson toured the country with her own basketball team and played exhibition baseball, billiards and golf. She also did the vaudeville circuit, where she ran on a treadmill, sang and played the harmonica—but we digress.

She took up golf and practised her swing until her hands bled. In 1935, she won the Texas women's championship. But when she promoted golf clubs named after her, she was banned from amateur golf competition until 1943. She waited, and then came back with a vengeance, winning 40 tournaments over the next 4 years.

Didrikson's fame gave instant credibility to the new LPGA and she became its first star. She amassed 41 pro wins overall, including 10 majors. She won her third U.S. Women's Open in 1954, just months after having a colostomy, but lost her battle with cancer and died in 1956. She had won the Vare Trophy two years before.

Astounded at her accomplishments in so many sports, an incredulous journalist once asked her, "Is there anything you don't play?" "Yeah," Didrikson shot back. "Dolls."

Carry On

Didrikson's death in 1956 left a vacuum in women's golf. No one could take the place of such a phenomenon, but three women did stand out on the fairway:

➤ Betsy Rawls (b. 1928) excelled in the classroom and on the links. She graduated from the University of Texas with a combined degree in math and physics. Her pro career started in 1951 and ended in 1975. The Texan notched 55 pro victories, including 8 majors. Rawls, who served as the LPGA's tournament director for six years, won the Vare Trophy once.

➤ Mickey Wright (b. 1935), who grew up in South Carolina, turned pro in 1955. She went on to claim 82 victories, including 13 majors, thanks to her swing, which was considered technically perfect. The soft-spoken Wright was a crowd favourite. She stopped playing full-time in 1969, with five Vare Trophies in her cabinet, and retired in 1980.

➤ Kathy Whitworth (b. 1939) had a career that spanned an incredible three decades. But it wasn't peachy from the outset. The shy Texan joined the Tour in 1958 and didn't win an event until 1962. However, she went on to win 88 tournaments, including 6 majors as a pro, more than any other golfer, male or female. She also served as LPGA president four times. Whitworth won seven Vare Trophies.

The Tour got a big boost in 1963 when the final round of the LPGA Championship was televised for the first time. But despite the efforts of Rawls, Wright and Whitworth, it was lacking a single, charismatic leader. That would soon change.

Sports Shorts

Betsy Rawls finished second to a woman named Jackie Pung in the 1957 U.S. Women's Open. But Rawls claimed victory when the unlucky Pung accidentally signed an incorrect scorecard and was disqualified from the tournament. It was Rawls's third U.S. Women's Open title. She won another one in 1960. Pung hasn't been heard from since.

Sweetheart Darlin'

Sports fans didn't notice Nancy Lopez (b. 1957) when she won her first pee-wee golf tournament by 110 strokes in 1966, but when Lopez won 9 tournaments as a rookie—a record 5 in a row—on the LPGA Tour in 1978, she became an instant celebrity. All of a sudden, people who didn't know a driver from a putter found themselves drawn to golf. The women's game surged in popularity, paving the way for today's big money winners from around the world.

Q & A

Q: What woman golfer's grandmother was the first female pharmacist in the state of Illinois?

A: Mickey Wright's. Her grandfather was an inventor.

Lopez's winsome smile and sparkling eyes silenced critics who dismissed female golfers as too masculine. Her role as devoted wife and mother altered the perception of female golfers as bra-burning feminists. But Lopez was no June Cleaver, polishing silverware and shopping for pearls to wear around the house—she was a serious competitor. In high school, she led an otherwise all-male golf team to the

Sports Shorts

When sportscaster Tim Melton interviewed Nancy Lopez at the Lady Keystone Open in Pennsylvania in 1979, he had more than her backswing on his mind. Love was in the air. They were married in no time, but split three years later—he reportedly wanted to her to quit pro golf—and she married baseball player Ray Knight. Nancy gave birth to three daughters, an undertaking that barely slowed her down.

Q & A

Q: Which household chore was Nancy Lopez excused from doing as a child?

A: Washing the dishes. Her father refused to let her near the kitchen sink after meals; he feared she might hurt her hands and, by extension, her golf game.

Let Me Explain

A driver is the club of choice for hitting balls for long distances; it has the longest shaft of all the clubs.

state championship. Later, in her freshman year at the University of Tulsa, she won the AIAW Golf Championship and was named an All-American.

In her first year on the Tour, the newcomer with the perfect swing won the Vare Trophy. She was also named rookie-of-the-year and player-of-the-year, the first player to win both awards in the same season. She was mobbed wherever she played.

Today, Lopez still plays on the Tour, with a trophy bag busting at the seams. As of November 2000, she had 48 pro career wins to her credit, including 3 majors and 3 Vare Trophies. She was tenth on the all-time career win list, having earned $5.29 million.

Supporting Cast

Lopez was the dominant force in women's golf through much of the 1970s and 1980s, but there were some other big names on the links:

➤ Pat Bradley (b. 1951) joined the Tour in 1974. Bradley had a stellar year in 1986, setting a single-season earnings record with $492,000. She went on to become the first woman to pass the $2-million mark in total career earnings. She passed the $3-million mark in 1990 and, just for good measure, added another million the following year. In November 2000, she was sixth on the all-time career money list with $5.74 million in earnings. She had 31 pro wins, including 6 majors, and 2 Vare Trophies. Not bad for an athlete who started her competitive life as a skier!

➤ Betsy King (b. 1955) joined the Tour in 1977 and struggled for seven seasons while Lopez became a household name. She rebuilt her game from the ground up and—ta da!—fell further into a slump. But she stayed the course and won her first pro tournament in 1984. After that, she started winning bigtime. As of November 2000, she had 33 pro wins, including 6 majors. She also had two Vare Trophies, and was first on the all-time career money list with $6.81 million in earnings.

➤ Beth Daniel (b. 1956) joined the LPGA in 1979, began winning tournaments immediately and was named rookie of the year. But she had no sooner been hailed as the "next big thing" before she fell into a slump. She spent much of the 1980s alienating caddies by screaming at them in mid-competition and throwing equipment hither and thither. The release of tension must have helped—she snapped out of her slump in 1990 and led the Tour in earnings, becoming the first woman to take home more than $800,000 in a single season. As of November 2000, she had 32 pro wins, including 1 major, and 3 Vare Trophies. She was fifth on the all-time career money list with $6.01 million in earnings.

Sports Shorts

Betsy King's first love wasn't golf. She preferred several other sports, including basketball and softball. In fact, she batted .480 as a shortstop on her high school team. She didn't take golf seriously until she injured her knee playing field hockey in college.

American women's domination of the LPGA Tour started with Didrikson in the 1950s and continued into the 1980s, but ended soon after.

World Domination

International players have been on the LPGA Tour from the outset, but they became a dominant force in the 1990s. In November 2000, four non-Americans were among the top ten money winners for the season.

Q & A

Q: What golfer did former LPGA Commissioner Jim Ritts once introduce as "the baby-faced assassin?"

A: Annika Sorenstam.

Jock Talk

"I can't deny it. I check her scores whether I'm playing or not. She's one of the best. And if you want to be the best, you've got to beat the best."

—Annika Sorenstam on Karrie Webb, the day before they teed off in the 2000 U.S. Women's Open.

The most prominent among them was Sweden's Annika Sorenstam (b. 1970). Sorenstam was a talented tennis player as a youngster but before she was old enough to drive a car, she abandoned the sport in favour of golf. It was a good career move. She excelled at the national level in Sweden and after watching compatriot Liselotte Neumann (b. 1966) win the U.S. Women's Open in 1988, Sorenstam set her sights on the LPGA Tour.

She joined the Tour in 1994 after successful stints at the University of Arizona and on the European Pro Tour where she won rookie-of-the-year honours. The following season she overcame bad nerves to capture a one-stroke victory in the U.S. Women's Open. But rather than retire, which she once vowed to do if she won the event, she honed her skills and continued her ascent to the top of the women's golf scene.

By November 2000, she had amassed 23 career victories, including 2 majors. She had won three Vare Trophies, and was third on the all-time money list, with earnings of $6.12 million.

For the past few years, Sorenstam has battled for supremacy on the links with Australia's Karrie Webb (b. 1974), who finished second to the Swede for the most LPGA victories the 1990s (Sorenstam finished the decade with 18 wins, 2 more than Webb).

Webb first swung a golf club when she was eight, and was a bona fide golf fanatic within three years. And what do you suppose she got as a gift for her twelfth birthday? A Culture Club album? Forget about it! She was sent to the Gold Coast (a resort region on the East Coast of Australia) to see star Australian golfer Greg Norman (b. 1955) compete in a tournament. She got his autograph and met him again five years later when several top junior players visited him in the United States. Webb must have heeded his advice; she had a stellar amateur career at home. She made a splash when she joined the LPGA Tour in 1996, winning top rookie honours. By November 2000, Webb had 23 career victories, including 3 majors and 2 Vare Trophies. She had climbed to second on the all-time money list, with earnings of $6.15 million.

While Sorenstam and Webb duked it out, another non-American player made her mark. England's Laura Davies (b. 1963) wasn't supposed to be the golf star in her family—it was supposed to be her brother, Tony, who was given a set of clubs for his birthday. But when his envious sister was appeased with a five-iron, it became obvious the little girl was headed for greatness. Davies won a number of amateur titles at home and soon joined the Women's Professional Golfers European Tour. But when she won the U.S. Women's Open in 1987, she could no longer put off joining the LPGA Tour (which she had done for years because she loathed straying far from home). Davies is now one of the Tour's top players thanks in part to her phenomenal strength. At 5-foot-10 and 180 pounds, Davies is the longest hitter in the game. She had 19 career victories, including 4 majors as of November 2000. She was eleventh on the all-time money list with earnings of $5.18 million.

Marvel at the accomplishments of Sorenstam, Webb and Davies, but don't overlook the Tour's other top international golfers:

➤ Liselotte Neumann excelled at tennis, soccer and basketball, but when she joined her parents on an outing to a nine-hole golf course, she discovered a new passion. The Swede won several amateur titles in Europe before turning pro in 1988. That year, she won the U.S. Women's Open and was named rookie of the year. By November 2000, Neumann had won 12 events, including 1 major. She was thirteenth on the all-time money list with $4.04 million.

➤ Se Ri Pak (b. 1977) was a track star in high school in South Korea, but golf—which she learned from her father—was her primary focus. Pak won 30 tournaments as an amateur before joining the LPGA Tour in 1998. She competed in 27 events that season, running away with the rookie-of-the-year award. She had chalked up eight career wins by November 2000, including two majors, and was thirty-fourth on the all-time money list with a cool $2.36 million.

➤ Lorie Kane (b. 1964), a native of Prince Edward Island, represented Canada at several international competitions before joining the LPGA Tour in 1996. Two seasons later, she recorded twelve top-ten finishes, including a tie for second and two third-place finishes. She blasted through 2000, winning three titles by November and moving up to twenty-eighth on the all-time money list with $2.60 million.

Q & A

Q: What famous woman golfer had to pump gas to make ends meet when she was an amateur?

A: Laura Davies, who also did time as a checkout girl at a grocery store.

Q & A

Q: Which golfer on the LPGA Tour has a dog named Happy?

A: Se Ri Pak. She also has two sisters, though she doesn't have to walk them twice a day!

Today's the Day

Stars couldn't afford to fly in the Tour's formative years and Kathy Whitworth had to spend part of the year living out of the trunk of her car. But times change, and lured by Nancy Lopez's award-winning smile, women's golf attracted more spectators who, in turn, brought new corporate sponsorships and television contracts. By the mid-1970s it was clear the LPGA's days as a player-run organization were long gone.

How's business today? LPGA commissioner Ty Votaw isn't complaining. He notes that total prize money on the Tour grew from approximately $15 million in 1990 to $39 million in 1999, and adds that 35 Tour events were televised in 2000—24 more than in 1990.

But despite the promising figures, observers insist the LPGA looks like a tinpot tour when compared to its male counterpart, the Professional Golf Association (PGA). In November 2000, Karrie Webb held the top spot on the season's money list with 1.86 million. It was a mere pittance compared to the $9.03 million that Tiger Woods (b. 1975) had earned.

Sports Shorts

Most well-known golf games focus on individuals but some emphasize teamwork. Every now and then, fans' attention turns to international women's competitions such as the Curtis Cup, which pits amateurs from the United States and Britain against each other, or the Solheim Cup, which is a contest between the best U.S.-born players and the best European-born players on the LPGA Tour.

This comparison makes women's golf fans cringe, as does continued speculation that their game has been hampered by a lingering image problem. There has long been whispers about the sexual orientation of women on the Tour—talk that many observers believe discourages sponsors. Whispers about lesbianism on the Tour is "the biggest problem facing women's golf today. If it can be sorted out somehow, sponsorship will increase," said James Barclay, author of *Golf in Canada: A History*.

Sadly, it seems not much has changed since CBS broadcaster Ben Wright caused a commotion during the 1995 LPGA Championship when he was quoted as saying, "Let's face facts here. Lesbians in the sport hurt women's golf." Not desperate to make new friends, he also said Davies was "built like a tank." But what the LPGA Tour needs is not a field of tried and true heterosexuals. What it needs is a shining star say observers, preferably one as appealing as tennis favourite Anna Kournikova, who has raised interest in her sport without so much as a singles title to her name. "The LPGA hasn't had that kind of sex appeal since the late 1970s and early 1980s when Jan Stephenson, Laura Baugh and Nancy Lopez among others had poster-girl looks," John Lindsay of Scripps Howard News Service has said (golfing babes Baugh and Stephenson were popular features in the LPGA annual magazine).

Regardless, golf has exploded in popularity as a pastime throughout North America, thanks in part to an increase in leisure time and aging baby boomers' fascination with Tiger Woods. Significantly, women have been taking to the links as well as men. "The are more women in the workplace, and the workplace promotes [participation in] golf," offers Peggy Grimsteed, national executive director of the Canadian Ladies' Golf Association.

Jock Talk

"I'm going to enjoy it. I mean, this will probably never happen again."

—Juli Inkster (b. 1960), after winning the 1999 LPGA Championship. She won the same event the following year. Inkster finished the 2000 season as one of the Tour's top players, with 25 career wins, including 6 majors.

The next Nancy Lopez may very well be wrapping her hands around her first nine-iron right now. Her rookie season on the Tour may be a long way off, but that's fine with commissioner Votaw. "I'm a glass is half full person, so I'm very bullish about our future," he told Scripps Howard. "If we need to improve on one thing, it's people's appreciation of our players' abilities. And I think we're doing that now. We just need to do a better job of it."

Table 6.1: Initiation of Major Worldwide Competitions

Event	Year
LPGA Championship*	1955–present
U.S. Women's Open*	1946–present
The Nabisco Championship (The Dinah Shore, 1972–1999)*	2000–present
The du Maurier Classic*	1979–2000
British Women's Open*	starts in 2001
Solheim Cup	1990–present
Curtis Cup	1932–present

*Years the competitions were deemed majors by the LPGA

The Least You Need to Know

➤ Some of golf's earliest enthusiasts were aristocratic women.

➤ Talented players made their mark before the LPGA was formed.

➤ The LPGA faced tough times in the beginning.

➤ Babe Didrikson brought instant credibility to the LPGA.

➤ Nancy Lopez's dazzling smile and fabulous swing made her a household name.

➤ The top players in women's golf are no longer Americans.

➤ The LPGA is thriving despite homophobic discrimination and comparisons to the more lucrative men's tour.

Run, Baby, Run: Track and Field

Marie-José Perec's frantic flight from Australia during the 2000 Sydney Games raised some pressing questions. Why did the French runner leave before her showdown with an Australian rival? Had she been stalked as she claimed, or was she just afraid of losing? And why had she arrived in Sydney wearing a ridiculous wig? These are just some of the inquiries raised by the kind of drama that has defined women's track and field over the centuries. One also wonders: Did runner Stella Walsh regret competing as a woman since she was technically a man? Would history have been different if sprinter Helen Stephens had accepted Adolf Hitler's invitation for a romantic getaway? We'll never know the answers. But the questions have helped to make women's track and field a riveting story.

Ancient History

The story begins in Ancient Greece, where people worshipped several athletic goddesses, including the independent and strong-willed Atalanta who wed the only man to beat her in a footrace. He won the contest through cunning—she paused to pick up some golden apples he had thrown in her path—because he could not outrun her. While Atalanta was held in great esteem thanks to her incredible exploits, the same cannot be said for mortal women, who were excluded from the Olympics not only as competitors but also as spectators. Women caught in an ancient Greek stadium were to be escorted to a nearby cliff and promptly thrown over.

Sports Shorts

At least one woman watched the ancient Olympics and survived. When her husband died while preparing their son to box in the 404 BC Games, the woman took over as coach and snuck into the stadium during the competition disguised as a man. When her son won, she leapt over an enclosure to congratulate him. Her clothes shifted in the commotion and her gender was revealed. She was spared the death sentence because her father and brothers had also been champions.

Let Me Explain

The javelin is a long, spear-like object that competitors throw as far as possible into a marked area. The one who throws the furthest, wins.

That rule may have given women pause for thought, but it didn't stop them from competing. All-women's games were held throughout Ancient Greece. Single women competed in the Heraia, a competition dedicated to the goddess Hera. They were divided into three age groups and competitors ran in knee-length tunics that exposed their right breasts. The track was shortened by a sixth for the female participants who competed in events over 160m and there were no lucrative endorsement deals for the winners. Instead, they were awarded crowns of olives and chunks of cow sacrificed to Hera.

By the time Roman legions were traipsing through foreign lands in the name of Emperor Augustus, women were taking athletic competition seriously. Three girls won so many races, their father erected a statue to each of them. These sisters were single of course—married women were forbidden to compete. Eventually, races for married women were included in the Sebasteia in Naples. Females—both single and hitched—raced in other competitions too, including the Capitoline Games and the Augustralia. A fourth-century mosaic depicts young women not only running but also throwing the javelin, the discus and doing the long jump. These pursuits were not recreational, as the women are also shown holding prizes. The artwork has been dubbed the "Bikini Mosaic" because its subjects are wearing two-piece outfits similar to Annette Funicello's swimsuit in the 1965 movie, *Beach Blanket Bingo*. Sadly, the women in the mosaic don't sport glorious piles of hair as Funicello did while she frolicked on the beach. Could there have been a Roman Empire shortage of super-hold hair spray?

Let Me Explain

The discus is a round metal object that looks like a dinner plate from a distance, and a miniature flying saucer up close. Competitors throw the discus into a marked-out area in a field, and the winner is the athlete who throws it the furthest.

Let Me Explain

In the long jump, competitors sprint down a runway and jump into a sand pit. The one who jumps furthest, wins. The triple jump is similar except that the approach to the sand pit includes a hop, a skip and a jump.

In the high jump, competitors try to jump over a horizontal bar supported by two vertical poles. The winner is the athlete who clears the greatest height without knocking the bar off its supports.

Smack Dab in the Middle

Track and field declined in popularity as the Roman Empire crumbled and the centre of civilization shifted north. It was too darn cold to be running outside in a tunic and, besides, athletic competition seemed frivolous to the Christians who celebrated the human spirit rather than the human body. Furthermore, life became more difficult during this era as the European continent became more populated and its inhabitants competed for resources. Who had the time to do wind sprints after a long day of land tilling and basket weaving?

But a few years later (give or take a few hundred), builders were erecting magnificent Gothic cathedrals, English wool traders were making a killing and footraces were popping up at rural fairs. The competitive element of these events was not emphasized; people indulged in one-legged races and other such pursuits just for fun. Women raced holding griddles in one hand and flipping pancakes with the other on Shrove Tuesday.

While these women elicited chuckles in competition, others drew leers. Some less fortunate women took part in races to win much-needed items of clothing. These events were held for the amusement of affluent male spectators who attempted to grab or knock over the scantily clad contestants as they ran past. These so-called smock races were banned in the late 1500s, but returned a few decades later and continued for centuries. Ultimately, they became more respectable.

Running Forward

Victorian women had a tough time breathing in their corsets let alone running in them, but footraces for females didn't disappear altogether in this rigid era. While many urban women risked skin welts, broken ribs and various abdominal injuries in the name of fashion, rural women wore much less restrictive clothing. These women, along with urban women who couldn't afford corsets, were much more inclined to run.

Also during this time, track and field was being introduced at colleges, several of which were established just for women. Some progressive educators saw athletic competition as a way for their female students to let off steam and to expand the boundaries of their restrictive Victorian lives.

Who's Playin' Games?

Women soon began to lobby for the right to compete in track and field at the Olympics. With their efforts stymied by the IOC, a Frenchwoman named Alice Milliat founded the FSFI and the organization established its own international competition.

The first Women's Olympics were held in Paris, France, in 1922. Some twenty thousand spectators gathered to watch the competition, which included participants from five countries. Four years later, the second Women's Olympics were held in Gothenburg, Sweden. That competition, which included women from 10 nations, kicked off with a grand ceremony that included the release of thousands of pigeons.

Those Olympics were successful enough to irritate the IOC and the International Amateur Athletic Federation (IAAF), which demanded the word "Olympics" be dropped from the official name of the competition. Milliat agreed, providing that the IOC include 10 women's events at the next Olympic Games. In the end, just five women's track and field events were included in the 1928 Amsterdam Games. Women's participation increased in subsequent years and they competed in 22 events at the 2000 Sydney Games—just two less than men did.

Sports Shorts

Kinue Hitomi (1907-1931) was one of the first international stars in women's track and field. The Japanese athlete set many world records, starting with the triple jump in 1924. She won two events at the 1926 Women's Olympics in Gothenburg, Sweden, and finished second in the 800m at the 1928 Olympics in Amsterdam, Holland. At the 1930 Women's World Games (the successor to the Women's Olympics), Hitomi won a gold medal in the long jump, a silver in the triathlon and two bronze, one in the 60m dash and one in discus, and was named the competition's best all-round athlete. She died of tuberculosis the following year at age 24.

Table 7.1: Initiation of Women's Olympic Track and Field Events

Olympics	Event(s)
1928	100m; 4x100m relay; high jump; discus; 800m*
1932	100m hurdles; javelin
1948	200m; long jump; shot put
1964	400m
1972	1500m; 4x400m relay
1984	400m hurdles; marathon; heptathlon
1988	10,000m
1996	5000m; triple jump
2000	20,000m walk; pole vault; hammer throw
Discontinued events:	10,000 walk (1992–1996); 3000m (1984–1992); pentathlon (1964–1980)

*Was then banned until 1960

Hit the Ground Running

Female athletes added drama to the 1928 Amsterdam Games. According to *The Complete Book of the Summer Olympics*, three Canadians (Fanny "Bobbie" Rosenfeld, Ethel Smith and Myrtle Cook) flustered male spectators by hugging and kissing each other for good luck before the 100m.

Sports Shorts

Canadian women were a dominant force at the 1928 Olympics in Amsterdam, Holland. Ethel Catherwood won the gold medal in the high jump while Bobbie Rosenfeld finished second in the 100m, one place ahead of Ethel Smith. These two runners joined Florence Jane Bell and Myrtle Cook on the 4x100m relay team. The women finished first in world-record time.

Jock Talk

"I'd rather gulp poison than try my hand at motion pictures."

—Canadian runner Ethel Catherwood, when asked if she would head to Hollywood after winning a gold medal at the 1928 Olympics in Amsterdam, Holland. The beautiful athlete was known as "The Saskatoon Lily."

And if that wasn't enough, some female runners collapsed at the end of the 800m run. True, men had been collapsing after races for generations, but that didn't matter to the reporters who filed sensational accounts of wild-eyed women gasping for air as they crossed the finish line. These reports sparked an international debate over the inclusion of women in the Olympics. Even the Pope argued that women were too frail to undertake such endeavours. In the end, women were not excluded from the Games entirely, but they were forbidden to run the 800m for the next 32 years.

I've Got You, Babe

While a debate over athletic competition for women raged among educators—some claimed it was beneficial and perfectly normal whereas others insisted it was a health hazard and even worse, unfeminine—working women were competing in industrial leagues established by companies to promote business and to boost their employees' morale. These competitions produced the earliest stars in many women's sports, including track and field.

First among them was Mildred "Babe" Didrikson (1913–1956), who displayed a knack for track when she raced streetcars for fun as a schoolgirl. In fact, she excelled at several sports and first pursued her passion for basketball, moving to Dallas to compete for an insurance company. After her first season, her employer encouraged her to take up track and field.

At the 1932 AAU track and field championships, Didrikson competed as a one-woman team representing her company and won six of the eight events she entered. She set

Jock Talk

"I am fed up to the ears with women as track and field competitors. Their charms sink to less than zero."

—Avery Bundage, who served as President of the AAU and later the IOC, in 1936, in *Nike is a Goddess*. Bundage was likely referring to the brash demeanour of Olympian Babe Didrikson, whom many people deemed "too masculine."

world records in the hurdles and javelin, and shared a new high jump world record with American Jean Shiley (b. 1911). Didrikson accumulated 30 points on her own, 8 more than the combined total of the 22 members of the second place team.

Jock Talk

"I could have won a medal in five events if they let me."

—American Babe Didrikson after winning medals in the only three events she was allowed to enter at the 1932 Olympics in Los Angeles, CA.

Due to a rule change, Didrikson could only enter three events at the 1932 Los Angeles Games. She chose the javelin throw, the 80m hurdles and the high jump. She won gold in the first two events (setting a world record in the hurdles), and won silver in the third. In fact, Didrikson and Shiley tied for first in the high jump, setting a world record in the process, but officials relegated Didrikson to second place because she had been using a technique in which her head cleared the bar before the rest of her body. The jump was illegal for women at the time, though not for men.

Didrikson was often called the "Texas Tornado" and her stellar accomplishments made her an international name. When the AAU suspended her from future competition for allowing an auto manufacturer to use her photo in an advertisement, Didrikson barnstormed the country with her own basketball team, toured with a men's baseball team and—just to prove she was well-rounded—played in exhibition billiards matches. She also pitched an inning for the Philadelphia Phillies in an exhibition game and then went on to become one of the world's top female golfers.

Sports Shorts

American Helen Stephens (1918–1994) defeated Stella Walsh (1911–1980) in the 100m at the 1936 Olympics in Berlin, Germany. Her victory was so shocking an upset, the Polish press requested confirmation of Stephens's gender (Walsh was competing for her native Poland after winning dozens of U.S. national titles). Stephens passed the test, but it was actually Walsh who had something to hide. An autopsy performed on her after she was murdered in 1980 revealed she had small male sex organs and no female sex organs at all.

Dutch Treat

Dutchwoman Fanny Blankers-Koen (b. 1918) didn't win a medal at the 1936 Olympics in Berlin, Germany, but her coach forgave her. In fact, he married her! The Olympics weren't held during World War II, so Blankers-Koen had to bide her time until the 1948 Olympics in London, England to pursue another chance at a medal.

By then she was a 30-year-old mother. In the months leading up to the event, she was dismissed as too old to compete and was chided for neglecting her son and daughter. Her husband assured critics that the athlete was "a real housewife" with an aptitude for cooking and cleaning.

Q & A

Q: The fourth place finisher in the women's high jump at the 1936 Olympics in Berlin, Germany was barred from competition two years later. Why?

A: Dora Ratjen was a hermaphrodite. In 1957, the German revealed that her name was really Herman and Nazi officials had commanded her to take part in the 1936 competition.

Jock Talk

"[Adolf] Hitler comes in and gives me the Nazi salute. I gave him a good old Missouri handshake. Immediately, Hitler gets a hold of my fanny, and he begins to squeeze and pinch and hug me up and he said, 'You're a true Aryan type. You should be running for Germany.' So after he gave me the once-over and a full massage, he asked me if I'd like to spend the weekend in Berchtesgaden."

—American runner Helen Stephens, describing her encounter with the German dictator after she won the 100m at the 1936 Olympics in Berlin, Germany, in *The Complete Book of the Summer Olympics*. Stephens turned down *Der Fuhrer*.

Q & A

Q: France's Micheline Ostermeyer finished first in the discus and shot put and third in the high jump at the 1948 Olympics in London, England. Her success jeopardized her job. What was it?

A: She was a concert pianist. When she returned to France after the Games, critics deemed her performances "too sporty." But she soldiered on. She performed in Lebanon after moving there with her husband, and a decade later she ended up teaching music at a conservatory outside of Paris.

Blankers-Koen shrugged off the criticism and went to work, winning four gold medals in London (80m hurdles, 100m, 200m and 4x100m relay) and establishing herself as one of the greatest female athletes in history. Her exploits were celebrated in the press. The headline in the *London Daily Graphic* read: "Fastest Woman in the World Is an Expert Cook."

Let Me Explain

A shot put is a metal ball that a competitor throws as far as possible into a marked field. The one who throws it furthest, wins.

Black Celebration

It's incredible that American Wilma Rudolph (1940–1994) ever managed to walk, let alone run. Rudolph was a sickly toddler who almost died from pneumonia and scarlet fever. A bout with polio forced her to walk with braces, but Rudolph underwent intense therapy and soon managed to walk unassisted.

She excelled in basketball—her high school coach called her "Skeeter" because she buzzed around the court like a mosquito—and also took up track. She was outstanding in cleats and went to the 1956 Olympics in Melbourne, Australia. She returned home with a bronze medal from the 4x100m relay.

Viewers around the world watched flickering images of the tall (5-foot-11) black athlete clinching three gold medals (100m, 200m and 4x100m relay) and breaking one world record (200m) at the 1960 Olympics in Rome, Italy; she became an instant celebrity.

Following a competition in Germany, fans stole her shoes and beat on the sides of the team bus until she waved to them. And you thought only Elvis and the Beatles inspired such devotion! American blacks, who had started to push for civil rights, also embraced the Black Gazelle (as she was dubbed by the European press). An activist as well as an athlete, Rudolph joined them routinely for sit-ins at whites-only restaurants.

Communism's Daughters

The Soviet Bloc's big red sports machine was firing on all cylinders by the mid-1970s, producing some top Olympians:

➤ Irena Kirszenstein Szewinska (b. 1946) represented Poland in five Olympic Games between 1964 and 1980, winning three gold (200m, 400m and 4x100m relay), two silver (200m and long jump) and two bronze (100m and 200m). She broke six world records and was the first woman to break the 50-second barrier in the 400m.

➤ Romanian high jumper Iolanda Balas (b. 1936) rose to prominence in the mid-1950s and went unbeaten for an entire decade, making opponents look as nimble as pregnant oxen. Balas became the first woman to jump 6 feet and she set 14 world records. She won gold medals at the 1960 Rome Games and the 1964 Olympics in Tokyo, Japan. Many of her competitors complained they had no chance against her because she was so tall (6-foot-1) and had incredibly long legs.

➤ The Soviet Union's Tatyana Kazankina (b. 1951) dominated middle distance events. She won two gold medals (800m and 1500m) at the 1976 Montréal Games, and one in the 1500m at the 1980 Olympics in Moscow, USSR.

Drugs in my Pocket

The phenomenal success of these athletes was sometimes tainted by allegations of drug use. Soviet Bloc states viewed the Olympics as a political forum in which to express their might and young athletes were recruited, trained and often given performance-enhancing drugs in the pursuit of gold medals.

The IOC banned doping in 1967 and athletes have been tested for performance-enhancing drugs ever since. But as scientists have developed new tests, athletes have developed new ways to avoid detection, and allegations of drug use continue to cast a pall over track and field. Nonetheless, the collapse of Communism in Eastern Europe "has helped level the playing field in women's track and field," says Jon Hendershott, associate editor of *Track & Field News*. "Overall, the level of performances have dropped but results are more realistic now, in keeping with natural progression."

Life in the Fast Lane

As Soviet Bloc dominance ebbed in the 1980s, American sprinters climbed to the top of the medal podium:

➤ Evelyn Ashford (b. 1957) finished fifth in the 100m at the 1976 Montréal Games, but hit her stride eight years later when she won a gold medal in the 100m at the 1984 Olympics in Los Angeles, CA, setting a world record in the event. As Ashford neared her thirtieth birthday in 1987, observers wondered if she was about to retire. "Oh no," she insisted, "I'm going to run until these legs fall off." She went on to finish second in the 100m at the 1988 Seoul Games. Ashford also won gold in the 4x100m relay at the Los Angeles Games, the Seoul Games and at the 1992 Olympics in Barcelona, Spain. She is now retired and has both her legs.

➤ Valerie Brisco Hooks (b. 1960) was a college track star when she married NFL player Alvin Hooks in 1981. After giving birth to their son a year later, she was 40 pounds overweight. But she embarked on an intense training regimen for the first time in her life and returned to top form in time for the 1984 Los Angeles Games. There, she became the first athlete ever to win both the 200m and 400m events at one Olympics.

➤ Gail Devers (b. 1966) advanced to the semifinals of the 100m hurdles at the 1988 Seoul Games even though she had been suffering from migraine headaches, sleeplessness and fainting spells. Her health continued to deteriorate and in 1990 she was diagnosed with Graves' disease, a thyroid disorder. Devers underwent radiation treatment and suffered horrible side effects, including infected and swollen feet. Doctors considered amputating her feet, but didn't—which was fortunate because she put them to good use. She returned to competition after sitting out two-and-a-half years and captured gold in the 100m at the 1992 Barcelona Games. She won the same event at the 1996 Atlanta Games, where she added another gold in the 4x100m relay.

Jock Talk

"I like to run like a man. I don't like to look like a man."

—American sprinter Florence Griffith Joyner, whose candy-coloured running tights and long, painted nails made as big an impression as her blazing speed.

Q & A

Q: Florence Griffith Joyner was thrown out of a mall when she was young. Why?

A: She strolled through the food court with a pet boa constrictor around her neck.

Colourful World

Of all the American sprinters who dominated in the 1980s, Florence Griffith Joyner (1959–1998) made the biggest impact, bursting onto the scene sporting one-legged running tights and six-inch fingernails. But she was more than a fashion icon. She was lightning fast.

"Flo Jo" won silver in the 200m at the 1984 Los Angeles Games. Then, four years later at the Seoul Games, she captured three gold (100m, 200m and 4x100m relay) and a silver (4x400m relay). In her ascent to the top she set two world records, in the 100m and 200m. Both records still stand.

Her incredible performances raised allegations of drug use and it didn't help that she had taken training tips from Canada's Ben Johnson, who was stripped of his gold medal in Seoul when he tested positive for anabolic steroids. Suspicion was heightened when she retired just before random drug testing was made mandatory in 1989. The world will never know definitively if this athlete's amazing accomplishments were aided by drug use. Griffith Joyner died in her sleep one night in 1998; an autopsy revealed she had suffered a seizure.

Nonetheless, Flo Jo's contribution to women's sports is undeniable. "She wore one-legged unitards and lace attachments when other women wore shorts, melding athleticism and glamour like no one else," said Tim Layden in *Sports Illustrated for Women*. Added Jon Hendershott: "Flo Jo changed public perception of female athletes. She made sweating glamorous."

The Wonder Years

While Flo Jo left competitors breathless at the finish line, her sister-in-law was recording jaw-dropping performances in the heptathlon, establishing herself as one of the best all-round athletes in track and field history.

Jackie Joyner-Kersee (b. 1962) ditched dancing when she discovered the joys of leaping off her front porch into a makeshift long jump pit. Within a decade she had climbed to the top of the track and field world. She won six medals over four Olympics from 1984 to 1996, including two gold and a silver in the heptathlon and a gold and two bronze in the long jump. At the 1988 Seoul Games, she set a world record (7291 points) in the heptathlon that still stands.

Let Me Explain

The heptathlon includes seven events contested over two days. On the first day, athletes compete in the 100m hurdles, high jump, shot put and 200m. The second day features the long jump, javelin and 800m.

The 1996 Atlanta Games saw her final and most dramatic Olympic appearance. Joyner-Kersee withdrew from the heptathlon with an injured thigh, but returned six days later to compete in the long jump. Languishing in sixth place as the competition wound down, the ailing athlete managed a decent final jump and limped away with the bronze medal.

Jock Talk

"Jackie Joyner-Kersee did for the heptathlon what Bruce Jenner did for the decathlon, taking an oddball mix of events and not only elevating them to great sport but also infusing them with high personal drama."

—*Sports Illustrated for Women.*

Sports Shorts

American Mary Decker Slaney (b. 1958) was a running prodigy who won her first international competition when she was 11 years old, and then set numerous world records at long distance events. She is best remembered for her showdown with Zola Budd (b. 1966), a native South African who got a British passport so she could compete internationally (South African athletes had been barred by the International Amateur Athletic Federation [IAAF] because of their government's apartheid policy). Midway through the 3000m race at the 1984 Olympics in Los Angeles, CA, the two women collided. Decker Slaney stumbled off the track, injuring a hip muscle. Budd, who was running barefoot, lost her composure and finished seventh. Decker Slaney blamed Budd for the collision. After the race, when the younger woman expressed regret over what had happened Decker Slaney responded, "Don't bother. I don't want to talk to you." Both went on to other triumphs, but neither has ever won an Olympic event.

Golden Girl

As Joyner-Kersee limped off the international stage, another American leapt into the spotlight. Marion Jones (b. 1975) won several junior national sprint titles as a high school student and was dubbed "the greatest sprint talent ever" by *Sports Illustrated*. She was equally passionate about basketball, however, and competed in both sports in university.

Jones focused on track after graduation and blazed a path to the 2000 Sydney Games, where she aimed to become the first woman to win five track and field gold medals at a single Olympics. "I'm going to run fast and jump far. All my preparation is pointed at that moment on October 1 when the Games are over and I have the satisfaction of having won all I've entered," she told *Newsweek*.

In the end, Jones won three gold (100m, 200m and 4x400m relay) and two bronze (4x100m relay and long jump) and promised to be back for more.

Up From Down Under

Jones might have been the biggest name on the track in the summer of 2000, but she wasn't the only woman in the spotlight. In the months leading up to the Sydney Games, international media focused on Australian runner Cathy Freeman (b. 1973), the reigning world champion in the 400m. Journalists anticipated her pending showdown with two-time Olympic champion Marie-José Perec (b. 1968) of France and, ever mindful of the human interest angle, emphasized Freeman's aboriginal background. The plot thickened when Perec fled Australia before the race, insisting that a stalker had threatened her at her hotel. Soon after, Perec posted a comment on her Web site: "The Games have hardly begun and already I wish they would end because I'm so scared—I get the impression everything is fabricated to destabilize me."

Observers noted that hotel security cameras didn't support Perec's story and accused her of running scared. Freeman kept her mouth closed and let her legs do the talking. She won the 400m before a crowd of 110,000 inside Stadium Australia. And then, just for good measure, she took on Marion Jones in the 200m. Freeman finished seventh, but before she crossed the finish line she had already secured her place as one of the brightest lights in Sydney.

Money (That's What I Want)

Jones and other top athletes have far more career options than their predecessors did. Over the last 10 years, track and field has become a true vocation. Top runners, jumpers and throwers can now earn a living through endorsements, government stipends and competitions like the Golden League.

In 1998, the IAAF launched this League, unifying the elite individual competitions held in Europe. The league consists of seven meets.

Table 7.2: Initiation of Major Worldwide Competitions

Event	Men	Women
Olympics	1896	1928
World Championships	1983	1983

The Least You Need to Know

➤ Ancient Greeks worshipped athletic goddesses, but had mixed feelings about active women.

➤ Running could be fun or frightening for women in the Middle Ages.

➤ Feminist and activist Alice Milliat was the first star of women's track and field.

➤ Babe Didrikson carved herself a niche as one of the best athletes in history, in large part due to her success in track and field.

➤ Fanny Blankers-Koen proved women could cook, clean, raise kids and *still* run like the wind.

➤ Wilma Rudolph's success inspired the American black community.

➤ Soviet Bloc countries used their female athletes as propaganda tools and made performance-enhancing drugs a front page story.

➤ Flo Jo won top billing in a great American show.

Chapter 8

Take the Long Way Home: Distance Running and Triathlon

In This Chapter

➤ A Greek legend inspires the creation of the marathon

➤ Women distance runners play hide-and-go-seek with race officials

➤ Female runners get organized

➤ The world's best female marathoners win medals at the 1984 Los Angeles Games

➤ African and Asian marathoners gain on Europeans and North Americans

➤ Women show steely reserve by testing themselves in the Ironman

➤ The Ironman triathlon produces its first crop of female stars, as do smaller triathlons

---

To women who compete in marathons and triathlons today, Kathy Switzer's ordeal seems as ancient as the gramophone. But just over three decades ago, the American entered the Boston Marathon as K. Switzer and ended up in a mid-race confrontation with an irate official. Despite his efforts to thwart her participation, Switzer finished the marathon and became an inspiration to a generation of female distance runners.

Drop Dead

When Phidippides (also noted as "Philippides" in some sources) completed a 24.2-mile (39km) run from the battlefield of Marathon to Athens in 490 BC, he could not have predicted the impact his feat would have on the future of sport. Nor could he have

Sports Shorts

Ancient messenger Phidippides has been immortalized by generations of poets and writers. But some modern scholars claim there has been a misunderstanding and insist Phidippides did not run 24.2 miles (39km) bearing news of victory from the battlefield of Marathon. For example, Charlie Lovett, author of *Olympic Marathon: A Centennial History of the Games' Most Storied Race*, claims the Athenians sent Phidippides to Sparta to enlist the city-state's help when the Persian army landed at Marathon. While he was away, the impatient Athenians attacked the Persians and emerged victorious. Lovett notes that historians writing around the time of the battle make no reference to the fabled run from the battlefield to Athens. Furthermore, if such a run did take place, Lovett is convinced the messenger was not Phidippides: "It is highly unlikely he would have made such a run after having just run to Sparta. If he had, contemporary historians would surely have noted it."

taken another step. The exhausted messenger announced, "Rejoice, we conquer," then dropped dead. It was an unfortunate event for his family and friends, but not for the successive generations of writers who drew inspiration from the legend of his feat.

Phidippides's saga also fascinated French historian and linguist Michel Bréal. In 1894, at a meeting on the revival of the Olympic Games, Bréal lobbied for the inclusion of a long distance footrace to commemorate Phidippides's heroics. Sure enough, the marathon was the centrepiece of the 1896 Olympics in Athens, Greece. Competitors ran the same route Phidippides had completed centuries before. The event captivated a group of American athletes, who held a similar race in their hometown the following year—the Boston Marathon has been an annual event ever since.

The marathon's official distance was extended to 26.2 miles (42.2km) at the 1908 Olympics in London, England because it was the exact distance from Windsor Castle to the royal box at White City Stadium.

In the following decades, several athletes would distinguish themselves in the marathon. None of them, however, were female. Women were banned from the event because they were considered too frail to run long distances. It was thought the strain could kill them or, worse, render them unable to bear children.

Sports Shorts

Women weren't allowed to compete in the first modern Olympics in Athens, Greece. But that didn't stop at least two from running the marathon. According to Charlie Lovett in *Olympic Marathon: A Centennial History of the Games' Most Storied Race*, Stamatis Rovithi became the first woman to run a marathon when she covered the proposed Olympic course from Marathon to Athens in March of 1896. Lovett also notes that a local woman named Melpomene tried to sign up for the event, but was turned down by organizers. But she would not be denied. She ran beside the course while the race was in progress. She fell behind but then, after stopping for a glass of water, started overtaking runners who dropped out of the competition exhausted. Melpomene finished the race about an hour and a half after the winner, but wasn't allowed to enter the stadium. She ran her final lap around the outside of the building. Her final time was approximately four-and-a-half hours.

Sneak Preview

Women got a little cheeky in the 1960s, burning their bras and demanding more rights. When officials refused to allow her to compete in the 1966 Boston Marathon, American Roberta Gibb ducked behind some bushes near the start line and then snuck into the race. She finished in 3 hours, 21 minutes and 25 seconds, but was disqualified.

Compatriot Kathy Switzer (b. 1947) entered the 1967 Boston Marathon as the gender neutral "K. Switzer." Organizers didn't realize they had allowed a woman in the race until it was well underway. An official lunged at her shouting "Get the hell out of my race!" but Switzer's boyfriend ran interference and she finished in 4 hours and 20 minutes. The following day, newspapers worldwide ran photos of the incident. It became a hot topic and was adopted by the feminist movement as a symbol of the injustice suffered by women. Activists agreed with Switzer that it was "time to change the rules."

Run to the Sun

In 1972, one year after Australian Adrienne Beames became the first woman to run the marathon in less than three hours, the Boston Marathon began accepting female applicants. Before long, all-women's marathons popped up in Western Europe and

Let Me Explain

Distance running has become incredibly popular over the years, and marathons are held around the world. The Boston Marathon and the New York City Marathon are the most prestigious races, attracting thousands of runners and spectators each year.

North America, and female enthusiasts organized themselves and lobbied for the inclusion of women's long-distance races in international competition.

In the early 1980s, the IAAF, the governing body for track and field, started including women's marathons at major competitions, including the new world championships, and recommended to the IOC that a women's marathon be included in the Olympics.

Leaders of the Pack

Sure enough, the women's marathon was included at the 1984 Los Angeles Games. The top three finishers just happened to be the era's brightest stars:

➤ American Joan Benoit (b. 1957) was passionate about skiing. But after breaking her leg on the slopes, she started a rehabilitation program that included running and never looked back. She won the Boston Marathon in 1979 and underwent foot surgery two years later. Benoit was back on her feet in time for the 1983 Boston Marathon, which she won in world-record time. She returned to hospital the next year for arthroscopic knee surgery. Few people expected her to compete in the U.S. trials let alone the Olympics, but she prevailed. In Los Angeles, she took the lead early in the race and never let up. She ended up winning the historic event.

➤ Norwegian Grete Waitz (b. 1953) excelled at middle distances as a teen and won several national titles. She ran the 1500m at the 1972 Olympics in Munich, Germany, and then set a world record in the 3000m. The grade school teacher entered the New York City Marathon in 1978, and wasn't half bad for someone who had never run a marathon before; she won the race, smashing the world record by two minutes.

Q & A

Q: What did Grete Waitz win aside from numerous marathons and the respect of millions of sports fans?

A: Five cross-country world titles.

Waitz went on to win the event eight more times. She won several other marathons, too, and headed into the 1984 Los Angeles Games undefeated in her previous seven outings. She had a strong finishing kick in Los Angeles but could not catch Benoit and had to settle for silver. By the time she retired in 1991, Waitz had also won a world championship title.

➤ Portugal's Rosa Mota (b. 1960) ran middle distances before taking up the marathon as an experiment. Mota won her first marathon at the 1982 European

Jock Talk

"When I came into the stadium and saw all the colours and everything, I told myself, 'Listen, just look straight ahead, because if you don't, you're probably going to faint.'"

—Marathon runner Joan Benoit, describing her triumph at the 1984 Olympics in Los Angeles, CA.

Sports Shorts

Swiss marathon runner Gabriele Andersen-Scheiss didn't win a medal at the 1984 Olympics in Los Angeles, CA, but she did capture headlines. Fifteen minutes after American Joan Benoit crossed the finish line to win gold, Andersen-Scheiss entered the stadium. "The crowd gasped in horror as [she] staggered onto the track, her torso twisted, her right arm straight and her left arm limp, her right knee strangely stiff," wrote Charles Lovett, author of *Olympic Marathon: A Centennial History of the Games' Most Storied Race*. Suffering from heat exhaustion, the runner turned away medical personnel who rushed to her aid. "For nearly six minutes [she] hobbled around the track, occasionally stopping and holding her head. She collapsed over the finish line in 37th place, into the arms of waiting medics." They released her two hours later, and she returned to the Olympic Village for something to eat. Two weeks later, Andersen-Scheiss finished fifth in a competition that required her to run 20 miles and ride a horse for another 18.

championships, and finished third at the Los Angeles Games. She soon rose to the top of the marathon world, winning races by large margins. Mota was exceptionally popular in her homeland. Her compatriots expected her to win a medal at the 1988 Seoul Games, and she didn't disappoint them; she became the first Portuguese woman to win Olympic gold. When she returned home, she was greeted by a huge crowd that included the country's head of state. Mota also won a world championship title and three Boston Marathons.

It's Too Darn Hot

Though a handful of women dominated international competition in the 1970s and 1980s, the playing field levelled out as more women got involved in subsequent years. African and Asian runners began to make their mark.

Q & A

Q: What is the difference in times for male and female marathon runners?

A: In general, the best men's times are about 2 hours and 7 minutes, 13 minutes faster than the best women's times.

Japan's Naoko Takahashi (b. 1972) started running track in junior high school and then switched to the marathon. Less than two years later, she was victorious at the 1998 Asian Games, finishing 13 minutes ahead of the second place runner in blazing heat and 90 percent humidity. Her time was just one minute short of the world record held by Kenya's Tegla Laroupe.

The weather was better for the marathon at the 2000 Sydney Games in Australia, where Takahashi broke Benoit's 16-year-old Games record. When she woke up the next morning, she put on her running shoes and hit the road. "I went to bed at 3:30 in the morning. When I woke, I felt like running and I did," she told Agence France-Presse. "I tried to run by myself without my coach as he was drunk."

Running alone was an adequate challenge for Takahashi and her rivals, but other women needed variety to get their competitive fires burning...

Table 8.1: Initiation of Major Worldwide Marathon Competitions

Event	Men	Women
Olympics	1896	1984
World Championship	1983	1983
Boston Marathon	1897	1972
New York City Marathon	1970	1970

Triple Threat

Many people were cycling in the 1970s, but the sport didn't have much of a following. Some California-based bicycle clubs tackled the problem by combining road races with other sports, most often swimming and running.

In 1978, an American Naval officer organized the Hawaii Ironman, a combination of three existing events: The Waikiki Rough Water Swim, the Oahu Bicycle Race and the Honolulu Marathon. The event's colourful name and images of toned, bronzed bodies glistening in the Hawaiian sun captured the imagination of sports fans and put triathlon on the map. Before long, the Ironman race was standardized to include a 2.4-mile (3.86km) swim, a 112-mile (189km) bike ride and a marathon-length run.

Iron Maidens

More women began entering this annual competition, and one of them unwittingly raised its profile. Thousands of television viewers watched as Julie Moss collapsed exhausted a few metres from the finish line, then crawled on her hands and knees to a second-place finish in 1982.

Refusing to be scared off by Moss's dramatic finish, women were soon competing in triathlons around the world. The sport's first female superstar hailed from Africa. Paula Newby-Fraser (b. 1962) devoted herself to ballet and swimming growing up in South Africa. But she was burnt out by the time she graduated from high school and turned down both a university swimming scholarship and an invitation to join a dance company. She enrolled at a community college instead, and made up for lost time in her social life. But before long she packed away her disco ball and bottle opener and slipped into a pair of jogging shoes.

Let Me Explain

Ironman triathlons and short-course triathlons—also called Olympic-distance triathlons—are the most widely known. But North American enthusiasts also compete in sprint triathlons. These range in distance, but generally average half the Olympic distance. Serious fitness fanatics strut their stuff in triathlons that are double—or even triple!—the distance of the Ironman.

Let Me Explain

The triathlon is the most popular multi-sport event, but not the only one. The duathlon has also attracted some attention. In the duathlon, competitors run, cycle, and then run again. And for those who love the elements, world championships have also been initiated for the winter triathlon and the aquathlon.

After watching a local qualifier for the Ironman in 1984, Newby-Fraser adopted a fierce training regimen. She finished third in the women's division of the Ironman in 1985. She won the competition the following year and then went on to dominate the event, winning eight Ironmans overall. Over the course of her career, she became the first woman to complete the bicycle course in less than five hours and the first to complete the entire course in less than nine hours.

Several other women trained relentlessly and became Ironman standouts, including New Zealand's Erin Baker (b. 1961), Canadian twins Sylviane and Patricia Puntous (b. 1960) and, later, Lorie Bowden.

Rough and Tumble

Training for this gruelling event while working full time proved too taxing for some fitness fanatics. They organized shorter triathlons, prompting the International Triathlon Union (ITU) to endorse a short-course format when the organization was founded in 1989. The format included a 1.5-km swim, 40-km bike ride and 10-km run. This more manageable triathlon became so popular with both sexes that it was included at the 2000 Sydney Games.

One of the competitors there was three-time world championship medallist Canadian Carol Montgomery (b. 1965), who also excelled in distance track events. She won silver and bronze in the 5000m and 10,000m respectively at the 1995 Pan American Games. But her career took a turn for the worse in 1999 when she started experiencing cramping and swelling in her left leg. Tests revealed a partially blocked artery. Montgomery underwent surgery and then made a remarkable recovery. Within five months she had qualified for Sydney in the triathlon and the 10,000m. "My running came back so fast it was unbelievable," she told *Maclean's* magazine.

Montgomery had anticipated becoming the first Canadian woman to compete in two sports at one Olympics, but it wasn't to be. In the cycling segment of the triathlon, a competitor crashed in front of her. She tumbled off her bike, shattering her helmet as her head hit the pavement. Montgomery emerged with a broken wrist, deep cuts and whiplash. She had been a medal favourite, but was out of contention. Worse, her back was too sore to compete in the 10,000m ten days later.

Switzerland's Brigitte McMahon (b. 1967) was more fortunate in Australia. She won the triathlon just ahead of Australian Michellie Jones (b. 1969), who had already claimed almost every title in the sport, including back-to-back world championships in 1992 and 1993. "It's unbelievable, I just can't express it... just fantastic," McMahon told Reuters. "When I got to that last turn and saw it was just Michellie and me I thought 'first or second, I can't lose,' but then tried to push it as hard as I could." Jones didn't seem too upset about the result; she was tired but exhilarated: "I *love* this sport," she said.

Table 8.2: Initiation of Major Worldwide Triathlon Competitions

Event	Men	Women
Olympics	2000	2000
World Championships	1989	1989
Ironman	1978	1978
ITU World Cup	1991	1991

The Least You Need to Know

➤ Phidippides, the first marathoner, ran himself to death.

➤ Women had to be wily in order to run marathons until the 1970s.

➤ The first women's Olympic marathon was a demonstration of true grit.

➤ Japan boasts one of the current top female marathoners.

➤ The first women to compete in the triathlon didn't drop dead, but some came close.

➤ Some of the world's best women triathletes have been Canadian.

Chapter 9

Let's Have a Ball: Baseball and Softball

In This Chapter

➤ Girls bat the ball around in the Middle Ages

➤ North American women start swinging

➤ Bloomer Girls take on men's baseball teams

➤ Women's professional baseball makes an impact

➤ Softball makes its mark on the Olympic Games

➤ Professionals pull out all the stops

➤ Softball's popularity soars

Few pitchers struck out Babe Ruth and Lou Gehrig in succession, but at least one had the honour and her name was Jackie Mitchell. The woman who threw fireballs past the two baseball greats in 1931 inspired dozens of other women, some of whom later played in the All-American Girls Professional Baseball League. Despite these impressive feats in baseball, females have made more progress in softball, which made its Olympic debut in 1996.

The Games People Play

Modern softball and baseball can trace their roots to stoolball, a bat and ball game played by milkmaids in medieval Europe. That game developed at a fast clip—what's 300 years in the bigger scheme of things?—and by the 1700s Brtish women were throwing balls at stumps in the ground. One of these early cricket games pitted married and single women against each other. It's not known whether the single women won the contest and carried off their opponents' husbands, but keep in mind that old adage about war—to the victor goes the spoils...

Two men named William Matthews and S.B. Lohman recruited almost two dozen women to play professional cricket in 1890. The matches drew thousands of spectators, but the men ran off with the money and left the women penniless.

Take Me Out to the Ball Game

On this side of the Atlantic Ocean, women took up baseball dressed in—what else?— blouses with high necklines and long sleeves and skirts that they had to hold up when they ran. If nothing else, these uniforms helped the players develop strong arms—the skirts weighed almost 30 pounds! Eventually, women took to wearing much more participant-friendly clothing, namely loose-fitting trousers, or bloomers.

Sports Shorts

In an era when major league teams didn't have farm systems, men such Rogers Hornsby—who would later be inducted into the Hall of Fame—honed their skills playing for Bloomer Girls teams. In fact, many of these teams included male players. In the early days, male "toppers"— named for their fake coiffs—took to the field wearing skirts and wigs.

Vassar College in Poughkeepsie, NY had three women's baseball teams by 1875. At Smith College in Northampton, MA, a student named Minnie Stephens had to steal a bat from a group of boys to in order to play. The college later saved female players from lives of crime by providing them with their own equipment.

A few years later, in the 1880s, a man named Harry Freeman tried to establish a professional women's league but his effort failed when it was rumoured he was recruiting attractive young women for prostitution rather than baseball. One girl's father even took him to court. That decade also saw two women's teams, The Blondes and The Brunettes, tour the United States Eastern Seaboard. There was no designated team for redheads.

The Pioneer Life

Women's baseball took a giant leap forward with the barnstorming Bloomer Girls teams, which competed against men in exhibition games for three decades starting in the 1890s. Bloomer Girls teams popped up in towns and cities all over, from Nova Scotia in Eastern Canada to Texas in the Southern United States.

Q & A

Q: What Olympic champion starred on a baseball team in the 1930s?

A: Babe Didrikson, who travelled around the U.S. with Babe Didrikson's All-Americans after winning international acclaim in track and field at the 1932 Olympics in Los Angeles, CA. She also played for a touring team called The House of David that included bearded members of a religious sect, but she soon gave up America's pastime to become one of the world's best female golfers.

Bloomer Girls started out wearing skirts but later competed in short-sleeved tops and—you guessed it!—bloomers. Their "scandalous" dress contributed to their risqué reputation; upstanding young women didn't attend Bloomer Girls' games, let alone join the teams. But women from small towns where opportunities other than manual labour were scarce seemed willing to put up with the derision, and a few made names for themselves. In 1898, Lizzie Arlington made news when she signed a contract with a men's minor league club whose owner thought a female pitcher would attract spectators. But his plan failed and Arlington was sent back to the Bloomer Girls circuit after just one inning.

A few women fared better than Arlington and distinguished themselves playing on men's teams. Lizzie "Spike" Murphy spent most of her two-decade career with a men's professional team that toured through New England and Eastern Canada. In 1922, she became the first woman to play for a major league team in an exhibition game when she took the field at Boston's Fenway Park.

In 1931, the Double-A Chattanooga Lookouts signed Jackie Mitchell who caused quite a stir when she pitched in an exhibition game against the New York Yankees. Mitchell struck out none other than Babe Ruth and then dismissed fellow legend Lou Gehrig in three pitches. Mitchell left the game to a standing ovation from the crowd of over four

Jock Talk

"She uses an odd, side-armed delivery, and puts both speed and curve on the ball. Her greatest asset, however, is control. She can place the ball where she pleases, and her knack at guessing the weakness of a batter is uncanny. She believes that with careful training she may soon be the first woman to pitch in the big leagues."

—*The Chattanooga News,* on Jackie Mitchell.

thousand. Was it a publicity stunt or the real deal? The world will never know. Before you could say "Batter up!" the baseball commissioner voided her contract, insisting that the sport was too strenuous for fair ladies.

All-American Girls

When men left for overseas battlefields during World War II, women replaced them on baseball diamonds at home thanks to Chicago Cubs owner and chewing gum mogul Philip Wrigley. He founded the All-American Girls Professional Baseball League (AAGPBL) in 1943, confident that the team's managers, former players such as the Hall of Fame's Dave Bancroft, Max Carey and Jimmie Foxx, would draw fans to the new league.

Sports Shorts

Canadian Mary Baker (b. 1918) played for the All-American Girls Professional Baseball League's (AAPGBL) South Bend Blue Sox. The former model was often asked to pose for publicity photos and her picture appeared in *Life* magazine. She also appeared on the popular television show *What's My Line?* Baker later returned to Regina, SK and became a radio sportscaster. Some 10 percent of the league's players were Canadian.

Organizers recruited women deemed "wholesome" and "attractive." A pamphlet called on ball players with "looks, deportment and feminine charm." Those selected were sent to charm school and were instructed to pack "beauty kits" and wear makeup. Their social activities had to be authorized. To add painful injury to insult, they competed in skirts that rolled back when they slid. Ouch!

The women of the league started off playing softball, but ended up playing baseball. Pitchers were throwing overhand by the league's sixth season when the league had expanded from four teams to ten and games were attracting two to three thousand fans on average. Some ten thousand people attended a doubleheader in South Bend, IN in 1946.

Sports Shorts

Toni Stone (1921–1996) distinguished herself as baseball's first top black female. Black women were excluded from the All-American Girls Professional Baseball League (AAGPBL), just as black men were excluded from the men's major leagues for generations. But Stone was talented enough to compete in the men's Negro Leagues. She was a solid hitter and over one 50-game stretch she sported a .243 batting average. In 1953, she singled off the legendary Satchel Paige. She retired the following year due to lack of playing time.

The AAGPBL waned in popularity when the war ended. Men returned to the baseball diamond and women, who were no longer needed in the workplace, returned to the kitchen (someone, apparently, had to mash the potatoes!). But the league soldiered on for almost a decade, long enough to produce stars such as Dorothy "Dottie" Kamenshek (b. 1925).

Also known as "Kammie," Kamenshek was the league's first truly big name. When she was 17 years old she travelled from her home in Cincinnati, OH to tryouts in Chicago, IL with the permission of her mother, who was convinced her daughter would be cut. But Kamenshek rebounded from the trauma of having her glove stolen upon her arrival and was among the 60 girls selected from a group of 250. She played first base for the Rockford Peaches and ended her nine-year career with a .292 batting average, one of the best in the league. In 1950, Rockford held a "Kamenshek Night" to honour their star player. According team manager Bill Allington, Kamenshek "had a good cry and three hits."

Q & A

Q: Where was the first day of tryouts for the All–American Girls Professional Baseball League (AAGPBL) held?

A: Under the bleachers at Chicago's Wrigley Field. It was raining and, oddly enough, the stadium didn't have a retractable roof!

AAGPBL Rules of Conduct

Players in the All-American Girls Professional Baseball League (AAGPBL) had to follow rules of conduct. A list of these rules appears on the league Web site—and below— courtesy of the Northern Indiana Historical Society.

1. ALWAYS appear in feminine attire when not actively engaged in practice or playing ball. This regulation continues through the playoffs for all, even though your team is not participating. AT NO TIME MAY A PLAYER APPEAR IN THE STANDS IN HER UNIFORM, OR WEAR SLACKS OR SHORTS IN PUBLIC.

2. Boyish bobs are not permissible and in general your hair should be well groomed at all times with longer hair preferable to short hair cuts. Lipstick should always be on.

3. Smoking or drinking is not permissable in public places. Liquor drinking will not be permissable under any circumstances. Other intoxicating drinks in limited portions with after-game meal only, will be allowed. Obscene language will not be allowed at any time.

4. All social engagements must be approved by chaperone. Legitimate requests for dates can be allowed by chaperones.

5. Jewelry must not be worn during game or practice, regardless of type.

6. All living quarters and eating places must be approved by the chaperones. No player shall change her residence without the permission of the chaperone.

7. For emergency purposes, it is necessary that you leave notice of your whereabouts and your home phone.

8. Each club will establish a satisfactory place to eat, and a time when all members must be in their individual rooms. In general, the lapse of time will be two hours

after the finish of the last game, but in no case later than 12:30 a.m. Players must respect hotel regulations as to other guests after this hour, maintaining conduct in accordance with high standards set by the league.

9. Always carry your employee's pass as a means of identification for entering the various parks. This pass is NOT transferable.

10. Relatives, friends, and visitors are not allowed on the bench at anytime.

11. Due to shortage of equipment, baseballs must not be given as souvenirs without permission from the Management.

12. Baseball uniform skirts shall not be shorter than six inches above the knee-cap.

13. In order to sustain the complete spirit of rivalry between clubs, the members of different clubs must not fraternize at any time during the season. After the opening day of the season, fraternizing will be subject to heavy penalties. This also means in particular: room parties, auto trips to out of the way eating places, etc. However, friendly discussions in lobbies with opposing players are permissable. Players should never approach the opposing manager or chaperone about being transferred.

14. When traveling, the members of the clubs must be at the station thirty minutes before departure time. Anyone missing her arranged transportation will have to pay her own fair.

15. Players will not be allowed to drive their cars past their city's limits without the special permission of their manager. Each team will travel as a unit via method of travel provided for the league.

Soft Touch

When the AAGPBL folded in 1954, the emphasis shifted to fastpitch softball, which had grown in popularity since it was developed a half century earlier by male ball players who wanted to hone their skills in the winter. They played the game indoors, but it soon moved outside where it was played recreationally across Canada and the United States.

The game was promoted as a safer alternative to baseball, and women's leagues sprouted up across the continent. In fact, some sports historians claim the game's former name, "Kitten Ball," was inspired by its many female participants. Women's softball spread in other lands, too. Australia won the first women's world championship in 1965. The event was staged by the International Softball Federation, which became active that year.

Let Me Explain

Softball and baseball are very similar games but in softball there are fewer innings, bigger balls, aluminum bats and shorter fields.

Sports Shorts

Baseball has been eclipsed in popularity by softball but it hasn't disappeared altogether. In 1984, a man named Bob Hope—no, not *that* Bob Hope—tried to create a women's team to compete in the Class-A Florida State League, but his bid was turned down. Ten years later he tried again, and thanks to a cash injection from the Coors brewing company, the Colorado Silver Bullets began play in 1994 with Hall of Fame pitcher Phil Niekro as manager. Three years later, Coors ended its sponsorship and the team folded. Nonetheless, there are several women's baseball leagues in operation today. Among them is the American Women's Baseball League, which was founded in 1992 and includes 600 players.

In 1976, former golfer Jane Blaylock and tennis great Billie Jean King teamed up with softball ace Joan Joyce to establish the International Women's Professional Softball Association (IWPSA). The league included ten teams from cities across the United States, but folded four years later due in part to lack of funds.

Q & A

Q: Why did Dot Richardson turn down an offer to play little league baseball when she was 10 years old?

A: The coach suggested she cut her hair short and adopt the name "Bob."

It's a Competitive World

Females had already been playing softball competitively for decades, at both the youth and collegiate levels, when it was included at the 1996 Atlanta Games. The United States dominated the tournament, winning its first five games before losing to Australia in the preliminary round robin.

In that game, American Dani Tyler (b. 1974) hit a homer in the fifth inning and was so ecstatic that she forgot to touch home plate and was called out. Nonetheless, her team went ahead 1–0 on an unearned run and received a stellar performance from star pitcher Lisa Fernandez (b. 1971), who retired 29 batters in a row and was just one strike away from a perfect game when Australia's Joanne Brown hit a homer. She and a teammate (who had started the inning on second base in accordance with softball rules) crossed home plate, giving the Australians a 2–1 victory.

The Americans had the last laugh, however, winning the tournament while the Aussies finished third. The Chinese team finished second after losing 3–1 to the United States in the gold medal game. U.S. team captain Dorothy "Dot" Richardson (b. 1961) deserved much of the credit for that win, hitting the game-winning homer. She had taken a one-year leave from her orthopaedic surgery residency at the University of Southern California (USC) to compete in Atlanta. Three days after winning gold, she was back in her hospital greens.

Up and Down Under

Richardson was also on the team that competed at the 2000 Sydney Games. Richardson didn't dominate in the Australian tournament and—amazing but true!—neither did her team. Instead, it flirted with disaster.

The Americans arrived in Australia boasting an incredible 112-game winning streak but then shocked the sports world by losing three straight games in the first round. Alarmed, the players searched for answers to their difficulties on the playing field and even engaged in some lighthearted "voodoo cleansing" in the shower.

Sports Shorts

At the 2000 Olympics in Sydney, Australia, Hayley Wickenheiser became the second Canadian woman to compete in both Summer and Winter Olympics. She won a silver medal with the Canadian hockey team at the 1998 Olympics in Nagano, Japan. In addition to her hockey skills, the Saskatchewan native is also good with a softball. She took up the sport as a seven-year-old because "there was nothing else to do in the summer on the Prairies," she told *Softball Canada*. The Canadians finished eighth in Sydney.

Having given the evil spirits the heave-ho, the Americans returned to form and advanced to the medal round. There they avenged their first-round losses, beating China and Australia and then toppling Japan 2–1 in the final. The Americans won gold, one spot ahead of Japan and two ahead of their Aussie hosts.

Now and For Always

The success of women's softball contributed to the popularity of the Women's Professional Softball League (WPSL), which was launched in 1997 thanks to the efforts of former college player Jane Cowles. Eight years earlier, she had pitched the idea to her parents, owners of the Cowles Media Company, who agreed to provide financial backing for the league. The WPSL includes four teams in the United States.

Odds are there will be no shortage of players to fill the league's rosters. Some 22.5 million females play softball worldwide, comprising 60 percent of the total number of players, many of whom are excellent. "The calibre of play is much better today," says Mike Trudeau, editor of *National Fastpitch* magazine. "The players are stronger." He attributes the higher skill level to the age at which females start the game. "It used to be that girls took up softball when they were 14 or 15 years old. Now they are already playing T-ball by the time they are five or six."

Table 9.1: Initiation of Major Worldwide Softball Competitions

Event	Men	Women
Olympics	n/a	1996
World Championships	1966	1965

The Least You Need to Know

➤ Girls were playing bat and ball games when Chaucer wrote *The Canterbury Tales*.

➤ The Bloomer Girls circuit produced several top-notch players.

➤ Women's baseball drew thousands of fans in the 1940s and 1950s.

➤ Olympic softball has produced some star players.

➤ Women now play softball professionally.

➤ Some 60 percent of the world's softball players are female.

Chapter 10

Get Your Kicks: Soccer

> ## In This Chapter
>
> ➤ Women kick the ball around just for fun
>
> ➤ Women's soccer soars to new heights in Britain
>
> ➤ Suburban girls put on their cleats and the game takes off
>
> ➤ Women play competitively in universities and colleges
>
> ➤ Women's competitive soccer steps onto the world stage
>
> ➤ The game produces a handful of stars and a household name
>
> ➤ Women's professional soccer gains momentum

British women had a ball playing soccer in the 1920s and one team even travelled to the United States, taking on some top men's squads. But the English Football Association forced these Dick, Kerr Ladies into a hasty retreat and women's soccer all but disappeared. It surfaced again in the 1970s, surging through North American suburbs, and is now played at the sport's highest level. When American Brandi Chastain ripped off her shirt in jubilation after scoring the winning goal in the 1999 World Cup final, she made women's soccer headline news—and sent sales of sports bras through the roof.

Q & A

Q: A piece of ancient artwork depicts women dressed in elegant silks, sweating like wildebeests while kicking a ball. Where is this artifact from?

A: China.

Fun and Games

People have been kicking balls around since the beginning of time, from North America to the Far East. Indeed, soldiers played soccer to prepare for battle in Ancient Greece and Rome.

In the Middle Ages, French and British women celebrated Shrove Tuesday with vigorous games of folk football, a forerunner of soccer. They played with men or on their own, often in matches that saw single and married women facing off against each other.

In England, women took up soccer at school in the late 1800s. When the game was introduced to female students at Girton College, Cambridge, school founder Emily Davies commented that "it would certainly shock the world if it were known," according to *The Women's Sports Encyclopedia*.

North American educators favoured basketball for their female students. Soccer was deemed a health risk to women as it was thought to cause sterility. Furthermore, it was identified with the working class men who had taken up the sport in increasing numbers.

The Battle of Britain

When British men left for foreign lands during the World War I, women replaced them in the factories at home. Just as the men had, the women worked long, hard hours and blew off steam by kicking a ball around during breaks. Women at an English weapons plant called the Dick, Kerr Company organized a team in 1917 and played a match before 10,000 spectators; the proceeds went to help wounded soldiers at the front. Soon women's teams were competing against each other in sold out matches across the country and women's soccer continued to soar in popularity after the war. In 1920, the Dick, Kerr Ladies played to a packed stadium of 53,000 in Everton, England; an additional 10,000 fans were turned away due to lack of space.

The following year the team set sail for North America. The players arrived in Québec to find all their Canadian games had been cancelled by the Dominion of Canada Football Association (now the Canadian Soccer Association [CSA]) and were told they would have to play men's teams in the United States because none of the women's teams were good enough. As it turns out, many of the men's teams weren't good enough, either. The Dick, Kerr Ladies won three matches and tied another three in a nine-game swing through the United States Eastern Seaboard. Rival teams boasting professional and semi-professional players still couldn't beat these ladies.

Despite this success, a storm was brewing back home in England. The English Football Association (FA) banned women's soccer from its playing fields in 1921. Male players, trainers and referees faced suspension if they were caught aiding and abetting women in their soccer pursuits. FA officials claimed that not enough of the gate at women's matches had gone to charity, an allegation which the players could not disprove since they had not managed the finances (that task had been left to a handful of men). FA officials also marched out a line of doctors who insisted that soccer could harm women's reproductive organs or lead to nervous disorders. The FA concluded that soccer was "quite unsuitable for females and ought not to be encouraged."

Skeptical historians note that the Dick, Kerr Ladies were drawing bigger crowds than men at the time and conclude that FA officials had acted out of self interest, trying to preserve what was left of men's soccer. From then on, the Dick, Kerr Ladies played far less often and only on unsanctioned fields. Crowd attendance dropped dramatically. In the end, the ban snuffed out women's soccer in Britain and wasn't revoked until 1969.

Jock Talk

"From what I saw [soccer] is no more likely to cause injuries to women than a heavy day's washing."

—British doctor Mary Lowry, whose opinion clashed with that of the FA in 1922, on the *Soccer Girls* Web site.

Suburban Life

In North America, soccer was included in school field days and as an intramural sport at elite colleges, but it was deemed too masculine for women to take seriously. That perception started to change in the 1950s and 1960s as countless families followed the scent of freshly cut grass to new homes in the suburbs. The wide open spaces there invited activity, and since cattle herding had fallen out of fashion, people started kicking a ball around. Within a few years soccer had evolved from a sport for working class men to one for young people of both sexes, who competed in leagues and at school.

After School Special

Many post-secondary schools started women's soccer clubs. Then, while their friends shopped for platform shoes and practised disco dance steps, a few women started playing soccer competitively. Women at Brown University in Rhode Island took the initiative, challenging club teams from across the continent. In 1978, the school won thirteen games and lost just one (to a Canadian team from Lake Champlain, QC). The next year it hosted an Ivy League championship and helped organize a regional championship.

Some 50 American universities had varsity women's soccer teams by 1981. They got support from the AIAW and held the first women's soccer national championship that year. The NCAA wrested control of women's soccer the following year and has held the national championships ever since.

That first AIAW title went to the University of North Carolina (UNC), whose coach had been laying the foundations of a dynasty. Anson Dorrance was aggressive in seeking out talent. He organized games against local club teams and recruited their best players. His efforts paid off. The UNC Tar Heels went on to win the national championship in every season but three between 1981 and 1999, becoming one of the great dynasties in the history of U.S. intercollegiate athletics and producing some scratch players, including Canadians Carrie Serwetnyk and Angela Kelly.

World in Motion

While Dorrance was travelling around the United States in search of talent, soccer was becoming the game of choice for women in other parts of the world. Women's competitive teams were popping up in Canada, Italy, Denmark, Sweden and Norway. Germany joined in the fun a few years later, followed by Brazil, Japan, New Zealand and China.

Many countries assembled women's national teams, including the United States, which fielded its first one in 1985. Canada followed a year later. There were 65 national teams worldwide by 1992. (English women, incidentally, have rebounded from the Dick, Kerr setback and now boast the only women's national team in the United Kingdom.)

Q & A

Q: What American television star described the U.S. women's soccer team as "Babe City" during the 1999 World Cup?

A: Talk show host David Letterman.

Quest for the Cup

The Fédération Internationale de Football Association (FIFA), the worldwide governing body of soccer, soon initiated plans to hold the first women's world championship. A dozen teams competed at the women's 1991 World Cup in China, where the American team notched six straight wins, including a 2–1 triumph over Norway in the final. Throughout the tournament, observers raved about three American players—April Heinrichs (b. 1964), Michelle Akers (b. 1966) and Carin Gabarra (b. 1965)—who spearheaded their team's attack. The trio was dubbed the "triple-edged sword."

Norway redeemed itself at the 1995 World Cup in Sweden. The Scandinavian team defeated the United States in the semifinals and then clinched the title with a dramatic

2–0 win over Germany. The competition received modest coverage in North America, but the interest generated by the event paled in comparison to the brouhaha that would surround the next installment.

The 1999 World Cup, which included teams from 16 nations, was a milestone in women's soccer; for three weeks the world was besotted with women in cleats. Almost 79,000 fans attended the opening game at Giants Stadium in New Jersey, cheering wildly as the Americans rolled to a 3–0 win over Denmark.

Q & A

Q: During the 1999 World Cup, American star Mia Hamm appeared in a Gatorade commercial with another top athlete. Who?

A: Basketball legend Michael Jordan. In the ad, the two squared off on a soccer pitch, on a track and in a fencing competition. Both escaped uninjured.

The final game between China and the United States at the Rose Bowl in California attracted a crowd of 90,185, the largest ever at a women's sporting event. Some 40 million viewers tuned into that game, making it the most-watched soccer match in the history of U.S. network television. Party hats and peanuts notwithstanding, the game was a thriller. Neither team scored in regulation time nor in overtime, so the contest was decided with penalty kicks. Each side made its first two shots before American goalie Briana Scurry (b. 1971) stopped an opponent's attempt. All the subsequent shooters scored, leaving American Brandi Chastain (b. 1968) with the chance to clinch it when she stepped up in the fifth round. She scored and then, in a perfect Kodak moment, ripped off her shirt—an exultant gesture popular in the men's game—fell to her knees and was mobbed by her teammates.

Jock Talk

"I grew up watching Magic Johnson and Kareem Abdul-Jabbar, men I could never emulate. Girls need role models."

—American soccer player Julie Foudy (b. 1971), during the 1999 World Cup, in *Sports Illustrated.*

The image of Chastain shouting in jubilation wearing cleats, shorts and a black sports bra appeared on the cover of newspapers and magazines around the world. The popularity of women's soccer soared—and so did sales of sports bras. It was a milestone in women's sports history.

My Michelle

Chastain wasn't the only woman who distinguished herself on the soccer pitch at the end of the millennium. Compatriot Michelle Akers also emerged as one of the game's top players.

Akers threw a pigskin around with her father and brothers as a youngster and was determined to make her mark in the NFL. When a killjoy teacher informed her women didn't play professional football, Akers turned her attention to her other passion—soccer.

She was a standout in high school and then at the University of Central Florida. She joined the U.S. national team in 1985. Six years later she led the squad to victory in the World Cup by netting ten goals, including five in a match against Taiwan and both American markers in the final against Norway. She emerged as the tournament's top scorer and as an ambassador for women's soccer.

She continued to play despite a series of medical setbacks. In 1993 she collapsed on the pitch and was diagnosed with Epstein-Barr virus. Doctors later identified the ailment as chronic fatigue syndrome. At the 1995 World Cup, Akers collided with a Chinese player and left the match with a concussion and a twisted knee. She left the next World Cup with a concussion after dominating most of the final game. Akers retired from international competition, just before the 2000 Sydney Games, having suffered a serious shoulder injury. "It is a rare thing for someone with her injuries and illnesses to battle as hard and long as she has to stay on the best women's soccer team in the world," Mark

Sports Shorts

Carin Gabarra joined the U.S. national team when Madonna was a fresh face on the music scene. Like the pop icon, Gabarra had the right moves. She answered to the name "Crazy Legs" at the 1991 World Cup, where she scored six goals, including three in one game, with dazzling footwork. After the 1996 Olympics in Atlanta, GA, Gabarra took time off to have a baby and went on to coach at the U. S. Naval Academy.

Adams, the American national team doctor, told NBC. "However, this combination of problems and setbacks makes it very difficult for Michelle to play to the level that she expects of herself."

But quit soccer altogether? Don't even think about it. At 34 years of age, Akers has plans to join a women's professional league scheduled to kick off in April 2001.

Games Without Frontiers

Akers's withdrawal on the eve of the Sydney Games was not entirely tragic. She had competed at the 1996 Atlanta Games where women's soccer made its Olympic debut. Almost 77,000 people gathered in a stadium outside Atlanta to watch the United States defeat China 2–1 in the final match.

Earlier that year, American goalie Briana Scurry had promised to run naked through the streets if her team won the gold medal. Hours after the win, the dutiful athlete sprinted down a street near the stadium wearing nothing but her gold medal. A friend captured the moment on video.

The Americans had less to celebrate at the next Games in Australia. They suffered a 3–2 overtime loss to Norway in the final and settled for silver.

Sports Shorts

April Heinrichs was a scrappy teenager who couldn't convince the University of North Carolina (UNC) or any other top soccer institution to take a look at her, so she accepted a basketball scholarship at another school in 1981 and continued to play for club teams in Colorado. She was soon noticed at a tournament, however, and recruited by Anson Dorrance. At UNC, she was heads and shoulders above her peers and so intense that her teammates often found her annoying. Nonetheless, they followed her lead and the team won three national titles during Heinrichs's four-year stint. When she left, the school retired her jersey number. Heinrichs also played a pivotal role on the U.S. national team. She was captain of the squad that won the first women's World Cup in 1991. She retired after that competition due to a degenerative cartilage problem, but continued her career in soccer. She coached at three universities and joined the coaching staff of the U.S. women's national team. She took over as head coach in January 2000.

Star Bright

By then, American Mia Hamm (b. 1972) had become the face of women's soccer. Her brilliant career started when UNC coach Anson Dorrance saw her play in a high school game. "On the opening play, I saw a player accelerate like she was shot out of a cannon," Dorrance told NBC. Hamm later enrolled at UNC, where she led the team to four national titles in four years.

She joined the American national team in 1987 and put on a spectacular show at the 1995 World Cup, where she played several positions, including goalie (Briana Scurry had been ejected in a match against Denmark).

Her popularity soared to new heights in 1996 following the Atlanta Games, when she appeared in advertisements for various products from Pert Plus shampoo to Nike sports gear (Nike actually named one of the buildings at its headquarters after her). She also appeared on several television talk shows. *People* magazine named her one of the world's 50 most beautiful people, but beneath the pretty face and signature brown ponytail lay the heart of a ferocious forward. In 1999 she became the all-time leading scorer in the history of international women's soccer, surpassing the 107 career goals notched by Italy's Elisabetta Vignotto.

Pro Team

The success of women's soccer in the last quarter of the twentieth century led to the establishment of top-flight leagues in many countries, including the W-league in the United States, but the only professional league was located in Japan and it attracted top players from around the world.

Sports Shorts

When the Women's United Soccer Association (WUSA) started recruiting players from outside the United States, one of the first athletes they signed was Charmaine Hooper (b. 1968), the best female soccer player in Canada. A member of the country's national team for some 15 years, Hooper competed in the 1995 and 1999 World Cups. She scored a goal in each of the five World Cup games she played in, and was twice named to the all-star team representing countries outside the United States. When she was approached by WUSA, she was Canada's all-time leading scorer (43 goals) and had already played professionally in Japan.

Sports Shorts

Many of the world's best players come from the United States, but certainly not all of them. Norway, for instance, has produced some talented competitors as well. In October 2000, the Women's United Soccer Association (WUSA) announced the signing of eight international players and four of them were Norwegian. Of the four, the most popular was Hege Riise, who scored the first goal against the United States in the gold medal match at the 2000 Olympics in Sydney, Australia. Riise was named the most valuable player in the 1995 World Cup. The WUSA called Riise "one of the best and most savvy players in the women's game" thanks to her ability to "deliver the perfect pass." The league also signed two top Swedish players, Ulrika Karlsson and Kristin Bengttson, as well as Charmaine Hooper of Canada and England's Kelly Smith.

But the new millennium brought an exciting announcement: a fully professional women's soccer league would kick off in April 2001. In the months preceding the first season for the Women's United Soccer Association (WUSA), officials scoured the world for talented women to fill the rosters of the league's eight teams to be based in Atlanta, Boston, New York, Philadelphia, Orlando, San Diego, San Francisco and Washington, DC.

Table 10.1: Initiation of Major Worldwide Competitions

Event	Men	Women
Olympics	1900	1996
World Cup	1930	1991

The Least You Need to Know

➤ Women have been in on soccer's fun for centuries.

➤ British women played matches before thousands of spectators 70 years before the first women's World Cup.

➤ The growth of the suburbs fostered the popularity of women's soccer in North America.

➤ The University of North Carolina is the epicentre of women's soccer.

➤ The 1999 World Cup was a defining moment in the history of women's sports—and in the history of sports apparel.

➤ Mia Hamm's name is synonymous with women's soccer.

Part 3

Cold Feet—Winter Sports

Most people endure the wind, ice and snow of winter; others thrive in it. Ever since Skadi—a mythological Scandinavian goddess—strapped on skis, picked up a bow and arrow and hunted down wild animals, exceptional women have been recording their greatest triumphs with runny noses and chapped lips. Take for instance Bobbie Rosenfeld, whose puck-handling skills were the envy of men in the 1920s, or speed skater Catriona Le May Doan, who is now on target to break the sound barrier. And don't forget Tonya Harding; she has the distinction of being the first figure skater in history to assault a lover with a hubcap.

Chapter 11

It's All Downhill From Here: Alpine, Freestyle and Nordic Skiing, plus Biathlon

In This Chapter

➤ Women strap on their skis and get down to business

➤ Europeans set the pace in alpine competition

➤ A few North Americans stand out on the slopes

➤ Snowboarding fosters a brave new world in alpine skiing

➤ Freestyle takes a flying leap

➤ Nordic skiing produces enduring female stars

➤ Women take a shot at biathlon

Sure, Picabo Street has an odd first name. But given the history of women's alpine skiing, her last name is a little strange too, as it's not Swiss, German, Austrian, Norwegian or Russian. While the ebullient American in the melon-coloured ski suit has made her mark with a few others from this continent, the slopes and trails have been dominated by Europeans since the goddess Skadi hunted on skis in an ancient Scandinavian myth. The exception is in freestyle skiing, which took off in the home of the free and has been ruled by the brave from that same land.

Winter Wonderland

A pair of skis, thought to be over five thousand years old, are on display at a museum in Stockholm, Sweden, a logical spot given that Scandinavian countries developed skiing

Let Me Explain

There are three kinds of skiing:

➤ Alpine skiing involves competitors racing down hills or mountains in speed and technical events.

➤ Freestyle skiing focuses on acrobatics and incorporates elements of ballet, figure skating and gymnastics.

➤ Nordic skiing includes: cross-country skiing, where skiers race along courses filled with hills and flats; ski jumping; and nordic combined, which includes a jumping event and a cross-country race.

for travel, battle and hunting. Rock carvings suggest that prehistoric hunters in the region fastened splintered logs to the bottom of their feet and slid over snowy slopes looking for prey.

When the industrial revolution provided transportation up the mountain in the form of rope tows and T-bars, wealthy Europeans began to spend winter vacations at posh ski resorts in Switzerland, Germany and Austria. In those days, skiers wore heavy wooden skis and flimsy boots.

Let Me Explain

The downhill race is the most prestigious event in alpine skiing, emphasizing pure speed. Competitors ski down a steep slope making long straight lines and sweeping turns. The winner is determined based on her performance in a single run. The women's downhill was introduced at the Olympics in 1948.

Let Me Explain

The slalom emphasizes control over speed. Competitors weave in and out of blue- and red-flagged poles, called gates. If a competitor misses a gate she is automatically disqualified. The winner is determined through her times on two separate runs. The women's slalom was introduced at the Olympics in 1948.

As skiing became more popular, ski clubs were formed and competitions were held for men and women. Men started competing in the 1880s, and women followed 30 years later on wooden skis with cable bindings. They tackled the slopes bundled in wool ski pants, bulky sweaters and jackets, flapper hats and leather boots. One of the first North American clubs to stage women's competitions was the Lake Placid Club, which introduced slalom and downhill events, along with one cross-country race.

Get It Together

The International Ski Federation (FIS) was founded in 1924, and staged world championships starting in 1931. Soon after, men and women hit the slopes at the 1936 Olympics in Garmisch-Partenkirchen, Germany.

Christel Cranz won a gold medal in the combined for the host country after two incredible slalom runs. This, of course, pleased Adolf Hitler who expected no less from his German athletes. The United States sent a women's team that had been formed in 1934 by members of the Amateur Ski Club of New York, but those skiers were no match for the mighty Europeans who dominated the event.

Let Me Explain

The combined, which includes the slalom and the downhill, was the only alpine ski event at the 1936 Olympics in Garmisch-Partenkirchen, Germany. It was discontinued at the 1952 Olympics in Oslo, Norway, and was reinstated at the 1988 Olympics in Calgary, AB.

Change Has Come

World War II brought top-level competition skiing to a halt, but technology developed during the war would ultimately improve the sport:

➤ Metals and alloys were used to construct chair lifts and rope tows.

➤ Wooden skis were replaced by metal skis, which were faster and lighter. They were designed for downhill and slalom.

➤ Lightweight synthetics like nylon replaced cotton and wool clothing.

These advances drew more people to the slopes, including some talented young women.

The Most Popular Girls in Town

Q & A

Q: What American skier flew airplanes?

A: Gretchen Kunigk Fraser. She learned to fly several small airplanes and won two races in an army jet trainer.

Gretchen Kunigk Fraser (1919–1994) was named to the U.S. ski team along with her husband in 1940, but worldwide competitions were cancelled due to the outbreak of World War II. Fraser stayed at home and won several national titles before retiring. Her husband later convinced her to try out for the team headed to the 1948 Olympics in St. Moritz, Switzerland. There, Fraser became the first American skier to win an Olympic medal, taking home a gold (slalom) and a silver (combined).

At the 1952 Olympics in Oslo, Norway, Andrea Mead Lawrence (b. 1932) became the first American skier to take home two gold medals from the same Games. She easily won the giant slalom and captured her second gold, in the slalom, with a comeback performance. She had taken a tumble in the first run, but managed to finish the course with the fourth best time. Her second run was two seconds faster than the rest of the field, which vaulted her into first place. She returned for the 1956 Olympics in Cortina d'Ampezzo, Italy, after giving birth to her third child, and fell just one-tenth of a second short of a bronze medal in the giant slalom.

Q & A

Q: What American skier's parents owned and managed a ski resort at Pico Peak, VT?

A: Andrea Mead Lawrence's. Mead Lawrence learned to ski when she was three years old.

Let Me Explain

The giant slalom's course is longer than the slalom's. Also, the corners aren't as sharp and the gates are farther apart. The women's giant slalom was introduced at the Olympics in 1952.

European Legacy

Alpine skiing became a major professional sport when the World Cup circuit was established in 1967, and European skiers have dominated ever since.

An Austrian who started skiing at the age of four on her father's hand-whittled skis became one of the sport's biggest stars in the 1970s. Annemarie Moser-Proell (b. 1953) won the overall World Cup title five times that decade. She won two silver medals (downhill and giant slalom) at the 1972 Olympics in Sapporo, Japan, and added a gold (downhill) at the 1980 Olympics in Lake Placid, NY—no small feat considering she had taken time off between Olympics to open a café and marry a soccer player.

Moser-Proell shared the spotlight with Germany's Rosi Mittermeir (b. 1950), who won two gold (downhill and slalom) and a silver (giant slalom) at the 1976 Olympics in Innsbruck, Austria. Also that year, she was the overall World Cup champion. But Mittermeir's talent wasn't limited to skiing—she also recorded an album of folk songs.

Q & A

Q: What European skier almost died at six months old when a goat crushed her baby carriage?

A: Germany's seemingly accident prone Rosi Mittermeir, who swallowed rat poison two years later. As an adult, the German athlete nearly blinded herself when she collided into a slalom pole and she broke her arm skiing into a tourist. Oh, and then there was that surfing accident in Hawaii...

Sports Shorts

Petra Kronberger (b. 1969) began skiing when she was two years old and later left home to live at a school for athletes. When she graduated from secondary school she worked as a bank clerk, earning far less than the $300,000 a year she would soon take in as a professional skier. The Austrian was the overall World Cup titleholder for three straight years (1990–1992). She also won two gold medals (slalom and combined) at the 1992 Olympics in Albertville, France.

Let Me Explain

The super giant slalom, or Super-G, combines downhill speed with giant slalom technique. The giant slalom course is shortened by a few hundred metres and gates are added to ensure a minimum thirty changes of direction for women. The winner is decided on a single run. The women's Super-G was introduced at the Olympics in 1988.

Jock Talk

"Everything now is about money. The Olympics should be about the athletes, not money."

—Austrian skier Alexandra Meissnitzer, responding to recent reports of bribery and corruption among International Olympic Committee (IOC) members, in *Sports Illustrated*.

Today the Austrian women reign supreme on the slopes. Alexandra Meissnitzer (b. 1973) won a silver (giant slalom) and a bronze (super giant slalom) at the 1998 Olympics in Nagano, Japan. The next year, she won the overall World Cup title by a huge margin. In 2000, her compatriots Renate Goetschl (b. 1975) and Michaela Dorfmeister (b. 1973) finished first and second respectively in the overall World Cup standings.

Exception to the Rule

It's true that European domination of women's alpine skiing is as old as the transistor radio, but a few North Americans have managed to make an impression:

➤ Canadian Nancy Greene (b. 1943) won the overall World Cup title in 1967, the circuit's inaugural year, and again in 1968. At the 1968 Olympics in Grenoble, France, she won gold (giant slalom) and silver (slalom). She had her coaches to thank for her triumph. They executed a brilliant plan to alleviate her pre-race jitters. Forty-five minutes before the giant slalom, they distracted her by taking her to a restaurant at the top of the slope, engaging her in a discussion about ski politics. When one of the coaches interrupted the conversation to announce the competition had begun, they rushed to the start hut to find the fifth skier already in the gate. Greene had no time to panic. She went down a few minutes later, staging a perfect run.

➤ American Tamara McKinney (b. 1962) was raised on a horse-breeding farm, but skiing was central in her life. In the winter, she and her six siblings travelled with their mother to various races, and were on the road so much that they had to be home schooled. In the 1980s, when skiing was booming on this side of the Atlantic Ocean, McKinney rose to the top of international competition. She joined the World Cup circuit in 1978 and, five years later, became the first American woman to win the overall World Cup title.

Jock Talk

"I took figure skating lessons for a while, but to me there was no action. You'd stand around and one person would twirl, then the next."

—Canadian skier Nancy Greene, in *Celebrating Excellence: Canadian Women Athletes.*

Q & A

Q: Who is the only skier from a non-German speaking country to win the women's downhill at the Olympics?

A: Canadian Kerrin Lee Gartner (b. 1966), who won the gold at the 1992 Olympics in Albertville, France.

Q & A

Q: What American skier's childhood included an extended trip through Central America, where she grew her own food, chopped wood and watched no television?

A: Picabo Street, whose flower child parents' attempt to name her "Baby Girl Street" was nixed by the government.

➤ Picabo Street (b. 1972) became a celebrity in the mid-1990s, and not just because of her hide-and-go-seek name. The American started the decade with decidedly less than a bang, getting tossed off the national team for being out of shape. But she bounced back to win a silver medal (downhill) at the 1994 Olympics in Lillehammer, Norway. She solidified her celebrity status by coming back from a serious knee injury to win gold (super giant slalom) at the 1998 Nagano Games.

Table 11.1: Initiation of Major Worldwide Alpine Competitions

Event	Men	Women
Olympics	1936	1936
World Championships	1931	1931
World Cup	1967	1967

Everybody's Talking About Revolution, Evolution

While Street was touring the talk show circuit as America's favourite skier, monumental change was underfoot in her sport. The change stemmed from a pastime whose original name, "snurfing," made it sound like an activity for preschoolers.

Snowboarding was developed in the 1960s in the United States, where a few hepcats explored the idea of surfing on snow. The sport soared in popularity in the 1990s, luring countless people away from skiing. The FIS sanctioned snowboarding in 1993, ending its status as a so-called "fringe" sport. Snowboarding made its Olympic debut in 1998 at the Nagano Games, where France's Karine Ruby (b. 1978) won the giant slalom and Nicola Thost (b. 1978) of Germany took home gold in the halfpipe.

The snowboarding boom was a wake-up call to the stagnant alpine ski industry, which rose to the challenge by creating shaped skis. In the past few years, these new skis "have breathed a whole new life into alpine skiing," says Alpine Canada spokesman Gordie Bowles. Wider at the front and back than in the middle, these skis make it easy to get an edge and carve through the snow, and have changed the way men and women ski. In races, competitive skiers can cut more tightly around gates than ever before. "Shaped skis are now a must among women on the World Cup circuit," claims Bowles.

At the recreational level, the new equipment means "skiing has become easier to learn, less daunting to women who, traditionally, have been more hesitant than men to take up the sport," acknowledges Lori Knowles, senior editor of *Ski Press* magazine. As an instructor, Knowles has noticed that "women are more excited about learning to ski and are more inclined to stick with it."

Let Me Explain

A halfpipe is a structure built for freestyle snowboarding. It has two opposing walls of the same height and size. Snowboarders ascend and descend the walls, alternating between the two, gaining momentum and utilizing the halfpipe to "catch air" and perform tricks.

Traditionally, 60 percent of alpine skiers have been men, but the revolution in ski equipment may well lead to a shift in demographics on the slopes.

Women have certainly not shied away from new-style skiing, which combines elements of freestyle skiing and snowboarding. Free skiing (formerly known as extreme skiing), for example, is popular with both sexes. One recent event in the Canadian Rockies saw over two hundred entries, both male and female, tackling dangerously steep slopes and hurling themselves off 70-foot cliffs—for fun!

There is no doubt about it, says Iain Macmillan, editor of *Ski Canada*, "there are more really good women skiers now." Some of them are now even executing twists and turns on the slopes that would make Gumby green with envy. Hot dog! They're freestyle skiers!

Free and Easy

In the 1800s, Norwegian nordic skiers learned to turn, jump and ski straight downhill at high speeds. Soon, they were taking instruction from teachers such as Mathias Zdarsky, an Austrian gymnast who taught simple acrobatics in the European Alps in the late 1800s and early 1900s.

125

Let Me Explain

A freestyle moguls competition is held on a straight, steep slope covered with moguls (bumps), which the skier must contend with while descending as fast as possible. The course also contains two ramps (also called kickers), which the skiers use to perform tricks.

This form of skiing was deemed useful for training, but too flamboyant and dangerous—it resulted in a few spinal cord injuries—to be a sport in its own right. That changed, however, thanks in part to Norwegian Olympic downhill champion Stein Eriksen, who performed aerials and other tricks at exhibitions in the United States in the 1950s.

While Eriksen was thrilling crowds with his feats, other skiers in North America were discovering the joy of tackling slopes filled with hard bumps of snow, and were starting their own mogul competitions. Finally, in 1971, moguls, aerials and ballet-type manoeuvres (i.e., acro) were included at the national championships of exhibition skiing. This "hot dog" or "show off" skiing got its biggest boost yet from a real live wire.

Suzy Q

In 1967, Suzy Chaffee (b. 1947) was the highest-ranked American woman in alpine competition. A year later, she was named captain of the American ski team at the 1968 Grenoble Games. After the Games, she abandoned alpine and took up freestyle skiing; it was well suited for her because she was quite proficient in classical ballet.

There were no women's freestyle competitions in those days, so Chaffee won several competitions (1971–1973) competing against the men. She was also one of the first freestyle skiers to perform with musical accompaniment. She worked tirelessly promoting the sport.

Sports Shorts

Suzy Chaffee was a babe on skis, with long blonde hair and a dazzling smile. Three decades before tennis player Anna Kournikova's sexy pout adorned billboards selling sports bras, Chaffee made money promoting Chap Stick lip balm. She also appeared semi-nude in a magazine photo spread.

Q & A

Q: What American freestyle skier was one of the first women to sit on the U.S. Olympic Committee Board of Directors?

A: Suzy Chaffee, who also helped form the Athletic Advisory Council of the U.S. Olympic Committee and lobbied to pass Title IX legislation and the Amateur Sports Act.

Serious Business

FIS sanctioned freestyle skiing in 1979, and a World Cup circuit and world championships were added over the next decade. The sport became so popular internationally that mogul skiing for men and women was included at the 1992 Olympics in Albertville, France. Aerials were added at the 1994 Lillehammer Games.

American Girls

Not surprisingly (given freestyle skiing's homegrown appeal), American women rose up to dominate the sport in the 1990s. First among them was Donna Weinbrecht (b. 1965), who had a background in both figure skating and alpine skiing. At the 1992 Albertville Games she captured gold (moguls) skiing in a snowstorm to the accompaniment of "Rock 'n Roll High School" by the Ramones.

Four years later, American Nikki Stone (b. 1971) injured her back and was told by doctors that she would never ski again. What did they know? She won the aerials in 1998 at the Nagano Games.

Let Me Explain

In a freestyle aerials competition, skiers launch themselves into the air off a ramp (kicker) to perform acrobatics.

Let Me Explain

In a freestyle acro competition, the skier performs linked acrobatic manoeuvres and steps performed to music with skis and poles, on a smooth, even slope.

Right Here, Right Now

While freestyle skiing is not considered a mainstream sport on par with alpine skiing, more and more kids are participating in it, according to Mary Fraser, manager of media relations at the Canadian Freestyle Ski Association—and that includes young girls! "In the past, males have been more active in freestyle skiing," explains Fraser. "The first enthusiasts were teenagers—and among teenagers there are fewer daring females." She adds that parents have been reluctant to see their daughters spinning head over heels in mid-air. Go figure. But she notes hopefully that new development programs are attracting both boys and girls, many of whom have a background as trampolinists or gymnasts and are drawn to aerials.

Table 11.2: Initiation of Major Worldwide Freestyle Competitions

Event	Men	Women
Olympics	1992	1992
World Championships	1986	1986
World Cup	1979	1979

Country Roads

Of course, not all skiers were risking life and limb on the slopes as the twentieth century drew to a close; some traditionalists stayed on well-travelled trails. Nordic skiing (cross-country) has been a pastime since it was developed in Norway in the mid-1800s. Norwegians held the first recorded race in 1843, and later introduced the sport to the rest of Europe in addition to Australia, New Zealand, the United States and Canada.

Male cross-country skiers started competing in the Olympics in 1924 and females joined the fun in 1952—16 years after they started competing in alpine events. Women's

Let Me Explain

Cross-country races range from 1km sprints to 50km marathons and include both individual events and team relays. Some races require skiers to use the traditional diagonal stride (classical) and others allow skiers to use any technique they choose, most often a quick skating stride (freestyle). Some relay races incorporate both techniques.

competition has been dominated by Norwegians and Russians. One of the most accomplished among them is Russian Raissa Smetanina (b.1952), who won four gold, five silver and one bronze in five Olympics between 1976 and 1992. She was the first athlete to win ten medals over the course of a career at the Winter Games. When Smetanina won gold (4x5km relay) at the 1992 Albertville Games twelve days before her fortieth birthday, she became the oldest female medallist in Winter Games history.

Smetanina's accomplishments were followed by those of compatriot Larissa Lazutina (b. 1965), who won five gold, one silver and one bronze in three Olympics between 1992 and 1998. During the 1998 Nagano Games, the Russian armed forces promoted Lazutina from officer to lieutenant in the Strategic Missile Forces sports club in recognition of her "outstanding success in sport." Lazutina was still competing at the end of 2000.

Sports Shorts

When they were youngsters, a friend persuaded Bente Martinsen-Skari (b. 1972) to take up cross-country skiing. She won the first race she entered and over the next decade rose to the top of her sport. She went to the 1994 Olympics in Lillehammer, Norway, but came home empty handed. "I don't remember anything from those Olympics, really." Martinsen-Skari told CNN/SI. "I was new there, so there were many new people. It was a little scary even." She fared better at the 1998 Olympics in Nagano, Japan, however, winning a bronze (5km classical) and a silver (4x5km relay). She won her twentieth World Cup race in February 2001.

Table 11.3: Initiation of Major Worldwide Nordic Competitions

Event	Men	Women
Olympics	1924	1952
World Championships	1925	1956
World Cup	1979	1979

Sports Shorts

As a demonstration sport, the men's biathlon was debuted as a "military exercise" in the 1924 Olympics in Chamonix, France, but was removed from the Games after World War II for political reasons. The modern biathlon (for men) reappeared at the Games in 1960.

Let Me Explain

Pentathlon is a summer discipline that includes shooting, fencing, swimming, equestrian show jumping and cross-country running under a scoring system similar to that of the decathlon/heptathlon.

Hit Me With Your Best Shot

While most skiers are satisfied tearing down hills or gliding across trails, others need something more to engage them. They strap on skis, sling rifles over their shoulders and compete in races requiring them to stop at various intervals and shoot at targets. This seemingly odd pastime, called biathlon, started out as means of survival in Northern Europe and later evolved into a component of warfare. Ski-bound Finnish soldiers defended their border from Soviet troops in 1939.

Skiing and shooting were taken very seriously, but not all the time. Employees from companies that guarded the Swedish-Norwegian border competed against each other in 1767, and the Norwegian military organized a race in 1912.

The sport became increasingly popular in the following decades. In 1958, the Union Internationale de Pentathlon Moderne et Biathlon (UIPMB) was established to oversee biathlon and modern pentathlon worldwide. The biathlon has been overseen by its own international governing body, the International Biathlon Union, since 1993.

The first world championships were held in 1958, and biathlon was included at the 1960 Olympics in Squaw Valley, CA. Those competitions were for men only. It didn't take women long to discover the sports and become serious about it, though. Female biathletes first competed at the world championships in 1984 and at the Olympics in 1992.

Canadian Rose

One of the sport's first female stars was German border guard Ursula Disl, who won one gold, three silver and two bronze in three Olympics between 1992 and 1998. Disl won three of those medals at the 1998 Nagano Games, becoming the biggest medal winner in the history of the Olympic biathlon. "To have a gold in the Olympics is the greatest thing one can have in one's life in sport," she told *The Washington Post* after winning the 4x7.5km relay. "I think this evening we have reason to party."

Another top competitor was Canadian Myriam Bédard (b. 1969), who took up biathlon when asked to join in a team competition as a cadet. The 15-year-old agreed, even though she didn't know how to cross-country ski. "It was three men and they needed a woman for the team and they asked me," Bédard said in *Celebrating Excellence: Canadian Women Athletes*. "I was on rental skis, I didn't really know how to do it." Nonetheless, Bédard's team finished first and she was hooked on a new sport.

She went on to win several international competitions and was ranked second in the world in 1991. She won a bronze (15km) at the 1992 Albertville Games and two gold (7.5km and 15km) at the 1994 Lillehammer Games. Not long after she was diagnosed with hypothyroidism, a condition marked by slow metabolism. She also suffered from chronic fatigue syndrome and discovered she was allergic to certain foods, including bananas, which provide an important source of energy for athletes. But instead of retiring, Bédard embarked on an intense training regimen that featured kayaking, cycling, running and weight training. She reached her goal of competing in the 1998 Nagano Games, but came home empty handed.

Q & A

Q: How did biathlete Ursula Disl change her appearance before the 1998 Olympics in Nagano, Japan?

A: She tried to dye her hair gold for good luck, but ended up with red tresses instead.

Q & A

Q: Why did Canadian biathlete Myriam Bédard sue Wrigley Canada Inc., in 2000?

A: The company used an unauthorized, computer-altered photo of her in a gum campaign. Bédard claimed the ad, which featured an androgynous rifle-bearing skier, made her look foolish. "I have always made a point of remaining feminine in a sport that is very demanding and, especially, very masculine," Bédard told The Canadian Press. She reached an out-of-court settlement with the company seven months after filing the suit.

Sports Shorts

Biathlon is rarely mentioned in mainstream media in non-Winter Olympic years, but it made headlines in 2000 when an enthusiast was attacked by a bear while jogging near a training centre outside Québec City, QC. Mary Beth Miller, 24, had gone to the Myriam Bédard Training Centre to pursue her interest in biathlon and receive some top-notch coaching. Tragically, Miller was fatally mauled during the attack. "She knew and understood and respected bears," her friend Kristine Saugen told *Maclean's* magazine. "She respected nature and spent a lot of time in it. And I think that's what makes this even harder." Miller had worked as a wildlife technician and had studied animals such as caribou and grizzly bears.

Table 11.4: Initiation of Major Worldwide Biathlon Competitions

Event	Men	Women
Olympics	1960	1992
World Championships	1958	1984
World Cup	1978	1984

The Least You Need to Know

➤ Women have been involved in competitive alpine skiing from the sport's outset.

➤ Alpine skiing originated in Europe, and women from that continent dominate the slopes to this day, with a few notable exceptions.

➤ Alpine skiing, driven by the evolution of snowboarding, has recently been undergoing dramatic change.

➤ Freestyle skiing grew into a bona fide sport in North America, home of many of today's top competitors.

➤ Russians and Norwegians have dominated cross-country skiing.

➤ One of the world's best biathletes is Canadian.

Chapter 12

Fire and Ice: Figure Skating

In This Chapter

➤ Britain's Madge Syers takes on male competitors—and wins

➤ Sonja Henie puts women's figure skating on the map

➤ North America produces its first star: Barbara Ann Scott

➤ Television turns women's figure skating into a big deal

➤ Katarina Witt makes women's figure skating sexy

➤ Tonya Harding vs. Nancy Kerrigan: The Thriller in Lillehammer

➤ Old and young stars shine bright

➤ Men and women make beautiful pairs

The famous pre-Olympic rivalry between Americans Tonya Harding and Nancy Kerrigan may have been the most violent in figure skating history—disputes involving weapons rarely end peacefully—but it wasn't the first. That honour goes to Norwegian glamour puss Sonja Henie and Canadian cutie Barbara Ann Scott. In the 1920s and 1930s, Henie turned figure skating into the dazzling, athletic pursuit it is today. She was adored the world over—Adolf Hitler counted himself among her devoted fans—and had the spotlight to herself until Scott began to strut her stuff in the 1940s. Since then, women's figure skating has seen many rivalries and colourful personalities, from American Dorothy Hamill, whose haircut became the look *du jour*, to German Katarina Witt, whose sensual performances bewitched a world leader.

Round and Round

When members of the English house of Stuart were exiled to Holland in the late 1600s, the Dutch took them to frozen canals and taught them to skate. When the Britons finally returned home, they brought their skates with them.

The British didn't have long canals to skate on, but they made the most of their ponds and small lakes. They skated in circles and became good at making tracings, or figures, on the ice with their skate blades. In 1772, Captain Robert Jones wrote *A Treatise of Skating*, the first written account of figure skating, which at the time was executed in a cramped and formal style. A decade later, U.S. dance master Jackson Haines introduced techniques based on dance movements.

Watch Out Boys—She'll Chew You Up!

The International Skating Union (ISU), the world governing body of ice skating, was founded in 1892, and world championships began four years later. Organizers intended it to be a male-only event but didn't make that stipulation official, so they couldn't prevent Madge Syers (1881–1917) from participating in 1902. The indignant judges reluctantly awarded the Englishwoman the silver medal for a performance that many observers considered the best of the competition. To prevent such embarrassment in the future, officials amended the rules to prohibit women from participating in subsequent world championships (their excuse...errr...explanation was that judges couldn't see the feet of the female performers because they wore ankle-length skirts).

Q & A

Q: Who did Madge Syers defeat at the British national championships in 1904?

A: Her husband, Edgar.

But it wasn't long before sisters were doing it for themselves. They competed in the first Women's World Figure Skating Championships in 1906. Syers won the event that year and the next. And, just to prove she was no flash in the pan, she won a gold medal at the 1908 Olympics in London, England. Also at those Games, Syers and her husband, Edgar, finished third in the pairs competition.

Puttin' on the Ritz

Germany's Charlotte Oelschlagel was able to put on a performance that Ed Sullivan might have described as a "really big shooooooooow." Oelschlagel was a musical prodigy who performed with the Berlin Philharmonic before she was old enough to play spin the bottle. But her budding musical career took its toll, and the little girl had a nervous breakdown.

She took up skating to calm her nerves and ended up appearing in Berlin theatres, skating to music and wearing elaborate costumes. Like all rising European stars, from Albert Einstein to Arnold Schwarzenegger, Oelschlagel took her act to the United States. A six-week stint at New York's Hippodrome in 1915 was such a success, her contract was extended for six years and she performed twice a day to packed houses. Oelschlagel's main contribution to skating—apart from boas and plumage—was adding a theatrical element to a dull, technical endeavour. Her success set the stage for the sport's first major star.

Superstar

Inspired by Russian ballerina Anna Pavlova, Sonja Henie (1912–1969) melded skating with dance, and combined athleticism, drama and costume into one incredible package. The Norwegian became an international celebrity who was mobbed wherever she performed.

When Henie started skating, women wore long skirts, not just to protect them from the cold, but also because it was not considered ladylike to expose one's legs. Henie made the short free-floating skirt fashionable in women's figure skating, and is credited with being the first skater to wear boots dyed to match her tights (and you thought skates had always been flesh-coloured).

Henie—who also won Scandinavian championships in tennis and skiing—skated in the 1924 Olympics in Chamonix, France, when she was 11 years old. Her last place finish may have had something to do with the fact that she stopped several times during a routine to get instructions from her coach. Henie learned to perform without consultations and went on to win gold medals at the 1928 St. Moritz Games, the 1932

Sports Shorts

One of skating star Sonja Henie's biggest fans was Adolf Hitler, who twice invited her to lunch at his home near Munich and (modestly) gave her an autographed photo of himself. According to *The Complete Book of the Winter Olympics*, Henie skated up to the German dictator at an exhibition in 1935, gave him the Nazi salute and shouted out, "*Heil* Hitler!" Her actions made her popular in Germany but not at home in Norway, where she was denounced as a traitor. Five years later the Germans invaded Norway and set up a puppet government.

Lake Placid Games and the 1936 Garmisch-Partenkirchen Games. Henie also won 10 consecutive world championships (1927–1936), surpassed only by Ulrich Salchow, who won 11 straight world titles. Henie captured one of those titles in New York, NY, where she was hailed as the city's "Scandinavian Sweetheart." Oh, and let's not forget that she won nine European titles, too!

She turned professional in 1936 after the Garmisch-Partenkirchen Games and became a movie star. Her first film, *One in a Million*, was a box office smash. Within two years, Henie rivalled Clark Gable and Shirley Temple in box-office popularity. Henie also toured Europe and the Americas with the *Hollywood Ice Revue*. She travelled with her own Zamboni ice resurfacing machine—she was one of only three people in the world who owned one at the time—and permitted just one man, Eddie Pec, to sharpen her skates. He often travelled great distances to work on her blades.

Henie became an American citizen in 1941. She married and divorced twice before settling down with her childhood sweetheart, a Norwegian ship owner. At the time of her death in 1969, Henie was worth an incredible $47 million.

Henie inspired scores of little girls across North America to lace up skates and a generation later, Canadians and Americans began to appear on medal podiums in international competitions.

Q & A

Q: What figure skater had her legs insured for $5000 a week, the most Lloyds of London would underwrite?

A: Sonja Henie.

Q & A

Q: What figure skater's father was a wealthy furrier?

A: Sonja Henie's. Her family owned the first automobile in Oslo.

Ba ba ba ba Barbara Ann

When Canada's Barbara Ann Scott (b. 1928) was nine years old, she met Henie who was performing in Montréal at the time, and was beside herself with glee. "Oh, what a thrill to see this beautiful lady who I had read about, seen pictures of," Scott is quoted as saying in *Celebrating Excellence: Canadian Women Athletes*. "She gave me a huge autographed picture. That is one of my great memories." One wonders if Henie would have been as warm to Scott had she known the little girl would end up stealing the limelight from her...

In her prime, Scott was petite and charming, but more importantly, she was the world's fastest spinner. Her star rose while Henie's faded, a situation made painfully obvious by

Let Me Explain

Skating programs feature several spins, including the standing spin, the camel spin and the sit spin, in which the skater sits low to the ice with the skating (spinning) knee bent and the non-skating (free) leg extended beside it. Most figure skating fans love the layback spin, in which the skater, spinning in an upright position, drops her head and shoulders backward and arches her back.

Scott's press agent, who once noted that Scott's legs were much more becoming than Henie's.

In 1947, Scott won the European championship and the world championship, where she competed in –30°C temperatures. She was the first North American to win a world title. She won both titles again the following year, and added a gold medal at the 1948 St. Moritz Games. There, Scott had to do her free skate on a surface that had been used for two morning hockey games. The ice was riddled with holes, ruts and brittle spots, so Scott was forced to rearrange her routine at the last minute. Nonetheless, she put on a solid show, skating in a hand-sewn, cream-coloured fur dress, and ended up on the medal podium in a blizzard.

She turned professional soon after, joining the *Hollywood Ice Revue*. She also accepted a complimentary car from her hometown of Ottawa, ON, in praise of her accomplishments; its license plate read "48-U-1."

Scott's legacy is that her success galvanized a dispirited nation after World War II. She also made another important contribution to society: she inspired the creation of a Barbara Ann Scott doll, one of Barbie's more athletic predecessors.

North American Starship

Scott's early success kicked off an era in which North American women dominated international figure skating:

➤ American Tenley Albright (b. 1935) won two world championships (1953 and 1955) and two Olympic medals, one silver (1952) and one gold (1956). She skated to victory at the 1956 Cortina d'Ampezzo Games in great pain, however. Less than two weeks before the competition, Albright had hit a rut in the ice and fallen, her left skate blade hitting her right ankle, slashing a vein and severely scraping the bone. Her father, a surgeon, had treated the wound. After she retired, Albright followed in his footsteps and went on to become a surgeon herself.

➤ American Carol Heiss (b. 1940) won five world championships (1956–1960) and two Olympic medals, one silver (1956) and one gold (1960). When Heiss won her silver in 1956 at the Cortina d'Ampezzo Games, her mother was terminally ill. After her death, Heiss vowed to win an Olympic gold medal in her mother's honour. She did just that in 1960, and then attempted to forge a career in Hollywood. But she was less successful in front of the camera than she had been on the ice. Heiss made just one film, *Snow White and the Three Stooges*, a movie described by film critic Leonard Maltin as "stodgy."

Despite Heiss's celluloid mishap, women's figure skating got a big boost on the big screen, thanks in part to Henie's acting endeavours. It was to get another boost, this time on the small screen.

Television People

In the 1950s, television broadcasts of skating competitions and exhibitions began to reach huge audiences. Thousands of viewers watched the women's singles event at the 1960 Olympics in Squaw Valley, CA, setting women's figure skating on a path toward the glamorous, high profile sport it is today. Thanks to television, figure skating is one of the few sports where the women's names are bigger than the men's.

Q & A

Q: What figure skater had cosmetic surgery to increase her chances of winning an Olympic medal?

A: American Linda Fratianne, who had a nose job before the 1980 Olympics in Lake Placid, NY. She also hired someone to teach her how to smile while skating. She finished second.

One of the biggest stars the sport has produced is Peggy Fleming (b. 1948), who was just 13 years old in 1961 when her coach died in a plane crash that claimed the lives of the entire U.S. figure skating team. Fleming vowed to win in his memory, and she did, capturing three world titles (1966–1968) and becoming the only American to win a gold medal at the 1968 Grenoble Games. The world watched—on live television via satellite—as she skated to Tchaikovsky's "Pathetique."

Fleming later skated with the *Ice Follies* and appeared in television commercials, selling items as diverse as vitamins and pantyhose. In 1998, Fleming was diagnosed with breast cancer and underwent successful radiation therapy and surgery.

American Dorothy Hamill (b. 1956) also became a household name thanks in part to television, winning gold at the world championships and the 1976 Innsbruck

Games. Her Olympic victory, where she skated to music from Errol Flynn movies, was a unanimous decision by the judges, and it was the last time someone would capture gold without executing a triple jump.

Not only did Hamill invent a skating move called the "Hamill camel" (the camel is an element in which the skater moves directly from a spin into a sit spin)—she also started a fashion fad. After the Innsbruck Games, girls across North America flocked to their hairdressers bearing pictures of the skater, wanting to emulate the style; Hamill's short hair spread out like a fan when she spun. (The style soon fell out of fashion, however, giving way to the luscious locks look sported by Farrah Fawcett. The hair craze sparked by the *Charlie's Angels* star secured the 1970s' place in history as the decade ruled by hairdressers.)

You Sexy Thing

In the 1980s, the emphasis in women's figure skating shifted from North America to the German Democratic Republic (GDR) or East Germany. The country produced one of the most popular and accomplished figure skaters of all time.

Katarina Witt (b. 1965) offered the perfect blend of art and athleticism, winning over audiences with talent and a beguiling smile. She won four world titles (1984, 1985, 1987 and 1988), six European championships (1983–1988) and was the first woman since Henie to win consecutive Olympic gold medals in singles competition.

With her victory at the 1984 Olympics in Sarajevo, Yugoslavia, Witt won the affection of East German leader Erich Honecker, who instructed the country's spy organization to keep close tabs on her sex life. No doubt Witt's sensual gold-medal winning performance to Georges Bizet's opera *Carmen* at 1988 Olympics in Calgary, AB tickled his fancy.

Sports Shorts

Canadian Elizabeth Manley (b. 1965) had the potential to be one of the world's best figure skaters, but tended to crumble under pressure. Pundits predicted she would finish no better than third at the 1988 Olympics in Calgary, AB, behind favourites Katarina Witt of Germany and American Debi Thomas. Despite battling strep throat for a week, Manley captivated the audience—and the judges—with an incredible free skate that included five triple jumps. She won the silver medal in front of an appreciative homeland crowd.

Meanwhile, American Debi Thomas (b. 1967), the only skater to beat Witt in five years, blundered in her free skate program and finished third. Her outing was a personal disappointment. Nonetheless, she became the first black athlete to win a medal at a Winter Olympics.

Witt turned professional after the 1988 Calgary Games. In 1990, she starred in the television special *Carmen on Ice*, becoming the first female figure skater to win an Emmy Award. In the same year, she helped develop a skating program that toured the United States and then joined *Stars on Ice* in 1994.

Despite her professional success, Witt couldn't get rid of her itch to compete at the amateur level. Thanks to new rules that allowed professionals to reclaim amateur status, she represented Germany at the 1994 Lillehammer Games where she finished seventh. She later returned to professional skating and made headlines in 1998 for appearing in a ten-page pictorial in *Playboy*.

Sports Shorts

American Kristi Yamaguchi (b. 1971) was born with her feet turned inward and, as an infant, wore plaster casts to correct the problem. She later wore corrective shoes. As a little girl she carried a Dorothy Hamill doll everywhere. Later she won two world titles (1991 and 1992) and a gold medal at the 1992 Olympics in Albertville, France. Before that competition, Yamaguchi was given a pep talk by Hamill (the person, not the doll). Yamaguchi also had a successful career in pairs skating, teaming up with Rudy Galindo to win the U.S. national title in 1989. Yamaguchi made headlines again in 2000, when she married National Hockey League (NHL) player Brett Hedican.

Battle Cry

A 1994 American broadcast of the women's technical program at the Lillehammer Games garnered the highest ratings of any show in 11 years and the sixth highest rating in American television history. The showdown between Tonya Harding (b. 1970) and Nancy Kerrigan (b. 1969), two Americans, had sports fans glued to their screens. To be fair, it was an event boosted by an epic tale of envy, treachery and a truncheon.

Harding was a little different from other figure skaters, with a father who taught her how to replace a car transmission and a mother who publicly berated her when she didn't perform well. In December 1993, her husband at the time, Jeff Gillooly, hatched a plot to have thugs injure her main rival, Kerrigan. After a practice session at the U.S. nationals in Detroit, a hired assailant whacked Kerrigan with a baton. He missed her kneecap by an inch and, unfortunately for Harding, Kerrigan recovered in time for the Lillehammer Games.

Performing in a red, sleeveless dance-hall dress and wearing as much makeup as Tammy Faye Bakker, Harding blew her medal hopes only thirty seconds into the technical program, botching a triple jump, a combination jump and a double flip. She finished tenth in the program, while Kerrigan ended up first. The free skate, held two days later, was the most-watched Friday night show in American history.

Harding was out of medal contention by then thanks to the technical program, but the drama wasn't over. In the middle of her performance she stopped, burst into tears and approached the judges, claiming that one of her skate laces had broken during warm-ups and that its replacement was too short. She started over, with a new lace, and skated a solid program to the theme from *Jurassic Park*, but it was too little too late. She would not win a gold medal.

Jock Talk

"This is so dumb. I hate it. This is the most corny thing I've ever done."

—Nancy Kerrigan, while posing with Mickey Mouse at Disney World shortly after the 1994 Olympics in Lillehammer, Norway.

But neither would Kerrigan. The wholesome American finished second, ahead of China's Chen Lu (b. 1976) and behind Oksana Baiul (b. 1977), the Ukrainian teenager who had been orphaned a few years earlier when her mother and both maternal grandparents died (at one point, Baiul had resorted to sleeping on a cot at the ice rink in her hometown). The medal ceremony was delayed almost half an hour while officials searched for a recording of the Ukrainian national anthem.

Kerrigan, who had won a bronze medal in 1992 at the Albertville Games, went on to become a wife and mother and earn millions of dollars doing endorsements. Harding was less fortunate. Stripped of her national title and banned for life by the United States Figure Skating Association (USFSA), she lapsed into obscurity. She remarried and divorced, but never gave up on love. In 2000, she re-emerged in newspaper headlines for attacking a boyfriend with a hubcap.

The dramatic events leading up to the Lillehammer Games will go down as a rather notorious reason for bringing figure skating to the fore of the sports world. "The [Harding-Kerrigan] episode raised the profile of figure skating permanently," acknowledges H. Kermit Jackson, publisher and executive editor of *American Skating World*. "But the sport has never been quite as popular as it was that year."

Jump Around

In 1994 at the Lillehammer Games, almost as much emphasis was placed on jumping as on broken laces and bruised shins. After all, Baiul was known for spending as much time in the air as she did on the ice during her routines. But times have changed.

Rather than pushing jumping to new heights, the world's top figure skaters are now putting less spectacular leaps together in new ways. In recent years there has been more emphasis on combination jumps, as well as innovative spins and non-jump technical elements. "The emphasis has shifted from jumping to packaging and overall program concept," observes Bill Bridel, marketing and communications director of the Canadian Figure Skating Association (CFSA). Jackson attributes this change to a "risk-benefit ratio." After all, is any skater's life worth a triple Axel?

But there has been a general increase in technical skills, including jumping, at the middle and lower levels of competitive figure skating, where observers have noticed more triple jumps. In August 2000, an American junior named Chrissy Lipscomb became the first woman to land a quadruple-revolution jump in competition when she completed a quadruple Salchow (both Tonya Harding and Japan's Midori Ito [b. 1969] had landed triple Axels years earlier).

Jock Talk

"It's a deplorable instance of age discrimination."

—John Nicks, coach of Naomi Nari Nam (who finished second at the 1999 U.S. Figure Skating Championship as an eighth grader) about ISU rules stipulating girls must be 15 to compete internationally, in *Sports Illustrated*.

Older and Bolder

This emphasis on jumping has led to the prominence of young, flexible girls whom Jackson describes as "figure-less" skaters. American Tara Lipinksi (b. 1982), for example, became the youngest athlete to win an individual Winter Olympic gold medal when she beat compatriot Michelle Kwan (b. 1980) at the 1998 Nagano Games. Lipinski was just 15 years old.

Determined to avoid the very trend that has led to criticism of competitive gymnastics, the ISU ruled that skaters must be 15 years old to compete internationally. Given recent trends in the sport, one wonders, "What's the rush?" Figure skating careers last longer today than ever before. Skaters are taking better care of themselves, and are discovering a world of opportunity once their competitive careers are over.

And while Olympic champions have always been able to skate professionally—look no further than Sonja Henie—their professional careers never lasted more than a few years, until now. Not only is Katarina Witt still skating in front of audiences a dozen years after winning her last Olympic medal, but so is Dorothy Hamill, who is old enough to be the mother of current world champion Michelle Kwan. "Figure skating has exploded on a professional level," observes Jackson. "The stars are just too big to go away."

Shinin' Stars

It remains to be seen which of today's stars will be remembered two decades from now, but there are a few good candidates:

➤ American Michelle Kwan (b. 1980), the so-called "paragon of womanly beauty," had won three world championships as of the summer of 2000 and had taken home a silver medal in 1998 from the Nagano Games.

Let Me Explain

Jumps, often executed as doubles or triples, are an integral part of figure skating:

➤ The Axel is considered the most difficult jump. The skater takes off from the forward outside edge and lands on the back outside edge of the opposite foot. A single Axel consists of one-and-a-half revolutions, a double is two-and-a-half revolutions and a triple is three-and-a-half revolutions. This jump, which was introduced by Norway's Axel Paulsen in 1882, is easy to recognize because it is the only jump in which the skater takes off from the forward position.

➤ The Salchow was developed in 1901 by—you'll never believe this—Ulrich Salchow. The complex jump requires accuracy and balance, so it's not for those of us who can't stand on one foot while putting a shoe on the other. The skater takes off from the back inside edge of one foot and lands on the back outside edge of the opposite foot.

➤ The flip is a toe-pick-assisted jump, in which the skater takes off from the back inside edge of one foot, and lands on the back outside edge of the opposite foot.

➤ In the Lutz, invented by Austrian Alois Lutz in 1913, the skater takes off from a back outside edge and lands on the back outside edge of the opposite foot. The skater approaches the jump on a wide curve, taps her toe pick into the ice and rotates in the opposite direction of the curve.

➤ The toe loop is a toe-pick-assisted jump that takes off and lands on the same back outside edge.

➤ Russian Maria Butyrskaya (b. 1972) won the European championship and the world championship in 1999. "I'm skating like a woman on the ice. Today I proved I'm the best skater in the world and age is not important," the 26-year-old skater was quoted as saying in *Sports Illustrated* after capturing the world title.

➤ Russian Irina Slutskaya (b. 1979) had won three European championships by the summer of 2000.

Table 12.1: Initiation of Major Worldwide Singles Competitions

Event	Men	Women
Olympics	1908	1908
World Figure Skating Championships	1896	1906

What a Lovely Couple

For almost four decades, the Russians have dominated pairs skating, winning 10 straight Olympic pairs competitions since 1964.

One Russian pair that stood out in the late 1980s and early 1990s, Sergei Grinkov (1967–1995) and Yekaterina Gordeyeva (b. 1971), won two Olympic gold medals and four world championships (1986, 1987, 1989 and 1990) as amateurs and several competitions as professionals.

Sports Shorts

Canadians Cecil Smith and Melville Rogers received such hearty applause for their pairs performance at the 1924 Olympics in Chamonix, France, newspapers reported the pair had won the competition. But in the end, the skaters finished seventh.

The duo developed a superb style that was elegant, fluid and precise. At 5-foot-10, Grinkov was over a foot taller than his petite partner, making lifts and throws look effortless. One throw in particular, the quadruple twist, was a crowd favourite.

The pair won the gold medal in 1988 at the Calgary Games, just three months after Grinkov, 21, had dropped his 16-year-old partner on the ice and sent her to hospital for six days. Two years after the Calgary Games, the pair retired from competition, but kept busy; they got married, started a family and they skated professionally, too. When Olympic rules were changed to allow professionals to apply for reinstatement as amateurs, the pair seized the opportunity and competed in 1994 at the Lillehammer Games where they won another gold medal.

But the story didn't end with the pair skating off into the sunset. In November 1995, while practising for a show in Lake Placid, NY, Grinkov collapsed and tragically died of a

Sports Shorts

Two Canadians duos have made a name for themselves in international competition. In 2000, Jamie Salé (b. 1977) and David Pelletier (b. 1974) won the pairs competition at the Four Continents Figure Skating Championships and finished fourth at the world championships. The year before, Shae-Lynn Bourne (b. 1976) and Victor Kraatz (b. 1971) won the dance event at the Four Continents competition and finished third at the world championships. The pair had won three other bronze medals at previous world championships and finished fourth at the 1998 Olympics in Nagano, Japan.

Let Me Explain

In pairs skating, there are several spirals, including the front and back spiral. But the one that draws the most attention is the death spiral, which is a required technical element in all pairs programs. In this move, the man spins in a pivot position while holding one hand of the woman, who is spinning in a horizontal position with her body parallel to the ice; the goal is to have the woman as low to the ice as possible.

heart attack. Three months later, Gordeyeva skated alone for the very first time, in a tribute to her late husband.

Table 12.2: Initiation of Major Worldwide Pairs Competitions

Event	Year
Olympics	1908
World Championships	1908

Let Me Explain

In the pairs competition, a man and a woman team up to perform lifts and jumps, separately and together. In ice dance, the couple skates innovatively, without performing conventional lifts and jumps.

Dancin' Feet

Russians have also dominated ice dancing, but one of the greatest ice dancing teams in history was British. England's Jayne Torvill (b. 1957) and Christopher Dean (b. 1958) earned across-the-board perfect scores for artistic impression at the 1984 Sarajevo Games. It was the first perfect score in the event's history.

Ten years after winning that gold medal, the pair decided to put their professional careers on hold to compete at the Lillehammer Games. They put on a great show that featured Torvill doing a reverse somersault up Dean's back and over his shoulder. The audience gave the pair a standing ovation, but the judges weren't impressed and accused Dean of breaking the rules by raising his hands above shoulder level during the move. They pair ended up with the bronze.

By the end of their competitive careers, the most famous denizens of Nottingham since Robin Hood had also collected four world titles (1981–1984) and four European titles (1981, 1982, 1984 and 1994).

Table 12.3: Initiation of Major Dance Worldwide Competitions

Event	Year
Olympics	1976
World Figure Skating Championships	1952

Judgment Day

Couples events have grabbed headlines in recent years for judging scandals. At the 1998 Nagano Games, for example, the ice dance competition was mired in a controversy that raised allegations of bloc judging (a practice where judges from certain countries agree to vote in a certain, pre-determined manner, to guarantee placement of particular competitors). At the world championships a year later, television cameras caught two judges exchanging glances and making foot signals during the pairs free skate event. The camera caught the Russian judge communicating with the Ukrainian judge, who nodded then wrote on a sheet of paper on his desk. On another occasion, the camera caught the Ukrainian looking at the feet of the Russian, who made two or three distinct kicking movements under his desk. The Ukrainian then looked up and made more notes.

Russians Yelena Berzhnaya and Anton Sikharulidze ended up winning the gold, even though Berzhnaya fell during their performance. China's Shen Xue and Zhao Hongbo won silver, even though they put on a spectacular performance that was free of any major errors. The Russian judge was banned for three years for the mark-fixing scheme, while the Ukrainian was suspended for two.

Questionable judging is more of an issue in couples events—especially in ice dancing—than single events, says Jackson, "because couples events are so technical and complicated. The things that separate one pair from another are minute, whereas in singles skating the differentiations are more clear."

The Least You Need to Know

➤ International women's figure skating competition started when Madge Syers humiliated her male rivals.

➤ Sonja Henie revolutionized women's figure skating.

➤ Both North America and Europe have produced top female figure skaters.

➤ Television and the Tonya Harding–Nancy Kerrigan saga raised the status of women's figure skating.

➤ The world's current star figure skaters have shifted emphasis back to non–jump elements in their routines.

➤ Pairs and dance competitions have been marred by judging controversies.

➤ Figure skating is one of the few sports in which women get top billing.

Chapter 13

Built For Speed: Speed Skating

In This Chapter

➤ Prehistoric hunters slide along the ice atop animal bones

➤ Skating becomes a pastime in the 1500s

➤ Soviet women dominate early competition but are soon eclipsed by German rivals

➤ North American woman make their mark, too

➤ Canadian and American women rule the roost in short-track until Chinese and Korean women take over

Russian skater Lydia Skoblikova may have met with Nikita Khrushchev (not long after he took off his shoe at the United Nations and pounded it on a podium for effect) but she had nothing on American Bonnie Blair, who could boast that police in her hometown in Illinois dubbed her their "favourite speeder." Not that it matters, but Blair also won five Olympic gold medals. Skoblikova, Blair and other women successful on the speed skating oval owe much to the prehistoric hunters who strapped animal bones to their feet and skated after prey.

On the Hunt

Sure it's fun to zip along the ice with chapped lips and a runny nose, but speed skating didn't begin as light entertainment. Northern European hunters sped across the ice looking for food—not thrills—in the prehistoric era. Nor was skating recreational for people who waxed wood and fashioned it into blades in the 1300s. Dutch men and women skated along frozen canals to the Amsterdam market; women often skated with eggs on their head (in baskets, of course).

However, Europeans *did* discover skating was fun when a Scotsman invented the all-iron skate blade in the late 1500s. Men and women took up skating for recreation and before long, it became competitive. The first recorded race was held in England in 1763 and contests soon popped up across the continent. Around that same time, speed skating took off on the other side of the Atlantic Ocean thanks in part to Philadelphian E.W. Bushnell, who introduced the all-steel skate blade in 1850. This blade was light and strong and, unlike the iron blade, didn't need constant sharpening.

Let Me Explain

Traditional speed skating (i.e., long-track) races are held on a 400m oval. The track is divided into two lanes and skaters compete two at a time, with one skater in each lane. The outer lane is longer than the inner lane so in the name of fairness, skaters switch lanes once every lap. Race distances range from sprints of 500m and 1000m to distances as great as 5000m (women) and 10,000m (men). In pack-style racing, six to eight skaters compete at the same time in a single lane. Pack-style racing is not included at major international events.

The Netherlands hosted the first world championships in 1889. The ISU was formed three years later and speed skating made its Olympic debut in 1924.

Back in the USSR

Like stag parties, early speed skating contests were just for men. Women didn't compete in the world championships until 1936 or in the Olympics until 1960. When they finally did enter the competitive arena, European women reigned supreme for several decades. The best female skaters hailed from Finland, Norway, the Netherlands, Germany and the former Soviet Union.

The oval's main attraction through much of the 1960s was a product of Siberian winters. Lidya Skoblikova (b. 1939) started speed skating at age 12. Her father, an engineer, recognized her potential and found her a top coach, Alexander Skoblik. Dad may have regretted the move when Lydia married him six years later. No matter, Skoblikova became one of the best speed skaters in history.

She won two gold (1500m and 3000m) at the 1960 Squaw Valley Games. Then, at the 1964 Innsbruck Games, she won all four women's races (500m, 1000m, 1500m and 3000m) to become the first athlete to win four gold medals at a single Winter Games and six overall. Skoblikova's numerous Olympic and world championship titles made her a hero in the Soviet Union, where she was honoured by Soviet Premier Khrushchev in 1964. He was thrown out of office later that year, but Skoblikova remained a crowd favourite.

Deutscher Girls

Soviet skaters were soon nudged off the medal podium by talented rivals; German skaters held sway for the last two decades of the twentieth century. In the 1980s, Dresden natives Andrea Mitscherlich Schone (b. 1960), Christa Rothenburger and Karin Enke (b. 1961) dominated the oval.

Enke started out as a figure skater but after placing ninth in the 1977 European championships, she discarded her sequined dress and slipped into a wind resistant body suit. Between 1980 and 1988 she won numerous world championship titles and eight Olympic medals, including three gold (500m, 1000m and 1500m), four silver (500m, 1000m, 1500m and 3000m) and a bronze (500m).

Enke was eventually surpassed by compatriot Gunda Niemann (b. 1966), who had arrived at a state sports school when she was 12 years old hoping to make her mark in volleyball or track and field. Niemann had fared well as a hurdler, but not well enough to keep her in cleats. She soon switched to speed skating. It was a smart move. Niemann won two gold (3000m and 5000m) and a silver (1500m) at the 1992 Albertville Games, and added a silver (5000m) and bronze (1500m) at the 1994 Lillehammer Games. She went on to win almost every major event between 1995 and 1997.

The blonde athlete underwent knee surgery in 1997 but dashed her rivals' hopes by making a full (and speedy—what else?) recovery. She set a world record in the 3000m two months before the 1998 Nagano Games and won a gold (3000m) and two silver (1500m and 5000m). Niemann tied the record for the most individual medals (eight) won over a career at the Winter Games.

By November 2000, Niemann had won 17 world championship titles and seemed poised to collect a few more. She started her fifteenth competitive season by winning two races (3000m and 5000m)

Q & A

Q: Gunda Niemann's success endeared her to German fans. What did they call her?
A: They dubbed her "Ice Queen," and meant it as a compliment!

151

at a World Cup event. She smashed her own world record in the 5000m. "The ice was super fast but my technique has improved enormously," Niemann told Dutch television. "I hope I can maintain this form and maybe even improve."

Jock Talk

"Looks like Charlie's family has just added another skater."

—The public address system at a competition in Yonkers, NY, where Charlie Blair was working the day his daughter Bonnie was born.

Jock Talk

Q: Who dubbed Bonnie Blair "Champaign's favourite speeder"?

A: Police in Champaign, Ill., which supported Blair financially when local businesses failed to do so.

Bonnie Lass

While German skaters were taking their bows, some North Americans were creeping onto the world stage. Indeed, the continent produced some of the best sprinters in the 1980s and 1990s.

The United States produced top sprinters such as Dianne Holum (b. 1951), Anne Henning (b. 1955) and Beth Heiden (b. 1959). But the country's most celebrated speed skating export was Bonnie Blair (b. 1964), who blended talent and charm to put the sport on the map in the United States. There's no doubt Blair was born to race on the oval; her five older siblings competed there and her father, Charlie, was so fanatical about the sport that he was working at a competition in Yonkers, NY the day Bonnie was born.

Blair started skating when she was still in diapers and was nationally ranked before she was old enough to drive. After extensive training in Europe, she qualified for the 1984 Sarajevo Games. She returned empty-handed, but the best was yet to come. Blair won a gold (500m) and bronze (1000m) at the 1988 Calgary Games. She won both events at the 1992 Albertville Games and the 1994 Lillehammer Games. It's a good thing for the speed skating world her 1989 experiment in competitive cycling failed!

Blair was a winner off the ice, too. She won many commercial endorsements and speaking engagements thanks to her congeniality and girl-next-door appeal. How could anyone resist a champion who ate peanut butter and jelly sandwiches before races?

Jock Talk

"We get together for weddings, funerals and the Olympics."

—Bonnie Blair's cousin Kathy Murphy, one of 50 relatives who cheered the skater on at the 1992 Olympics in Albertville, France. The vocal group was dubbed "The Blair Bunch."

Oh, Canada

Jock Talk

"You could sell a lot of toothpaste with that smile."

—A Canadian athlete at the 1998 Olympics in Nagano, Japan, on teammate Catriona Le May Doan, in *Maclean's* magazine.

As Blair skated off into the sunset in 1995, a skater from north of the border began her ascent to the top of the skating world. Born in Saskatoon, SK, Catriona Le May Doan (b. 1970) was just 10 years old when she discovered speed skating was a great way to pass the long, cold prairie winters. She showed great promise when she and her sisters started skating competitively, and her career switched into high gear when she began training as a sprinter.

She competed at the 1992 Albertville Games and at the 1994 Lillehammer Games, but failed to win a medal at either. However, she regrouped and won gold in the 500m at the 1998 Nagano Games, one spot ahead of compatriot Susan Auch (b. 1966), who had won silver in that event four years earlier. Le May Doan added a bronze in the 1000m in Nagano.

She started the 2000–2001 season intending to break her own world record in the 500m sprint, and succeeded in January. She was the only woman in the world to have skated that race in less than 38 seconds.

Let Me Explain

In the 1980s, Dutch enthusiasts started using the clap skate. The blade is attached to the toe of the boot with a hinge so at the end of each stride, the skater's heel lifts off the ice while the blade does not, decreasing drag. When the revolutionary skate gained worldwide acceptance in the late 1990s, competitors' times began to drop dramatically.

Table 13.1: Initiation of Major Worldwide Long-Track Competitions

Event	Men	Women
Olympics	1924	1960
World Championships	1889	1936
World Cup	1986	1986

Short and Sweet

At the time Le May Doan was learning to walk, more and more skaters were strapping protective pads to their knees and elbows and lining up on a track a quarter the size of the traditional 400m oval. They raced against each other, in groups of four to eight, rather than against the clock. Stranger still, they shoved and bumped one another around as they jockeyed for position. Having gotten its start decades before, short-track speed skating gained worldwide popularity in the 1970s. Shag rugs have come and (thankfully) gone, but the pastime remains.

The ISU soon sanctioned short-track events, and the sport made its Olympic debut at the 1992 Albertville Games. Canadian women dominated competition at the time, but were soon surpassed by Chinese and Korean skaters.

Two Chinese women combined to win all five events at the 1999 world championships. Their names? Yang Yang A and Yang Yang S. "Their names, though pronounced the same, are written differently in Chinese and translate differently into English," explained *Sports Illustrated*. "A's means Flying Flag; S's means Sunshine. When the Chinese team was asked to come up with a way to help Westerners distinguish between the two skaters, coaches decided to call them L for large and S for small, though the

Yangs are, in fact, about the same size. The older Yang said she liked neither the large designation nor the coaches' other suggestion of O for older. She chose A as an inoffensive alternative. The younger Yang stayed with S." In November 2000, Yang Yang A was the world record holder in the 1000m, but South Koreans had set the world's best times in three of the remaining four events.

Table 13.2: Initiation of Major Worldwide Short-Track Competitions

Event	Men	Women
Olympics	1992	1992
World Championships	1976	1976
World Cup	1998	1998

The Least You Need to Know

➤ Skating was invented for work, not pleasure.

➤ Europeans took up skating as recreation before North Americans did.

➤ The Soviet Union produced Lidya Skoblikova, the first star in women's speed skating.

➤ German skaters have dominated long-track speed skating for decades.

➤ American Bonnie Blair and Canadian Catriona Le May Doan made their mark in shorter distances.

➤ China and Korea are currently producing the best skaters on the short track.

Chapter 14

Living in the Ice Age: Hockey

In This Chapter

➤ Women and men start playing ice hockey together

➤Women's hockey enjoys a golden era before lapsing into obscurity

➤Thanks to a few fearless females, the sport stages a comeback

➤The women's game produces controversies and stars

➤Women's hockey soars in popularity

➤The game reaches new heights at the 1998 Olympics

Competitive hockey for girls was virtually non-existent in the 1950s, so Canadian Abigail Hoffman cut her hair short and joined a first-rate league posing as a boy. "Ab" was good enough to make the all-star team, but when the league discovered its top defenceman was a girl, Hoffman was pushed out. Ultimately she had to choose between a middling girls' league or another sport. She ended up becoming a world-class runner. Women's hockey has since emerged from the dark ages—too late for Hoffman, but not for the women who competed at the 1998 Nagano Games.

Pass the Puck

Ice hockey may be the quintessential Canadian game, but some historians believe it was developed by the people responsible for tweed jackets and Mr. Bean. They claim modern hockey evolved when British soldiers stationed in Canada in the 1850s blended

Sports Shorts

In 1894, female students at Queen's University in Kingston, ON defied the school's archbishop and formed a hockey team. They called themselves the Love-Me-Littles.

Sports Shorts

Lord Stanley of Preston, one-time Governor General of Canada and namesake of the Stanley Cup, flooded the grounds of Government House in 1889 and spent hours playing hockey there with his whole family, including his wife and two daughters.

elements of lacrosse, field hockey and rugby into one ice sport. Other historians contend the game was developed a couple of decades earlier when Nova Scotia university students established rules to govern raucous games of "ice hurley," which featured stick-wielding players swatting at a hard ball. No matter what the origins, however, women were enthusiastic from the outset and often skated alongside men.

One of the earliest photographs of a hockey game shows women dressed in long skirts and hats chasing after the ball. In the 1880s, organized games were being held across Canada and in the northern United States. As the emphasis on competition heightened, however, the sport became segregated. Men ended up forming several leagues, including one that evolved into the prestigious National Hockey League (NHL). Women were left to their own devices.

Sports historians agree the first all-women's game took place in the early 1890s, but the consensus ends there. Most experts claim the historic game was held in Barrie, ON, 97 kilòmetres north of Toronto, in 1892. But according to USA Hockey, that game featured women playing men *dressed* as women (is it possible the first female hockey players tested their mettle against puck-chasing cross-dressers?). The organization claims the first actual all-women's game was held a year earlier, and cites an 1891 news report in the *Ottawa Citizen* as proof.

Golden Era

Fourteen years after the controversial all-women's game, Bobbie Rosenfeld (1903–1969) moved to Barrie from her native Russia. Rosenfeld, who excelled at half a dozen sports as a child, moved to Toronto in 1922 and took a job in a chocolate factory. The urge to sample the products must have been great, but Rosenfeld resisted temptation and retained her fighting form. Good thing, too. She became the country's premier female runner, winning five events and finishing second in two others at the 1925 Ontario Ladies Track and Field Championships. Three years later, Rosenfeld won gold (4x100m relay) and silver (100m) at the 1928 Amsterdam Games.

Sports Shorts

Canadian Bobbie Rosenfeld won a few medals on the track at the 1928 Olympics in Amsterdam, Holland, and also won friends and admiration along the way. Rosenfeld started the 800m run along with compatriot Jean Thompson, who was a specialist in that distance. When Thompson fell behind in the race due to a leg injury, Rosenfeld moved up from the back of the pack and ran beside her, spurring her on. Thompson finished fourth, with Rosenfeld right behind her in fifth. Many observers believed that if not for concern for her teammate, Rosenfeld could have won a medal in the race if she had wanted.

Jock Talk

"In Bobbie Rosenfeld and Casey McLean, the Pats have two players who could earn a place on any [men's] junior team. Both are speedy and good stickhandlers and pack a shot that has plenty of steam on it. Miss Rosenfeld was the best player on the ice but she spoiled her effectiveness around the net by failing to pass the puck."

—"The Toronto Star," reporting on a 1927 game, in *Proud Past, Bright Future*.

Rosenfeld also distinguished herself in organized softball and tennis, but was most enthusiastic about hockey. She starred on a dominant amateur team, the Toronto Patterson Pats, and helped form the Ladies' Ontario Hockey Association (LOHA).

Rosenfeld was fortunate to have played during the golden era of women's hockey, when dozens of teams competed at the local, regional and national level.

Dream Team

One of the era's best teams was formed on a dare. In 1930, the Preston Rivulettes girls softball team met in an arena in the town known today as Cambridge, ON. While

Sports Shorts

Canadian Elizabeth Graham, a goaltender at Queen's University in Kingston, ON, donned a crude wire fencing mask in 1927. Was it daring move or one of self-preservation? Either way, it was historic: Graham was the first goaltender to wear a mask. Thirty-two years later, the Montréal Canadiens' Jacques Plante became the first National Hockey League (NHL) goalie to wear a mask regularly.

discussing plans for the future, one woman suggested forming a hockey team. A male onlooker balked at the prospect and challenged the women to follow through.

They did just that, and became one of the best sports teams in Canadian history. The Rivulettes played an estimated 350 games between 1930 and 1940, winning all but 5. They won 10 provincial, 6 regional and 6 national titles. The team became so well known it was scheduled to tour Europe in 1939. The outbreak of World War II put an end to those plans—and to the golden era of women's hockey. Teams and leagues disbanded as North Americans turned their attention to more serious matters overseas.

Dark Ages

Following the war, more and more Canadians started to settle in urban centres. Hockey moved from ponds to indoor arenas, forcing teams to battle for limited ice time. Guess which teams lost out? While men's hockey thrived after the war, women's hockey fell into obscurity. These were desperate times that called for desperate measures.

One girl's passion for the sport led her to compete incognito on a local boys' team. Nine-year-old Abigail Hoffman (b. 1947) cut her hair short and started the 1956–57 season as "Ab." She became one of the top defencemen in the league. When she was named to the all-star team, officials inspected her birth certificate. They thought "Ab" had submitted a sister's birth certificate by mistake. But there was no mistake about it: Hoffman was busted! The story made headlines across the country. League officials let her finish the season—and assigned her a private dressing room—but they persuaded her to join a girls' league the following year.

The competition was mediocre and the games were infrequent in that league, so Hoffman quit hockey and focused on running. Like Rosenfeld before her, Hoffman became a world-class runner. She won several international competitions and competed in four Olympic Games. She was the Canadian team's flag bearer for her last Olympic appearance, at the 1976 Montréal Games.

Rise Up

While Hoffman was honing her skills in middle-distance running during the 1970s, women's hockey began a rebuilding phase. Leagues and organizations started to reappear in Canada. Women's hockey also flourished in northern parts of the United States and in Switzerland, Germany and Scandinavian countries. Women even started playing hockey in Japan.

By the 1980s, women were striding into boardrooms—often in suits with shoulder pads so wide they had to enter sideways—and into political office. In this new environment, hockey officials stopped dismissing female hockey players as cranks and obliged their request for more ice time. It helped, of course, that ice time was becoming more available due to a declining interest amongst boys. (As violence in organized hockey escalated, so did parents' concerns. An increasing number of them kept their sons away from the rink during the 1980s. The decade also saw boys start taking up other sports like soccer.) By decade's end, some 40,000 females were playing organized hockey in North America—that was eight times more female participants than in 1983.

The People's Court

Hockey's governing bodies had advocated segregation in hockey for decades. Abigail Hoffman didn't challenge their policy but, three decades later, someone else did.

Sports Shorts

Canada's Angela James (b. 1964) excelled at several sports growing up, including softball, soccer and basketball, but hockey was her favourite. "I think, living in Canada, Ontario especially, we had a lot of outdoor arenas. That's what we did for entertainment in the winter, otherwise we'd never get out of the house," she said in *Celebrating Excellence: Canadian Women Athletes*. James joined a senior level team when she was 15 years old, and tried out for the national team headed to the first world championship in 1990. She didn't make the team initially, but coaches reconsidered and added her name to the roster a week later. It was a wise decision. The forward paved the team's way to gold by scoring a team leading 11 goals and 2 assists in 5 games. She led the national team to several more first place finishes before being cut in advance of the 1998 Olympics in Nagano, Japan. James left competitive hockey in January 2001.

In 1985, Justine Blainey (b. 1973) took the Ontario Hockey Association (OHA) to court in a bid to play in a boys' league. Four years later, the Supreme Court of Canada ruled in her favour. She continued to play on a boys' team until she enrolled at the University of Toronto and joined the women's varsity team.

Let It Grow

While Blainey was still awaiting a decision, the Ontario Women's Hockey Association (OWHA) organized an informal world tournament that included teams from North America, Europe and Japan. The 1987 tournament was so successful, the International Ice Hockey Federation (IIHF), the game's international governing body, sanctioned the first world championship for women.

The eight-team tournament was held in Ottawa, ON, in 1990. Canada skated to gold, just ahead of the United States and Finland, wearing shocking pink and white uniforms designed by a Finnish sportswear company. *Ottawa Sun* writer Jane O'Hara described the uniforms as "the wussiest" she had ever seen, and many observers agreed with her. The uniforms were different but the final results were the same in the following five world championships, in 1992, 1994, 1997, 1999 and 2000.

Let Me Explain

In 1996, Canada, the United States and Finland established an annual competition called the Three Nations Cup. Sweden joined the competition in 2000 making it—you guessed it—the Four Nations Cup. Canada won the tournament four times in its first five years. The United States won once.

International competition brought heightened exposure, which, in turn, fostered an explosion in women's hockey worldwide. Registration numbers soared in the 1990s, increasing threefold in Canada and fourfold in the United States alone. In fact, the women's game became so popular one of its stars attracted attention from the NHL.

Girl Meets Boys

Canadian Manon Rheaume (b. 1972) started her career as a goaltender dodging her brothers' slapshots in the basement of their family home. She started in net for the minor league team coached by her father soon after and, in 1991, caused a commotion by playing in a game in the Québec Major Junior Hockey League. She allowed 3 goals on 13 shots. It wasn't a brilliant performance, but it captured the attention of Phil Esposito, former star player and general manager of a new NHL franchise, the Tampa Bay Lightning.

Sensing a good news story, Esposito put her in net in a pre-season game; she stopped seven of nine shots. Rheaume signed a contract with the team but was soon demoted to the International Hockey League (IHL).

She never distinguished herself in men's hockey, but Rheaume was a dominant player in the women's game. She joined the national team in 1992 and, six years later, represented Canada in the most significant tournament in women's hockey history.

Q & A

Q: What major U.S. magazine wanted to run a pictorial on star goalie Manon Rheaume?

A: *Playboy* asked the netminding hottie to pose nude. She declined.

Game Day

In the wake of Rheaume's NHL debut and the first two world championships, women's hockey created a buzz that extended to Lausanne, Switzerland, the headquarters of the IOC. In November 1992, the IOC decided to include women's ice hockey as a full medal sport at the 2002 Olympics in Salt Lake City, UT and gave organizers of the 1994 Lillehammer Games and the 1998 Nagano Games the option of including the competition in their programs. Norway declined, but Japan accepted.

Sports Shorts

A few hours after winning the gold medal at the 1998 Olympics in Nagano, Japan, 10 American team members were driven to a television studio by employees of *The Late Show with David Letterman*. There, the hockey players read a Top Ten List entitled "Cool Things About Winning an Olympic Gold Medal." (Number One: "Get to do Jell-O shots with Dave's mom.")

Jock Talk

"My favourite quote of the week comes from Allison Mleczko, the first left winger I've ever had a crush on. Mleczko, a forward on the gold medal–winning U.S. women's hockey team, said she began her life on skates not as a hockey player, but as a figure skater. But one day it dawned on her, 'It's time to trade in the little white tutu for a hockey stick.' Amen, A.J., amen."

—Michael Wilbon, *The Washington Post.*

The first women's Olympic hockey tournament featured teams from six countries, including host Japan, but only one was expected to win. Who else but the Canadians, the four-time world champions? Surprise! The American team, not willing to settle for second this time around, defeated Canada twice in the tournament to win gold. After the medal ceremony, the Canadians retreated to their dressing room and sang "O Canada." Or at least they tried. Most of them dissolved into tears before getting to "our home and native land." Canadian captain Stacy Wilson (b. 1965) explained the situation to the *Edmonton Sun*. "At first, it was kind of disbelief. This was a dream for so many years. And it's over. I thought of my friends and family and all of Canada. You get your medal, and you see it's silver and the feelings kick in pretty quick." Added teammate Judy Diduck (b. 1966): "They played better. Hats off to them."

Q & A

Q: Canadian national team player Hayley Wickenheiser had a famous cousin. Who was he?
A: Doug Wickenheiser, who played in the NHL (National Hockey League) for 10 seasons starting in 1980. He died of cancer in 1999.

Quick Wick

Unfortunately for the Canadians, their top player was skating injured. Forward Hayley Wickenheiser (b. 1978), routinely described as "the best female hockey player on the planet," suffered a strained medial collateral ligament in her right knee. Still, Wickenheiser was no slouch. She notched two goals and six assists in the six-game tournament. Wickenheiser, who joined the team in 1994, impressed more than her teammates and fans with her grit and talent.

She also impressed Bob Clarke, former superstar and president and general manager of the NHL's Philadelphia Flyers, who invited her to the team's rookie camp that

Jock Talk

"I always thought my first Olympics would be in softball because there were no girls' leagues for hockey [when I was growing up.]"

—Canadian Hayley Wickenheiser, who competed in the Winter Olympics with the hockey team and in the Summer Olympics with the softball team, to the *Ottawa Citizen.*

summer. Wickenheiser seized the opportunity as a chance to hone her skills not, as she assured anyone who would listen, to make the team.

After the camp, she returned to the national team, leading it to two more world championship titles, then traded in her skates for cleats and joined the national softball team at the 2000 Sydney Games. She became the second Canadian woman to compete in both Summer and Winter Games (Sue Holloway finished seventh in cross-country skiing in 1976 and won silver and bronze medals in kayak in 1984). Wickenheiser didn't come home with a medal this time; Canada finished eighth.

She took a five-month break and then laced up her skates and rejoined talented national squad teammates such as forward Danielle Goyette

Jock Talk

"Can you imagine being 6-foot-6 and not done growing? I wish!"

—Canadian star Hayley Wickenheiser, reporting on her peers at an NHL (National Hockey League) rookie camp in 1998, to CBS *Sportsline.*

(b. 1966), who had notched eight goals and one assist in Nagano, defenceman Geraldine Heaney (b. 1967), who had added two goals and four assists at the tournament and defenceman Cassie Campbell (b. 1973). The team has shifted its focus to the 2002 Salt Lake City Games, determined to avenge its loss in Nagano.

Sharpshooter

The Canadians will have their work cut out for them in Salt Lake City. The American squad has become a formidable one, featuring a star player with hockey in her blood. Cammi Granato (b. 1971) played hockey with her brothers growing up in Illinois. Her eldest brother, Tony, became a top NHL player and played on the American team at the 1988 Calgary Games. His participation inspired his younger sister, who went to college

Jock Talk

"The invitation to participate in the [game] demonstrates how far Granato in particular, and women's hockey in general, has come since the U.S. triumph in Nagano."

—*CNN/Sports Illustrated*, on American star Cammi Granato's appearance in the 1999 NHL Heroes of Hockey Game.

on a hockey scholarship and scored 256 points in 99 games. Not surprisingly, she joined the national team in 1990 and established herself a sharpshooter. She became team captain and, in time, emerged from the shadow of her famous brother.

A year after winning gold at the 1998 Nagano Games, she skated alongside retired NHL stars such as Rod Gilbert and Darryl Sittler in the Heroes of Hockey Game during the NHL All-Star Weekend. "I was a little bit intimidated. I didn't know how they would accept me, being the only girl, but they were very welcoming," she told USA Hockey.

At the end of 2000, the forward went to Lake Placid, NY to prepare for the 2002 Salt Lake City Games. She was joined by talented teammates such as forward Karen Bye (b. 1971), who had notched 100 goals and 64 assists in 87 games at the University of New Hampshire. While the outcome of the showdown in Salt Lake City Games remains undetermined, the status of women's hockey is not. "For years they've put up with ill-fitting skates, lousy ice times and equipment made for men," *Chatelaine* magazine reported in 1998, "Now suddenly, women hockey players are hot."

Table 14.1: Initiation of Major Worldwide Competitions

Event	Men	Women
Olympics	1920	1998
World Championships	1930	1990

Q & A

Q: How did American national team player Karen Bye get the nickname "K.L.?"

A: When she played for a boys' team as a 14-year-old, she put her initials rather than her full given name on the program so "people wouldn't know there was a girl on the team."

The Least You Need to Know

➤ In the beginning, men and women played hockey together.

➤ During the 1920s and 1930s, women's hockey was almost as popular as it is now.

➤ Women's hockey was one of the casualties of World War II.

➤ The sport was reborn in the 1970s and has since soared in popularity.

➤ The growth continues thanks to the game's inclusion in the Olympics and the emergence of star players.

Chapter 15

Love on the Rocks: Curling

In This Chapter

➤ Curling is invented. But by whom?

➤ Scottish enthusiasts develop the game and make it a hot export

➤ Women join men on the ice

➤ Two female curlers stand out in the crowd

➤ Curling becomes an Olympic sport

➤ The game loses one of its most popular players

Odds are, the sixteenth-century merry-makers who threw the rocks that ended up at the bottom of a Scottish lake weren't women. Nonetheless, women got in on the fun a few centuries later, and now compete in curling competitions at every level, including the Olympics. From the Canadian prairies to the Scandinavian peninsula, women love to curl. Their devotion is nothing short of rock solid.

The Battle of Evermore

If you're looking for a definitive answer to an intriguing question, ask an historian who assassinated U.S. President John F. Kennedy. Do *not* ask a curling enthusiast who invented the game; the topic has been hotly debated for years.

All curling buffs acknowledge that small flat stones dating from the early 1500s have been found in dried-out and drained lakes in Scotland. But consensus ends there. While some enthusiasts claim the stones prove the Scots invented the game, others claim these "loofies" prove only that the game was *played* in Scotland. This camp believes curling was introduced to Scotland by Flemish immigrants in the 1500s.

While the question of who invented the game may be uncertain, one thing is clear: the Scots made curling a national pastime. For three hundred years starting in the 1500s, the game was played in various Scottish communities, each with its own set of rules. When improved transportation allowed enthusiasts from various communities to meet for an end or two in the 1800s, rules gradually became uniform. The Grand Caledonian Curling Club was established to oversee competition in 1838. Five years later, the organization received royal patronage and became the Royal Caledonian Curling Club.

Jock Talk

"When [we] first went on-line, we included a brief history of curling. We quickly received a number of messages about our information, some agreeing with our facts and others disputing them. Since then, the comments have continued to come in, and all we have to say is ... 'How the hell did we manage to stir up this hornet's nest?'"

—International Curling Information Network Group, on the challenge of coming up with a definitive account of curling's origins.

Scotch Rocks

The Scots were soon exporting the game like so much toffee and single malt scotch. Scottish immigrants played the game where they settled and large numbers of them ended up in Canada, where the ice sport was a natural fit for the long, cold winters. Little wonder then, that Canadian curlers have become some of the best in the world and introduced many of the techniques and strategies that define the sport today.

Curling caught on in other parts of the world in the mid-twentieth century with the introduction of artificial rinks, where enthusiasts could hone their skills on smooth ice and play year round.

The sport eventually became more organized and governing bodies were established in several countries, including Canada. The Dominion Curling Association, later renamed the Canadian Curling Association (CCA), was founded in 1935. The United States

Curling Association (USCA) was founded in 1958. The International Curling Federation was founded in 1966. It is now known as the World Curling Federation (WCF).

Girls Just Wanna Have Fun

These organizations sanctioned local, regional and national events. The competitions were originally for men, but it didn't take long for women to get in on the action. In the mid-1900s, an increasing number of women began playing against each other (usually during the day, when ice was available because men were otherwise occupied) or with their spouses in mixed leagues.

In 1961, female curlers started competing in a national championship in Canada. In 1977, women in the United States followed suit. The first women's world championship was held in 1979, two decades after the first men's world championship. By the 1980s, there were almost as many women sliding down the ice, rock in tow and broom in hand, as men.

A few women distinguished themselves at the international level during the 1980s and 1990s, including Norwegian Dordi Nordby and Canadian Marilyn Bodogh (b. 1955), both of whom led their respective teams to two world titles. But two women generated more excitement in the sport.

Let Me Explain

The Scott Tournament of Hearts is the women's national championship in Canada. It's held every February.

Star Appeal

Sweden's Elisabet Gustafson (b. 1964) discovered curling watching the 1977 men's world championship. "I was fascinated from the games on television and wanted to try curling," Gustafson told *Sweep!*. She took up the sport in high school and became a top skip while moving up through the ranks.

In 1992, Gustafson and her teammates (Katarina Nyberg, Louise Marmont and Elisabeth Persson) represented Sweden at the world championship. The team lost to the defending champions from Norway in an early game, but regrouped and rolled to the world title without losing another game. The

Q & A

Q: Elisabet Gustafson's husband, Tomas, is famous in Sweden in his own right. Why?

A: The former speed skater won a gold and a silver at the 1984 Olympics in Sarajevo, Yugoslavia and two gold at the 1988 Olympics in Calgary, AB.

171

Let Me Explain

Each curling team consists of four players: the lead, the second, the third and the skip, who is usually the team captain and most experienced player, determines strategy. All four players are involved in every shot.

Q & A

Q: What is the off-rink profession of Swedish curler Elisabet Gustafson?

A: She is a surgeon.

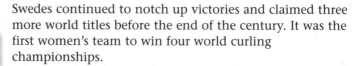

Swedes continued to notch up victories and claimed three more world titles before the end of the century. It was the first women's team to win four world curling championships.

Despite her success, Gustafson didn't have the spotlight to herself. She shared it with a rival from Saskatchewan, the Canadian province that has twice as many curlers as the entire United States. Sandra Schmirler (1963–2000) learned to curl when she was 12 years old and, soon after graduating from university, formed a team with compatriots Jan Betker, Joan McCusker and Marcia Gudereit. The four women forged a close friendship and became one of the world's best female teams, winning three national titles and three world titles.

Five-Ring Circus

Gustafson and Schmirler both competed at the 1998 Nagano Games, where curling made its debut as a full medal event (curling had been a demonstration sport at previous Olympics, in 1924, 1932, 1988 and 1992).

Gustafson and her teammates stepped up their training regimen well in advance of the tournament in Japan, taking months at a time off their jobs to practise and compete (the team received substantial financial support from the Swedish Olympic Committee). In the autumn before the Games, the Swedes trained in Canada. "During that season we spent 12–14 hours per week training on ice, and 6 hours per week on physical training," Katarina Nyberg told *Sweep!*. "We met 19 or 20 weekends for either competitions or training camps." But despite their efforts, Gustafson and her teammates ended up settling for bronze while their Canadian rivals took home the gold.

"Schmirler the Curler" led her teammates to one win after another in Nagano. The women dissolved into tears and hugged each other after squeaking past Britain in the semifinal game, then regained their composure and coasted past Denmark in the final.

Victory was sweet for the women, but it didn't ease the pain of separation from their children. All four members had infants at home in Canada. When asked about the challenge of combining curling with motherhood, Schmirler told reporters that her daughter was the "most important thing" in her life.

Q & A

Q: How does Swedish curler Elisabet Gustafson keep fit?

A: She adheres to a demanding training regimen that includes *a lot* of running. She has competed in the Stockholm Marathon a few times and takes part in orienteering, a competitive sport where participants use a map and a compass to make their way across varied, rugged terrain—no off-road vehicles allowed.

Jock Talk

"Our eyes just doubled in size when we found out we had an Olympic trial berth. That's huge. If we had thought about everything that was on the line, we wouldn't have made a shot."

—Nova Scotia skip Colleen Jones, after her team won the national title and, with it, a berth at the Canadian trials for the 2002 Olympics in Salt Lake City, UT. Jones is well known to Canadian television viewers as a broadcaster.

Sad Farewell

Just over a year later, Schmirler gave birth to a second daughter. Successful at combining family with a career on the ice, Schmirler seemed destined for a long and happy life. But it was not to be. She was diagnosed with cancer and died a few months later, in March 2000.

Hundreds attended her funeral and some 8000 fans gathered at the curling club Schmirler and her team

Let Me Explain

A curling tournament is called a bonspiel.

had called home. In Saskatoon, the Labatt Brier, the Canadian men's national championship, was delayed so players and fans could watch the funeral proceedings on giant screens set up in the facility.

In his eulogy, friend Brian McCusker paid tribute to Sandra Schmirler the person and, of course, the athlete. He noted that Schmirler had been a devout fan of the game. "If Sandra's watching here today and I think she is, she's saying 'C'mon, McCusker, let's get this over with. Don't you know the Brier's on this week? I don't want to miss the first rock.'"

Table 15.1: Initiation of Major Worldwide Competitions

Event	Men	Women
Olympics	1998	1998
World Championships	1959	1979

The Least You Need to Know

➤ The origins of curling have been debated for centuries.

➤ The Scots introduced curling to various countries, including Canada.

➤ Women's competitions followed hot on the heels of the men's.

➤ Elisabet Gustafson and Sandra Schmirler have been the biggest names in the women's game.

Part 4
The Water's Fine— Water Sports

When you hear the term "water sports," do you envision a pale, heavy-set man leaping off a diving board to land the first belly flop of his summer vacation? If so, give your head a shake. Others have made a bigger impact in the water (though not in the literal sense). Among them are remarkable women like Ethelda Bleibtrey, who was thrown in jail when she exposed her legs at a beach in 1919 (and then went on to be an Olympic champion) and Gertrude Ederle, the first woman to swim the English Channel. Such stories of grit and determination have inspired generations of water-loving women. Almost seven decades after Ederle dove into the frigid water, a piece of wood ripped through the leg of rower Silken Laumann. She suffered a fractured bone, cut muscles and sustained nerve and tissue damage. Ten weeks later she won an Olympic medal. How's that for making a splash?

Take a Dip: Swimming

Olympian Jenny Thompson made waves when she got her nose pierced in 1998, but the reaction paled in comparison to the uproar caused by another American swimmer decades earlier. In 1919, Ethelda Bleibtrey was thrown in jail for nude bathing; she had removed her woollen stockings before swimming at a beach in Manhattan Bay, NY.

Despite their antics, these women aren't misfits in the annals of swimming. From the time women raced on France's Seine River in 1885, many of the top female swimmers have been, well, unconventional...

Q & A

Q: What American woman became an Olympic champion in 1920, after being released from jail?

A: Ethelda Bleibtrey, who was fined and incarcerated when she exposed her legs at a beach. She was released due to public support. From then on, women could go to the beach without fear of being handcuffed and thrown behind bars.

Let Me Explain

The breaststroke is a complicated stroke that demands perfect synchronization of simultaneous arm and leg movements. The breaststroke was popular in late 1600s and remained the stroke of choice for almost 200 years.

In the Beginning

Ancient artifacts and texts suggest that women began swimming at the same time as men, and that swimming was part of a daily routine. The first humans imitated animals, using their limbs to propel themselves through the water. One mythic female of that period merits special attention. Wadjet, the goddess of swimming, was worshipped by the Ancient Egyptians, whose lives were geographically and culturally centred on the great Nile River.

But women's swimming then disappeared from the annals of western history. Female citizens of Ancient Greece and Rome bathed indoors and access to natural bodies of water was restricted. Swimming was *de rigeur* for men, but not for women.

Swimming fell out of fashion altogether as people started settling in the chilly, nether regions of Europe. Furthermore, an epidemic of bubonic and pneumonic plagues swept through the continent in the Middle Ages, discouraging the few remaining healthy souls from spending time at the lake.

Water Babies

In the 1700s water was deemed therapeutic, and men and women of means spent hours at the spa, sipping herbal potions while soaking in mineral springs. They weren't swimming, true, but at least they were getting their feet wet!

Within a few decades, people were being taught to swim at the YMCAs that had popped up around the world. Country clubs and athletic clubs were adding swimming pools and teaching the skill. In England, aquatic clubs were organized and competitions started in the 1870s under the auspices of the National Swimming Society in Britain. In 1875, The Dolphin Club of Toronto sponsored a race. The Montréal Swim Club did the same the following year. The New York Athletic Club followed suit and held a U.S. championship in 1883.

Men and women alike were swept up in the physical fitness craze in late 1800s. While society had little tolerance for competitive female cyclists or—good heavens!—female

Sports Shorts

In the early days of women's swimming, efforts were made to keep lascivious men at bay. In the 1890s, men were prevented from watching women's competitions in Germany. A few years later, they were allowed in, but had to sit at least 30 yards from the contestants.

Jock Talk

"[At the turn of the last century] women did not compete in strenuous athletics. It was not considered healthy for girls to overexert themselves or to swim as far as a mile. People thought it was a great mistake, that we were ruining our health, that we would never have children, and that we would be sorry for it later on."

—American swimmer and diver Aileen Riggin.

boxers, competitive female swimmers were more or less accepted. In 1885, for example, both sexes competed in a race on the Seine River in France. The event had been advertised in a poster displayed at kiosks around Paris. It showed a young female swimmer floating down the Seine with bare calves, bare arms and—of all things—a pair of shoes! As it turns out, female participants in the race wore full-skirted knee-length outfits and woollen socks, but skipped the footwear. However, a few daring women discarded those cumbersome outfits in favour of swimming suits that exposed their flesh and caused a stir.

Q & A

Q: What American statesman gave swimming demonstrations in England's Thames River?

A: Benjamin Franklin.

Women's swimming also caused a stir in medical circles, where doctors warned that the activity was bad for the womb and would inhibit conception. Those female swimmers who managed to conceive were cautioned to stay out of the water lest swimming damage the fetus.

Let Me Explain

The front crawl is the ideal stroke for sprinting and is the most popular in freestyle races. In a freestyle race, competitors technically may use any stroke they wish. In 1845, Native Americans Flying Gull and Tobacco travelled to Britain for exhibition races and won using a rudimentary front crawl. The stroke then became popular in the 1890s, when John Trudgen introduced it to Europe.

The Race is On

Female swimmers were not allowed to compete at the 1904 Olympics in St. Louis, MO. But four years later, swimming enthusiasts organized the Fédération Internationale de Nation Amateur (FINA) and through its efforts, women's swimming was introduced at the 1912 Stockholm Games.

Australia's Fanny Durack (1894–1955) set a world record in her heat for the 100m freestyle, breaking the one set by Briton Daisy Curwen. In the semifinals she beat Curwen, who then went straight to hospital for an emergency appendectomy. Durack went on to capture the gold medal in the event. Her compatriot, Mina Wylie, took home the silver.

In 1914, the AAU in the United States sanctioned competitive swimming for women, thanks in part to the efforts of a court reporter named Charlotte Epstein. Three years later, Epstein rented a small pool in the basement of a hotel in Brooklyn, NY and formed an organization called the Swimming Association of New York, that prepared women for competition. This club, along with the Illinois Women's Athletic Club, produced most of the United States' top female swimmers in the 1920s:

➤ Sybil Bauer (1903–1927) broke the men's world record in the backstroke, and asked to swim against men in the Olympics. Games officials turned down her request.

➤ Aileen Riggin (b. 1906) won her first Olympic medal at the 1920 Antwerp Games when she was 13 years old. She competed successfully in both swimming and diving for more than a decade.

➤ Ethelda Bleibtrey (1902–1978) became the first American woman to win a gold medal and the only person to win all the women's swimming events at a single Olympics. She won three gold (100m freestyle, in which she set a world record; 400m freestyle and another world record; and 4x100m freestyle relay) at the 1920 Antwerp Games, even though she said swimming in the pool's poor-quality water was like swimming in mud.

Led by Bleibtrey, American women dominated the Antwerp Games, taking four of five gold medals in swimming and diving. It was the first time American women swam in the Olympics and they went on to dominate the next two Games as well.

Q & A

Q: What American swimmer was thought to swim like a man?

A: Martha Norelius (b. 1902). She swam with her head high and her back arched and used a heavy kick to help her hydroplane over the water. She was the first female swimmer to win gold medals in two different Olympic Games, claiming victory in the 400m freestyle in 1924 (in world-record time) and again in 1928.

Sports Shorts

American officials were so determined to preserve the moral integrity of their female swimmers at the 1924 Olympics in Paris, France, that the young women were housed outside the city and had to spend five to six hours a day travelling to and from the Olympic pool. Despite this inconvenience, U.S. swimmers won gold, silver and bronze in the 100m freestyle.

The Glamorous Life

Within a few decades, women's swimming was more than acceptable—it was absolutely glamourous. A handful of female swimmers became as popular as movie stars, and magazines devoted full-length articles to their exploits. Some of these glamour girls also appeared in advertisements, paving the way for today's lucrative endorsement deals.

Gertrude Ederle (b. 1906)

This American learned to swim during family outings to the New Jersey shore, joined the Women's Swimming Association of New York when she was 15 years old and then became one of the most famous female swimmers in history. Ederle won one gold (4x100m freestyle relay) and two bronze (100m freestyle and 400m freestyle) at the 1924

Paris Games. Between 1921 and 1925 she set 29 world records at distances ranging from 45 metres to one 1 kilometre.

Ederle wanted more than just world records, however. She wanted to make an indelible mark in the history books. Swimming the English Channel seemed like just the ticket. She failed at her first crossing attempt in 1925, but succeeded the following year. Slathered in Vaseline, olive oil and lanolin, Ederle swam from Cape Gris-Nez, France, to Kingsdorn, England in 14 hours and 31 minutes, smashing the previous record (set by a man) by more than two hours. Ederle was the sixth swimmer and first woman to cross the Channel.

Ederle's feat was celebrated worldwide; two million people attended a ticker-tape parade in her honour in New York, NY. But her success came with a price. Ederle's ears had

Sports Shorts

In the wake of Gertrude Ederle's crossing of the English Channel, dozens of women took up marathon swimming. In 1951, Canadian Winnie Leuszler (b. 1926) won a cash prize for swimming across the Channel in an event organized by an English newspaper. A parade was held in her honour when she returned to Toronto.

Three years later, the Canadian National Exhibition offered American Florence Chadwick $10,000 to swim from Youngstown, NY, to Toronto, ON. Leuszler and compatriot Marilyn Bell (b. 1939) were not included in the offer, but took the plunge anyway "for the honour of Canada." Chadwick dropped out nauseous and exhausted, and Leuszler called it quits, too; she had gotten lost in the water and then suffered severe cramps from the exertion. But Bell persevered and finished the swim in 20 hours and 59 minutes. She became a hero overnight. The next year, Bell became the youngest swimmer to cross the English Channel.

Her exploits inspired a generation of Canadian marathon swimmers. In 1977, Cindy Nicholas (b. 1957) became the first woman to accomplish a double crossing of the English Channel. The Toronto native swam the English Channel 19 times, including three two-way crossings in 1981.

Vicki Keith qualified for the *Guiness Book of World Records* for several feats, including setting the record for swimming in a pool for 129 hours and 45 minutes in 1986. She crossed all five Great Lakes in 1988 and, a year later, became the first person to cross the English Channel using the butterfly stroke. She also swam for more than 13 hours in Australia's Sydney Harbour, and swam across California's Catalina Channel.

been damaged in the Channel crossing and she was left completely deaf by 1933. She suffered a nervous breakdown a few years later and then sustained a serious back injury falling down a flight of stairs. The steely Ederle would not be broken, however. She was able to regroup and became a swimming instructor for deaf children.

Annette Kellerman (1888–1975)

Kellerman was the first motion picture mermaid and thrilled her audiences by diving into aquariums and executing balletic moves in the water. Her novelty acts drew large crowds; a swim down the Seine River attracted some 500,000 spectators.

Q & A

Q: What famous swimmer was arrested for indecency?

A: Australian Annette Kellerman. In 1907, she appeared on a beach in the United States in a one-piece bathing suit.

Eleanor Holm (b. 1913)

In 1939, American entrepreneur Billy Rose launched the travelling swimming extravaganza, *Billy Rose's Aquacades*. He hired attractive swimmers to perform in his shows. One such performer was Johnny Weissmuller (better known as Tarzan). Another was Rose's second wife, Eleanor Holm, who was introduced to the audience wearing silver high heeled shoes, a swimsuit covered in silver sequins and a matching cape.

The American earned a gold medal in the 100m backstroke at the 1932 Los Angeles Games. She crushed the world record by several seconds, and went on to break every world record in the backstroke at every recorded distance.

After marrying a bandleader in 1933, she trained for the 1936 Berlin Games during the day and sang with her husband at night. On her cruise *en route* to the Berlin Games, she drank and gambled until dawn. She was removed from the team upon arrival in Germany, and was barred from Olympic competition for the rest of her life.

Soon after her first marriage ended in 1938, she married Rose. She starred in the *Aquacades* until 1940, when she was replaced by another famous swimming beauty named Esther Williams.

Esther Williams (b. 1923)

As a national swimming champion, Williams could have earned a spot on the U.S. team for the 1940 Olympics, but the Games were cancelled due to World War II. Williams ended up signing on with the *Aquacades* instead. Unfortunately, the show folded promptly after her arrival. Williams then signed on with MGM and starred in

Jock Talk

"I can't sing, I can't dance, I can't act."

—Esther Williams, when she was approached by talent scouts after her short-lived career in the *Aquacades*. Despite her protests, she had all the trappings of a Hollywood star.

extravagant movies. By the early 1950s, she was one of the highest paid actors in Hollywood.

From a Land Down Under

In the 1950s, competitive swimming became more popular than the show biz variety. At the 1956 Melbourne Games, women constituted just 16 percent of their country's contingent, yet they won more than half their team's gold medals and led Australia to a third-place finish (behind the United States and the Soviet Union).

Q & A

Q: What Australian swimmer once dreamt she was competing in a pool full of spaghetti?

A: Dawn Fraser. She had that dream the night before the finals of the 100m freestyle at the 1956 Olympics in Melbourne, Australia. Thankfully, the pool was filled with water on race day. Fraser won the gold.

Australian Dawn Fraser (b. 1937) won a gold (100m freestyle, which she swam in world-record time) and a silver (400m freestyle). She was also part of Australia's gold-medal-winning 4x100m freestyle relay team. Six years later she became the first woman to swim the 100m freestyle in under a minute. She won gold in the same event at the 1960 Rome Games and at the 1964 Tokyo Games, where she was referred to as "Granny" due to her "advanced" age of 27. She won her third gold medal in Tokyo, just six months after her mother was killed in a car accident. Fraser had been driving the car and suffered a chipped neck vertebra. Doctors put her in a cast and predicted she would not swim again. What did they know?

Despite her success, Fraser wasn't your garden-variety sports icon. Her fondness for beer upset Australian swimming officials, who were none too pleased with her refusal to wear a regulation suit in Tokyo. Fraser claimed the suit was uncomfortable and hindered her performance. And the hijinx weren't over. Also at those Games, Fraser marched in the opening ceremonies even though she had been ordered to rest, and climbed a fence at Emperor Hirohito's palace and stole the Japanese flag. Fraser wasn't shot on the spot but she was arrested and later released. The Emperor gave her the flag as a gift but her joke fell flat with her own country's swimming officials, who banned her for 10 years. The ban was lifted four years later, but it was too late—Fraser's career was over.

Serious Business

Few people in swimming circles shared Fraser's fun-loving approach to the sport. In the 1950s and 1960s, swimming became serious. New conditioning techniques were introduced and training intensified. Swimsuits were streamlined. Records were being smashed left, right and centre.

The women's swimming program started to expand in this era and hasn't stopped since. The Olympic swim program now includes 16 women's events—a few more than the 2 events contested in 1912. (The men's program also includes 16 events.)

Let Me Explain

In the individual medley, athletes swim each stroke for at least one length of the pool. The strokes are: breaststroke, backstroke, butterfly and freestyle, which can be any stroke but one of the first three (swimmers invariably use the crawl).

Table 16.1: Initiation of Women's Olympic Swimming Events

Olympics	Event(s)
1912	100m freestyle; 4x100m freestyle relay
1920	400m freestyle
1924	100m backstroke; 200m breaststroke
1956	100m butterfly
1960	4x100m medley relay
1964	400m individual medley
1968	200m freestyle; 800m freestyle; 200m backstroke; 100m breaststroke; 200m butterfly; 200m individual medley
1988	50m freestyle
1996	4x200m freestyle relay

Q & A

Q: What female swimmer became the first female sportscaster for an American network television, in 1965, and the first women to do commentary for the Olympics on American television, in 1968?

A: Donna de Verona, who helped found the Women's Sports Foundation.

Teeny-Boppers

Though Fraser ushered in an era in which Americans and Australians dominated international competition, she wasn't the only star at the 1964 Tokyo Games. A group of American teenagers also grabbed headlines. Dubbed "Water Babies" due to their youthfulness, they won seven of the ten women's swimming and diving events. Donna De Verona (b. 1947) won two gold (400m individual medley and 4x100m freestyle relay), which was poetic justice for the 17-year-old American. Four years earlier she had come home empty-handed from the Rome Games, where she had been the youngest member of the American team. Her event, the 400m individual medley, had been cancelled.

At the 1972 Munich Games, Australian Shane Gould (b. 1956) won three gold in world-record time (200m freestyle, 400m freestyle and 200m individual medley), a silver (800m freestyle) and a bronze (100m freestyle). Her dominance led hopeful American swimmers to sport t-shirts bearing the slogan, "All that glitters is not Gould." Wishful thinking!

Handy Dandy Controversy

At the 1976 Montréal Games, a new power emerged in women's swimming: the German Democratic Republic. East German women didn't win a single gold medal in swimming until the Montréal Games, where they won 11 of 13 events and set 8 world records. Their exploits shocked the American team, which was loaded with stars.

German Kornelia Ender (b. 1958) stood head and (very broad) shoulders above her competitors. She set 23 world records during her career. When she was 11 years old, Ender was enrolled in a school for gifted athletes where she swam 7 miles a day under the supervision of a coach and a team doctor. Two years later, she was 5-foot-11 and 167 pounds.

At the 1972 Munich Games, she was anchor of two relay teams, both of which won silver. Ender picked up a third silver medal on her own (200m individual medley). Four years later in Montréal, Ender captured four gold (100m freestyle, 200m freestyle, 100m butterfly and 4x100m medley relay) and one silver (4x100m freestyle relay). She won two of those medals within the space of 28 minutes and every one of her times broke a world record.

American Shirley Babashoff (b. 1957)—who was beaten by East German swimmers in every event at the Montréal Games and had to settle for five silver medals—first refused to congratulate Ender, and then complained that GDR swimmers, with their suspiciously broad shoulders and deep voices, were using performance-enhancing drugs (i.e. steroids). Her complaints were dismissed as sour grapes.

Ender herself denied using drugs. "I don't think I was the type who needed something, she was quoted as saying in *Sports Illustrated*. "I didn't lift weights much. I was agile, naturally strong. I did drills. I had a naturally perfect freestyle stroke. I was used as an example to others." Nonetheless, after the fall of the Berlin Wall in 1989, Ender admitted she had been given injections without being told what they contained. Several eminent coaches from the former East Germany also confirmed that use of anabolic steroids had been prevalent among the country's female athletes in the 1970s. And recently, more revelations have surfaced.

Let Me Explain

In the butterfly, the arms are lifted forward and pulled back symmetrically for propulsion. The shoulders stay horizontal and parallel to the water surface. The legs also move in unison in the dolphin kick. The butterfly was introduced in the 1930s. However, it was deemed too strenuous and remained a novelty until the 1950s when it became a competitive stroke.

In 2000, Manfred Ewald, former head of the GDR's Gymnastics and Sports Federation, and Manfred Hoppner, the doctor who administered the illegal substances to the country's top athletes, were convicted of aiding and abetting bodily harm. They received suspended sentences, however, much to the disappointment of affected female athletes, many of whom had suffered side effects from the drugs, ranging from excessive body hair to liver, kidney and menstrual problems.

Sports Shorts

Canada's Anne Ottenbrite (b. 1966) won gold (200m breaststroke) at the 1984 Olympics in Los Angeles, CA, an incredible feat given her history of mishaps. In May 1984 she dislocated her kneecap while showing off a new pair of shoes; she missed the Canadian trials, but was placed on the team anyway. Just before the Games she suffered whiplash in a car accident. While recuperating, she strained a thigh muscle playing video games.

Sports Shorts

American Summer Sanders (b. 1972) was one of the most popular athletes at the 1992 Olympics in Barcelona, Spain, where she won two gold (200m butterfly and 4x100m medley relay), one silver (200m individual medley) and one bronze (400m individual medley). She won product endorsements, too, and appeared as a guest star on *All My Children*. Unfortunately, she was never able to improve on her times from 1992 and she failed to qualify for the 1996 Olympics in Atlanta, GA.

American Bandstand

Many observers deemed Tracy Caulkins (b. 1963) one of the best swimmers of all time. She qualified for the 1980 Moscow Games, but the ensuing American boycott barely dented her career. She went to the University of Florida and won 48 national long- and short-course titles—the most ever by a swimmer in U.S. history—and broke 62 national records. She excelled at all distances.

Caulkins trained five hours a day, six days a week heading into the Los Angeles Games in 1984. She won the 400m individual medley on opening day and went on to win two more gold (200m individual medley and 4x100m medley relay). She retired later that year at 21 years of age.

American swimmer Janet Evans (b. 1971), noted for her unorthodox windmill stroke, took her place at the top of swimming world at the 1988 Seoul Games, where she won three gold (400m freestyle, 800m freestyle and 400m individual medley). The swimmer, once ridiculed for her diminutive size—she weighed just 95 pounds—won her fourth gold four years later at the Barcelona Games (800m freestyle) and added a silver (400m freestyle). Three of her world records (400m freestyle, 800m freestyle and 1500 freestyle) still stand.

Q & A

Q: What Canadian swimmer was inspired by American champion Janet Evans?

A: Canada's Joanne Malar (b. 1975), who finished fourth in the 200m individual medley at the 1996 Olympics in Atlanta, GA, and fifth in the same race at the 2000 Olympics in Sydney, Australia. Evans's success convinced Malar that size isn't everything in the water. Malar was just 5-foot-1 when she joined the Canadian national team in 1989. She grew seven inches over the next few years.

Stay in the Pool, Drugs Aren't Cool

In the 1990s, the Chinese women dominated the freestyle sprints and were widely believed to be taking performance-enhancing drugs. Indeed, the Chinese swim program was tainted by several positive drug tests. As a result, China was banned from taking part in the Pan Pacific Games in 1995, but no Chinese woman had ever tested positive for steroids in Olympic competition.

Controversy exploded at the 1992 Barcelona Games when China's Zhuang Yong was the surprise winner in the 100m freestyle. With a deep voice, heavy muscles and bad acne, Zhuang fit the profile of a steroid user like a glove, but she was not tested for drugs after her controversial victory (FINA's policy at the time was to test randomly only two of the top four finishers, whereas all other sports tested all medallists). She passed a doping test five days later, but doubts about her drug status lingered.

Suspicion heightened two years later at the 1994 world championships in Rome, when Chinese swimmers won 12 of the 16 women's races. China's Lu Bin won the 200m individual medley and tested positive for steroids four weeks later. FINA reacted to the ensuing outcry by stepping up out-of-competition testing. Chinese dominance soon ended and only one Chinese swimmer, Le Jingyi, won a gold medal (100m freestyle) at the 1996 Atlanta Games.

Allegations of drug abuse also swirled around Irish swimmer Michelle Smith (b. 1970), who rose from obscurity to capture three gold (400m freestyle, 200m individual medley and 400m individual medley) and a bronze (200m butterfly) at the 1996 Atlanta Games.

In 1993, Smith met her future husband Erik de Bruin, a Dutch discus thrower who had tested positive for drugs. Under his guidance, her times dropped dramatically and she began winning international events. She also became increasingly difficult to track down for out-of-competition drug tests.

Her exploits in Atlanta made her a hero in Ireland. Irish president Mary Robinson greeted the swimmer at the airport upon her return from the Games and a folk song was written in Smith's honour. Less than two years later, two FINA officials showed up at her

Let Me Explain

Swimmers held their arms straight through the entire backstroke until the 1950s when they realized they could gain speed by bending their arms during the underwater part of the stroke.

Jock Talk

"[The 1994 world championships] is when the Chinese team broke all the records and the rules by using steroids."

—American swimmer Jenny Thompson, in *Women Who Win.*

Sports Shorts

Hungary's Krisztina Egerszegi (b. 1974) was 99 pounds and 14 years old at her first Olympics, in 1988. She won gold (200m backstroke) and silver (100m backstroke). Four years later, at the 1992 Olympics in Barcelona, Spain, she won three gold (100m backstroke, 200m backstroke and 400m individual medley). She picked up another gold (200m backstroke) and a bronze (400m individual medley) at the 1996 Olympics in Atlanta, GA. There, she became the first woman in any sport to earn five gold medals in individual events. Not surprisingly, she became known as the greatest backstroker of all time and she retired after the Atlanta Games. Her best time in the 200m backstroke still stands as a world record.

home in Ireland and requested a urine sample. The sample was found to contain a level of alcohol that would be fatal if consumed by a human. FINA concluded that the alcohol had been added to the sample to act as a masking agent and suspended Smith for four years, effectively ending her career.

Jock Talk

"Doping is an explosive issue in swimming because there is a tradition of purity in the sport. When one female swimmer is caught taking performance-enhancing drugs we're outraged."

—Phil Whitten, editor of *Swimming World* magazine.

Old World, New World

Drugs continue to be an issue at the top level of women's swimming. While officials now test for some drugs, including anabolic steroids and erythropoietin (EPO), they do not test for others such as human growth hormone (HGH). It's commonly held that science hasn't yet advanced to the point where these chemicals can be detected, and some observers charge that swimming's governing bodies want to keep it that way; proof of illegal drug use would damage the credibility of the sport and that would be bad for business. But there's no doubt that doping exists in swimming according to Phil Whitten, editor of *Swimming World* magazine. The difference is it's no longer state sanctioned, he adds. It's now done on an individual basis.

Getting Better All The Time

Doping problems notwithstanding, there are bright spots in swimming today. Take, for example, the incredible longevity of female swimmers' competitive lives. Once upon a time, female swimmers retired in their late teens. But today, swimmers in their late twenties and early thirties are dominant, especially in the sprints. People used to believe that a female athlete peaked in her late teens, but some recent tests indicate that women get stronger as they get older.

Female swimmers are also encouraged to lengthen their competitive careers by an age-old motivator: money. Top female swimmers can now earn a decent living plying their trade thanks to money from endorsements, government stipends and bonuses. No female swimmer in the world can hold a candle to Tiger Woods in terms of marketability, but a few make substantial amounts of money.

Golden-Haired Surprise

American Dara Torres (b. 1967) made a splash in international swimming when she won gold (4x100m freestyle relay) at the 1984 Los Angeles Games and added a silver (4x100m medley relay) and a bronze (4x100m freestyle relay) at the 1988 Seoul Games. She captured another gold (4x100m freestyle relay) at the 1992 Barcelona Games, and then retired.

Years later, she was working as a model when a conversation with a friend touched on the Olympics. Within months, Torres had donned a bathing cap and goggles and plunged back in to competitive swimming. "Someone planted the seed in my head, and the seed grew," she said, explaining her comeback at age 32. "The age factor was a concern of mine," she admitted before the U.S. trials in 2000 for the Sydney Games. "But I feel that I'm in better shape now than ever before. I'm having a blast."

The festivities continued as Torres won two gold (4x100m medley and 4x100m medley relay and 4x100m freestyle relay) and three bronze (50m freestyle, 100m freestyle and 100m butterfly) in Australia. There, Torres became the first American to swim in four Olympic Games.

Other Old Timers

Torres was in good company as several other "grannies" made a splash at the 2000 Sydney Games:

➤ Jenny Thompson (b. 1973) is the most decorated American woman in Olympic history with her ten medals, eight of them gold. That total includes three gold (4x100m medley relay, 4x200m freestyle relay and 4x100m freestyle relay) and a bronze (100m freestyle) from the Sydney Games. Before that competition, Thompson acknowledged two big influences in her career: Wonder Woman and Miss Piggy. "They were my role models growing up," she told the Sydney Organizing Committee for the Olympic Games (SOCOG). "They are mentally strong, feminine and kick some serious butt." Haaaa-ya!

➤ Amy Van Dyken (b. 1973) swam at the 1996 Atlanta Games where she won four gold medals. The American added another one (4x100m freestyle relay) at the 2000 Sydney Games. Not a bad showing for a woman who suffers from asthma. When Van Dyken began swimming as a 12-year-old, she didn't have enough wind to swim the length of an Olympic-sized pool. Even now she gets just 65 percent of a normal person's oxygen intake—on a good day. But what she lacks in lung capacity she makes up for in attitude. Before races, Van Dyken intimidates opponents by spitting into their lanes.

➤ Susie O'Neill (b. 1973) won gold, silver and bronze at the 1996 Atlanta Games and added a gold (200m freestyle) and three silver (200m butterfly, 4x100m medley relay and 4x200m freestyle relay) in Sydney. This Australian holds the world record in the 200m butterfly.

➤ Penny Heyns (b. 1974) won two gold in Atlanta and added a bronze (100m breaststroke) in Sydney. The South African holds three world records (50m backstroke, 100m breaststroke and 200m breaststroke).

Let's Go Dutch

Torres & Company performed well in Sydney, but someone else stole the show. Four years earlier, a Dutch woman known as "Inky" qualified for the Atlanta Games but her lack of motivation infuriated her coach, who kicked her off the team. Inge de Bruijn (b. 1973) spent an agonizing week watching the 1996 Games on television and then changed her tack. She returned to the pool with a vengeance.

She hooked up with American coach Paul Bergen, who had coached Tracy Caulkins, and embraced a training regime that included rope climbing, weight lifting, martial arts and, sometimes, swimming with shoes on. "I needed to be tougher mentally," she told SOCOG before the Sydney Games. "Before, I never was. I was scared. Today, I'm not scared of anyone. I feel invincible." And she was. She won three gold (50m freestyle, 100m freestyle and 100m butterfly) and a silver (4x100m freestyle relay) in Sydney. She set world records in all her individual events to accompany the one she set in the 50m butterfly a few months previous.

It's a good thing for swimming fans that de Bruijn didn't take up water polo like her brother and sister who have played for the Dutch national teams—hey would have missed out on some spectacular performances!

Present Day

While the careers of de Bruijn, Torres and other top swimmers won't likely last another two decades, there will be others to take their places. In Canada and the United States alone, swimming exists in almost every town and city, from the recreational summer league level to the competitive year-round circuit. It is a varsity sport in many high

Sports Shorts

In recent years the swimming world has seen the development of a new hydrodynamic swimsuit that enhances speed. The full-length suit, which was developed based on a study of shark's skin, is more water resistant than others. A debate has raged over the legality of using such suits in competition. The Fédération Internationale de Nation Amateur (FINA) sanctioned them in 1999 over loud protests in swimming circles. "If these claims [of enhanced speed] are genuine, and I think they are, it is a direct violation of FINA rules," Phil Whitten, editor of *Swimming World* magazine, said. "It is forbidden equipment."

schools, colleges and universities. Girls start swimming competitively at five years old and compete into their seventies in masters' swimming programs.

In the United States, there are substantially more competitive swimmers now than there were when Kornelia Ender burst on the international swimming scene in 1976. A decade later, in 1986, there were 170,000 competitive swimmers—both men and women—racing in the United States. By 1999, that number had increased to 250,000. The increase can be attributed to new fitness movements and to American Olympic success, according to Cathy Durant, member services coordinator at USA Swimming Inc. Of the current total number, 60 percent of the participants are women.

Table 16.2: Initiation of Major Worldwide Competitions

Event	Men	Women
Olympics	1896	1912
World Championships	1973	1973

The Least You Need to Know

➤ Women have been in the water since time began.

➤ Some top entertainers have emerged from the water.

➤ Australia has produced top-rate swimmers (not to mention the United States and several European nations).

➤ Cold War politics spawned strapping swimmers and gave rise to controversy about drug use in the sport.

➤ Today, women are swimming much better—and for much longer.

Dive In: Diving and Synchronized Swimming

When Pat McCormick visited her doctor in 1951, he noticed she was covered in welts and had scars on her head. Had the young housewife been moonlighting as a lion tamer or had she just returned from the front lines of the Korean War? Neither. McCormick had been spending hours upon hours plunging into the water, perfecting her dives. The American went on to win four gold medals in two Olympics and set the standard for future generations of divers, including her daughter. Likewise, bathing beauty Esther Williams inspired countless synchronized swimmers.

Fancy Diving, Too

McCormick wasn't the first person to leap into the water with the greatest of ease. At least one person was diving by the time the Greeks and Persians were battling for

Sports Shorts

Bungee jumping wasn't an option for thrill seekers in the late 1800s and early 1900s so they climbed to the side of pools or docks and leapt into the water. Oh, and the fun didn't end there! Once submerged, merry-makers would hold their breath and glide under the water as far as possible for as long as possible. The sport was called plunging, and it was included at the 1904 Olympics in St. Louis, MO. The event wasn't a hit with spectators, who had time enough to prepare their tax returns while waiting for the contestants to surface. The event soon disappeared.

supremacy in Asia Minor; a 2500-year-old tomb in Italy depicts a man plunging off a platform.

In the 1800s, gymnasts in Germany and Sweden combined business and pleasure by moving their equipment from a gymnasium to a beach. Using flying rings, trapezes and springboards mounted on high platforms, the trendsetters flipped and twisted into the water attracting crowds with their "fancy diving."

Before long, organized competitions began to pop up in Britain. Many of the contests were held in ponds, with divers pausing as rows of ducks skittered by. Spectators weren't treated to aerial acrobatics at these contests; the competitive dive *du jour* was a simple plunge that resembled the basic entry of today's swimmers. Very quickly, however, divers developed pike and tuck positions and made somersaults commonplace.

Let Me Explain

Two distinct diving events emerged in the early 1900s. Those platform and springboard events endure as the basis of diving competition today. Platform divers take off from a rigid platform ten metres above the water whereas springboard divers leap off a narrow, flexible board ranging from one to three metres above the water. In Olympic competitions, the springboard is three metres above the water.

Diving became an Olympic sport in 1904 when men started competing in platform diving. Men's springboard diving made its debut four years later. The women's platform event was added in 1912 and the women's springboard event made its debut in 1920. FINA was established in 1908 to oversee diving along with swimming and water polo.

Let Me Explain

In the pike position, the diver's body is bent at the waist and her legs are straight. In the tuck position, her body is bent at the knees and hips and her knees are held together against her chest.

Arc of a Diver

German and Swedish competitors dominated the sport in those early days of competition. But when Swedish coach Ernst Brainstem immigrated to the United States and introduced dry-land training, American divers began to make their mark. The United States soon became the top diving nation. Indeed, one of the best divers in history hails from the land of suntan lotion and bikinis.

Sports Shorts

American Aileen Riggin was just 14 years old when she won the springboard event at the 1920 Olympics in Antwerp, Belgium. But her size drew more attention than her youthfulness. The smallest athlete at the Games, Riggin stood 4-foot-7 and weighed 65 pounds. At the 1924 Olympics in Paris, France, she won a silver in springboard diving and a bronze in the 100m backstroke. Riggin went on to star in a popular aquatic show and become one of the first female sportswriters in the United States. She was still swimming competitively as she neared her ninetieth birthday.

Born in California, Pat McCormick (b. 1930) was impressed by the swimmers and weight lifters she saw on a childhood outing to famed Muscle Beach. But she was captivated by the divers, and was soon jumping off a float herself. When she started winning diving competitions, a coach convinced her to join his aquatics club in Los Angeles.

She became a fierce competitor, practising one hundred dives a day, six days a week. The training took a toll. During a physical examination, a doctor examined her cracked bones and scars and told her, "I've seen worse casualty cases, but only where a building

Jock Talk

"I was a tomboy, always trying to keep up with my brother. I remember playing football when I was 10 years old. I threw a pass and somebody said, 'Block that dame.' I was completely wiped out because it was the first time I realized I was a girl. Girls didn't play football back then, and I went crying to my brother."

—Diver Pat McCormick, in *Women Who Win*.

caved in." Before long, McCormick was performing dives so daring, they were prohibited for women in international competition. When the ban was lifted, McCormick went to town.

She won both the platform and springboard events at the 1952 Olympics in Helsinki, Finland. Then, eight months after giving birth to her son, she headed to Australia for the 1956 Melbourne Games. She won both events again, becoming the first diver to do so in successive Olympics.

McCormick later made her mark outside the pool with charity work, and by giving birth to a daughter who would also become an Olympic diver.

Chinese Water Torture

In the 1960s, American divers started to share the spotlight with Europeans. Germany's Ingrid Kramer (b. 1943) won two gold (platform and springboard) in 1960 and one gold (springboard) in 1964.

A new diving superpower emerged in the 1980s, however. Chinese women won every Olympic diving event from 1984 through 1996 except for the springboard competition at the 1984 Los Angeles Games, which was won by Canada's Sylvie Bernier (b. 1964).

Q & A

Q: Fu Mingxia's success led to a rule change in competitive swimming. What was it?

A: The Chinese diver won the world platform title when she was just 12 years old. Diving officials thought she was too young to be hurtling through the air in pursuit of a perfect plunge and introduced age restrictions to international competition. Divers must now be at least 14 years old to compete in a given meet. The only exceptions are competitors who will turn 14 later in the year of the competition in question.

One Chinese diver stood head and shoulders above the rest though she was just five feet tall. Born in one of the country's poorest regions, Fu Mingxia (b. 1978) caught the attention of government officials, who plucked her out of her parents' home when she was nine years old and shipped her to a sports school to be moulded into a champion diver. The homesick girl cried for months, but her misery didn't hinder her performance. She was soon diving with such gusto, her short hair sometimes brushed the end of the platform during her descent.

Fu arrived in Spain for the 1992 Barcelona Games with high hopes and a teddy bear, which she clutched between dives. She won gold in the platform event by a huge margin. Fu returned to China and continued her demanding training regime, seeing her parents just once a year. She grew a few inches, gained 30 pounds and qualified for the 1996 Atlanta Games. There she won both the platform and springboard events.

Fu then retired, citing mental exhaustion. What next? Not yet 20 years old, she was too young to purchase a condominium in Florida or take up lawn bowling. Instead, she enrolled at Beijing's prestigious Qinghua University to study economics management. She grew her hair long and developed a fondness for snug-fitting t-shirts, baggy pants and unlaced running shoes. She also started dating a soccer player. Diving was the furthest thing from her mind.

But while daydreaming during a lecture in 1998, Fu decided she missed the sport. She mounted a comeback and beat out dozens of tough young competitors to qualify for the 2000 Sydney Games. She won gold in the springboard event and silver in the springboard synchronized event, a new addition to the Games' diving program.

Sports Shorts

The springboard diving competition at the 1984 Olympics in Los Angeles, CA, had been promoted as a battle between China's Li Yihua and American Kelly McCormick, the daughter of Olympic legend Pat McCormick. But in the end, their thunder was stolen by a Canadian diver with a reputation for folding under pressure. Sylvie Bernier ignored the standings during the competition. According to *The Complete Book of the Summer Olympics*, she drowned out the public address system by listening to the soundtrack from *Flashdance* on her walkman. When she finished all her dives, her coach informed her she would win gold if McCormick scored under 70 points on her final dive. Minutes later, McCormick scored 67.20 and Bernier became the first Canadian to win an Olympic diving event. McCormick took home the silver and won bronze in the same event at the 1988 Olympics in Seoul, South Korea.

Fu's success in Australia made her one of just three divers to win four gold medals—Americans Greg Louganis and Pat McCormick are the two others—and the only woman diver to win five medals. "Standing on the medal podium, I felt that all the roads I've walked since I returned to diving until now were just a small part of my life," she told the *Minneapolis Star Tribune*. "I'm just an ordinary person who accomplished a miracle."

Table 17.1: Initiation of Major Worldwide Diving Competitions

Event	Men	Women
Olympics	1904	1912
World Championships	1973	1973
World Cup	1979	1979

Sports Shorts

Synchronized diving made its Olympic debut at the 2000 Olympics in Sydney, Australia. Men and women competed separately on the three-metre springboard and the ten-metre platform. In synchronized diving, a pair of divers form a team that dives simultaneously from the same height.

Thinking Outside the Glass Bowl

While McCormick was taking flying leaps in the 1950s, Canadian and American women were giving international demonstrations in synchronized swimming. They had a tough time convincing the world it was a bona fide sport. After all, it was rooted in the campy aquarium shows of the 1930s. Today, the participants' nose plugs, hair gel and makeup are the butt of jokes, but there is no doubt synchronized swimming is an athletic pursuit. Competitors are as muscular and flexible as the men who practised underwater gymnastics in ancient times.

4 Men

Yes, the first synchronized swimmers were men. According to the *Encyclopedia of World Sport*, old Japanese wood-block prints show men performing somersaults and other manoeuvres in the water. Men were still getting their aqua kicks centuries later. A men's "scientific and ornamental swimming" competition started in England in 1892. Six years later, a similar competition was launched for Canadian men.

Brave New Waves

Women drifted in floating patterns during the late 1800s but soon mobilized, plucking the plugs from the men's noses and turning synchronized swimming into a female pastime.

Australian swimmer Annette Kellerman set the ball rolling in 1907, when she dove into a glass tank filled with water at the New York Hippodrome and enthralled crowds with "water ballet" demonstrations. In the 1920s, a group of Canadian women, led by top water polo player and diver Margaret Sellers, developed "ornamental swimming" from life saving and swimming techniques.

Meanwhile, under the guidance of a former gymnast named Katharine Curtis, University of Chicago students were doing figures in the water to musical accompaniment. The Kay Curtis Modern Mermaids performed three times daily at the 1933–1934 World's Fair in Chicago, attracting up to ten thousand spectators a show.

American swimmer Eleanor Holm performed a similar routine at the 1939 World's Fair in New York. She made a splash, but didn't didn't really bring synchronized swimming into the limelight. That task was left to another glamour girl.

There's No Business Like Show Business

The world was introduced to so-called water ballet by Esther Williams (b. 1923). The American started swimming as a child and went on to win national breaststroke and freestyle titles. Williams was expected to win Olympic gold, too, but the 1940 Games were cancelled due to the outbreak of World War II. The end of her competitive days marked the beginning of a career in show business.

Showman Billy Rose noticed the tall, attractive athlete and recruited her to appear in *Aquacades*, a Broadway musical featuring hundreds of swimmers and divers and breathtaking special effects. (True, the productions didn't feature digital imaging, but Steven Spielberg wasn't born until 1947!) Williams (Aquabelle No.1) performed choreographed duets with Olympic champion Johnny Weismuller (Aquadonis No. 1).

MGM executives offered Williams a screen test and a star was born. In *Bathing Beauty*, Hollywood's first swimming movie, Williams performed in a special pool built on the MGM lot. It had hydraulic lifts,

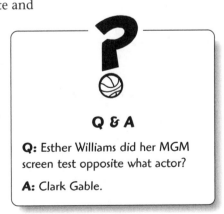

Q & A

Q: Esther Williams did her MGM screen test opposite what actor?

A: Clark Gable.

Q & A

Q: Johnny Weismuller starred with Esther Williams in the *Aquacades* but is best remembered for what movie role?

A: Tarzan.

Jock Talk

"They were going off high platforms in swan dives and hitting the water, getting water in their sinuses and sinking to the bottom."

—Esther Williams, on the perils of doing underwater sequences in her movies with women who knew how to dance but not swim, in *The Saturday Evening Post.*

hidden air hoses and special camera cranes for overhead shots. "No one had ever done a swimming movie before so we just made it up as we went along," Williams recalls on her Web site. "I ad-libbed all my own underwater movements." Williams appeared in 26 movies from the early 1940s to the end of the 1950s and became an international celebrity.

Down to Competitive Business

Williams's underwater antics fanned the flames of men's desire and made an impact on women, too. When *Bathing Beauty* became a box office hit in 1945, girls started writing to Williams asking her how they could "swim pretty like [she] did in the movies," reported *The Saturday Evening Post.* Williams had unwittingly breathed life into synchronized swimming.

The United States held its first national synchronized swimming championship the following year, and Canada did the same in 1948. Around that time Canadians started winning competitions south of the border, fostering a decades-long rivalry.

Despite their competitiveness, swimmers from both countries teamed up to stage demonstrations at international swimming meets, including five consecutive Olympics Games. Their efforts paid off; FINA sanctioned synchronized swimming in 1954. The level of competition gradually improved, and the sport made its Olympic debut in 1984 with solo and duet competitions. In 1996, the solo and duet events were dropped from the Games and the team event, which includes eight swimmers, was added. The duet was reinstated in 2000.

Some Kind of Wonderful

Canadians and Americans emerged as a world power in the synchro pool, taking all the gold and silver medals possible at major international meets up to 1998. One of the first international stars in synchronized swimming was a woman from Beaconsfield, QC. Carolyn Waldo (b. 1964) almost drowned as a kid when she followed two older sisters into a lake, and was afraid to put her face in the water for years. But she overcame her aversion and, in fact, learned to submerge herself for more than a minute at a time.

Waldo rose to the top of her sport, winning silver (solo) at the 1984 Los Angeles Games and two gold (solo and duet) at the 1988 Seoul Games.

Settling a Score

Waldo seemed a distant memory at the 1992 Barcelona Games as sports fans got caught up in controversy involving American Kristen Babb-Sprague and Canadian Sylvie Frechette (b. 1967), who was the gold medal favourite heading into the Games.

Q & A

Q: Sylvie Frechette suffered a personal tragedy weeks before the 1992 Olympics in Barcelona, Spain. What was it?

A: Her live-in boyfriend committed suicide.

In figures, a round of competition that counted for 50 percent of the final score, Frechette received excellent scores from all but one of the judges, who gave her 8.7 (out of a possible 10). Seconds later, Brazilian judge Ana Maria da Silveira claimed she had made a mistake and tried to change the score. She said she had pressed the wrong button. But it was too late—the score had already been made public. As a result, Babb-Sprague came out of the figures with a lead and, after the free routine, won the gold medal. If de Silveira had been allowed to make her score higher, Frechette likely would have won.

The outcome angered Canadian sports fans who started booing Toronto Blue Jays third baseman Ed Sprague because he was married to the woman who took home the gold. Fans forgave him when the Blue Jays won the World Series, but the swimming dispute lingered. Canada's Dick Pound, a member of the IOC, led a crusade to overturn the official results. In the end, FINA awarded Frechette a gold medal and allowed Babb-Sprague to keep hers as well.

Taste Test

The 1996 Atlanta Games were also marked by controversy. In the months before the event, the French team created a performance based on the Holocaust. In the routine, swimmers goose-stepped into the pool as Nazis and then assumed the identities of female victims being led to their execution. The musical score? What else but the soundtrack from *Schindler's List*. The French government stepped in, ruling that all allusions to the Holocaust had to be removed from the routine.

The French Swimming Federation was disappointed since the swimmers had been practising for months. "The program was created to denounce not only the Holocaust in particular, but all forms of racism and intolerance that we see rising," one Federation official told *Time* magazine. Nonetheless, the ruling pleased many people including

Haim Musicant, executive director of the Council of Jewish Institutions in France. "There are certain subjects you just cannot deal with in a swimming pool," he said.

Dawn of a New Era

Top swimmers from Canada and the United States retired in the late 1990s, sending both countries into a rebuilding phase and allowing swimmers from other countries to scale the medal podium. Russia became a contender in synchronized swimming, as did Japan and France. At the 2000 Sydney Games, Russia won two gold (team and duet), Japan won two silver (team and duet) and France won a bronze (duet). The Canadians managed a bronze in the team event.

The competitors' hair gel elicited some snide remarks during the Sydney Games, but far less than in previous years. Evidently, more people have come to view synchronized swimming as pure athleticism and agree with Esther Williams, who once said, "it is a gruelling sport. You have to train for years; you have to be precise, skilled and athletic."

Table 17.2: Initiation of Major Worldwide Synchronized Swimming Competitions

Event	Year
Olympics	1984
World Championships	1973
World Cup	1983

The Least You Need to Know

➤ Diving has roots in gymnastics—not swimming.

➤ American Pat McCormick was the only superstar in women's diving until China's Fu Mingxia arrived on the scene.

➤ Synchronized swimming started out as a male pastime.

➤ Synchro gained fame and recognition through Hollywood movies.

➤ Synchro finally established itself as a bona fide sport, replete with rivalries and judging controversies.

Chapter 18

Pretty Maids All in a Row: Rowing

In This Chapter

➤ In ancient times rowing is for business, not pleasure

➤ The first competitions are held, but for men only

➤ Women start rowing competitively halfway through the twentieth century

➤ Soviet Bloc countries take the helm

➤ Canadian women climb onto the medal podium

For many years, female rowers at Yale University had nowhere to bathe after practices though their male counterparts showered in a boathouse. Determined to rectify the situation, the women marched into the office of the school's athletic director one day in 1976, and took off their clothes. On their bare torsos they had painted the words "Title IX," a reference to U.S. government legislation that mandated equal treatment for both genders in educational programs. The school official got the message and a women's wing was added to the boathouse soon after. For the past hundred years, women have fought hard to make inroads in competitive rowing. They have had much success—even with their clothes on.

Slave to the Rhythm

Rowing didn't start with women's full participation. Men were using boats for exploration, commerce and war thousands of years ago. The Ancient Egyptians and Romans used low, single-decked vessels in battle. These galleys had oars manned by criminals or slaves. (Think of Charlton Heston in *Ben Hur*, looking dapper in a loincloth while pulling on an oar.) Later, Scandinavian traders and pirates (i.e. Vikings) travelled around the Atlantic in long, narrow warships manned by rowers.

Riverboat Gamblers

Modern racing began in England, where watermen ferried people up and down the Thames River. Goaded on by bet-placing passengers, the men started racing each other. These contests were spur of the moment at first, but later became organized. A race from the London Bridge to Chelsea was held in 1715. It was called the Doggett's Coat and Badge, named after Irish actor Thomas Doggett who provided a sum of money in his will to be awarded to the winning crew. Still held annually, the race is recognized as the oldest rowing contest in the world.

Let Me Explain

A regatta is an event that includes a series of boat races.

In the early 1800s, boating clubs popped up across Europe and North America and members started competing in international competitions. Because these regattas offered prize money and involved betting among the spectators, they became rife with corruption. The sport developed a shady reputation.

But a rowing revival took shape a few decades later, when the sport became popular at elite universities on both sides of the Atlantic Ocean. Harvard and Yale started an American tradition by holding a race in 1852. Oxford and Cambridge held a regatta in an English town called Henley in 1829. Ten years later the Henley Regatta was officially established. The contest features the world's best rowers to this day and is known as the Henley Royal Regatta.

Soon, rowing enthusiasts got organized. The National Association of Amateur Oarsmen (NAAO) was founded in the United States in 1872, followed by the Canadian Association of Amateur Oarsmen (CAAO) eight years later. An international governing body, the Fédération Internationale des Sociétés d'Aviron (FISA), was founded in 1892. Rowing was supposed to be included in the first modern Olympics four years later, but bad weather prevented that from happening. Instead, rowing made its debut at the 1900 Paris Games with a handful of men's events.

Women in the Front Row

Female rowers were not included at the Olympics or other major competitions at that point, but they had already discovered the joys of dipping their oars in the water and going for a ride. Some four hundred years earlier in Venice, Italy, some 50 peasant girls marked the arrival of dignitary Beatrice D'Este by competing against each other in a boat race that was more spectacle than sport. Wearing short linen skirts, the women upstaged the men who raced afterwards.

In the late 1800s, noted English philologist Frederick James Furnivall espoused the benefits of rowing for women, who started joining clubs and holding competitions across Europe. The pastime became especially popular among women in Germany and the Scandinavian countries.

Meanwhile, women started rowing at clubs and progressive universities in North America. A collegiate rowing club for women was founded at Wellesley College in Massachusetts in 1875. Not that these members' outings would leave them sweating like prizefighters—their events emphasized grace, not speed. At the school's annual regatta, participants sang as they rowed and were judged on appearance and form.

Sports Shorts

When Henry Fowle Durant founded Wellesley College in 1875, he rejected accepted notions of female frailty. "The physical idea of womanhood is a noble, beautiful form, healthful, vigorous [and] graceful, not pretty," he said, "not a confused compound of vanity and sentimentality and shams." Female students were encouraged "to row on the lake, take long brisk walks, and exercise in the gymnasium."

Land of Competition

The downplaying of competition didn't sit well with all women. An American named Ernestine Bayer grew bored resting on the riverbank watching her husband and his peers compete in the 1930s. Why, she wondered, couldn't women do the same? When her husband failed to come up with a good explanation, she and some friends formed the Philadelphia Girls Rowing Club (PGRC), and he began giving them lessons. The PGRC entered three boats in a local regatta in 1938.

Meanwhile, women were taking up rowing further west. Three decades earlier, four women had gone exploring on the water in a butcher boat in California and decided to form their own club.

Q & A

Q: Ernestine Bayer's husband was an accomplished oarsman. What was his major achievement on the water?

A: He won a silver medal at the 1928 Olympics in Amsterdam, Holland.

When the president of the San Diego Rowing Club offered them a six-oared barge that had once sunk, the ZLAC Rowing Club was founded.

Female rowers worldwide were also pressing forward. Women's clubs in Germany, Denmark, Norway and Poland persuaded FISA to include women's events at the European championships starting in 1954 (the championships had been held since 1893).

American women formed the National Women's Rowing Association (NWRA) in the early 1960s, and started competing in national championships in 1966. The organization melded with the NAAO in 1982, forming the United States Rowing Association (USRowing). In Canada, women started competing at national championships in 1972 and were recognized as full members in the CAAO two years later. The organization changed its name to Canadian Amateur Rowing Association (Rowing Canada Aviron).

Sports Shorts

When the NAAO refused to send a women's crew to the prestigious European championships on the grounds that it would be humiliated, Ernestine Bayer set out to prove the American women were tough enough. She staged a battle of the sexes at a regatta in St. Catharines, ON, in 1967. There, the best U.S. women's crew raced against a boat full of men who were former Olympians and national champions. The women won the race and headed to France for the championships.

Women started competing in the world championships in 1974, a dozen years after the men. Two years later, women's rowing made its Olympic debut in Montréal, QC.

European Legacy

Soviet Bloc countries won all six women's rowing events at the 1976 Montréal Games, and dominated the sport for the next decade and a half. By methodically recruiting and developing athletes, these states produced dozens of world-class rowers, including two Romanians who made their mark in the mid-1980s.

Let Me Explain

Rowing has two distinct forms. The first is called crew racing or sweep-oar racing. Here, two or more rowers sit facing the back of the boat and each rower pulls on one oar. Crews of two, four or eight rowers are the most common. In crews of eight (often referred to as "eights") the boat is steered by a coxswain who sits facing the others. The coxswain barks out orders like a substitute teacher but, in fact, she isn't interested in teaching multiplication tables or confiscating peashooters. She is responsible for establishing and maintaining the rhythm of the rowers' strokes. Sculling is the other form of racing. Scullers race alone or in crews of two or four. Each sculler faces the back of the boat and pulls on a pair of oars. Coxswains are never used in sculling.

Veronica Cogeanu-Cochela (b. 1965) won numerous medals including two gold (eights), three silver (two in double sculls and one in quadruple sculls) and one bronze (quadruple sculls) over four Olympic Games, starting in 1988.

She was a stroke behind compatriot Elisabeta Oleniuc-Lipa (b. 1962), who won four gold (one in single sculls, one in double sculls and two in eights), two silver (both in double sculls) and one bronze (quadruple sculls) over five Olympic Games, starting in 1984.

Sports Shorts

American Anita DeFrantz (b. 1952) won a bronze medal on the eights team at the 1976 Olympics in Montréal, QC, but she has won more recognition for her accomplishments on shore. DeFrantz was one of the first women to advance to the upper echelons of sports governance. She was appointed to the International Olympic Committee (IOC) in 1986, and joined its executive board six years later. Also, she was elected vice president of the Fédération Internationale des Sociétés d'Aviron (FISA) in 1993. DeFrantz lobbied for an increase in women's involvement in this area. "It's very important for the future of sports that we have more female leadership," she said in *You Go Girl! Winning The Woman's Way*. "Wherever I have been the first, I make certain I am not the last."

Smooth as Silken

European communist regimes collapsed in the early 1990s, changing the course of history and ending their stranglehold on international rowing competition. Athletes from other countries began to make their mark, especially those from Canada.

In 1992, a Canadian named Silken Laumann (b. 1964) did the impossible: she pushed hockey off the front page of newspapers across the nation. It didn't take much—just an epic tale of trial and tribulation, with a measure of blood and gore.

Q & A

Q: Silken Laumann won a bronze medal in double sculls at the 1984 Olympics in Los Angeles, CA. Who was her teammate?

A: Her sister, Daniele, who had piqued Silken's interest in rowing years earlier.

Laumann won a bronze in double sculls at the 1984 Los Angeles Games, and then won the single sculls event at the 1991 world championships. She was favoured to win gold in that event at the 1992 Barcelona Games. But 10 weeks before the competition, her boat was rammed by another in the warm-up area at a meet in Germany. A piece of wood ripped through her lower right leg, fracturing the bone, cutting muscles and causing nerve and tissue damage. "It was like being cut with two hundred knives," she said in *You Go Girl! Winning The Woman's Way*, "and when I looked down my muscle was hanging outside my ankle and I could see my bone." No wonder the two men who rushed to her aid fainted after surveying the damage.

Doctors said Laumann would need half a year to recover, but she was determined to compete in the Olympics. Five operations later, she arrived in Barcelona walking with a cane. She had been instructed not to stand up for more than 15 minutes at a time, so she sat out the opening ceremonies. It was a wise move. She finished second in her qualifying heat and then won her semifinal race. Laumann went on to win a bronze medal in the final. Her success stunned the sports world, including sleep-deprived Canadians who watched the race live in the wee hours of the morning. Laumann added a silver in the same event at the 1996 Atlanta Games.

Canadian Girls Rule

Several other Canadians shared headlines with Laumann in the 1990s. Among them were Marnie McBean (b. 1968) and Kathleen Heddle (b. 1965), known as "the odd couple" because of their contrasting personalities. McBean was as gregarious as Heddle was shy.

At the 1992 Barcelona Games, the two teamed up to win gold in the coxless pairs and then joined six compatriots and a coxswain to clinch the women's eights. Heddle retired after the Games but came back in 1994. She and McBean joined forces for the 1996

Atlanta Games, this time in the double and quadruple sculls. They won the former—becoming the first Canadians in any sport to win three gold medals—and finished third in the latter.

McBean then set her sights on the 2000 Sydney Games. She was to scheduled to compete in the single sculls but it wasn't to be. McBean threw out her back while training days before the race and had to withdraw from the competition. She stayed in Australia to cheer on her teammates, travelling from place to place stretched out in a backseat or on a van floor. A month later she underwent surgery to remove 30 percent of a disc in her lower back. Her future in rowing was uncertain, but one thing was clear: she had made her mark. With 12 Olympic and world championship medals in her trophy cabinet, she was the third most decorated woman in the sport's history.

Jock Talk

"[Thyroid cancer] is a good kind of cancer if you want to choose one. It's 97 percent curable."

—Canadian Emma Robinson (b. 1971), to NBC. Robinson won her third straight world pairs title in 1999, less than six months after having her thyroid removed. At the 2000 Olympics in Sydney, Australia, Robinson won a bronze in the eights. She had already won a silver in that event at the 1996 Olympics in Atlanta, GA.

Table 18.1: Initiation of Major Worldwide Competitions

Event	Men	Women
Olympics	1900	1976
World Championships	1962	1974

The Least You Need to Know

➤ In Ancient Rome, most rowers were prisoners or slaves.

➤ Competitive rowing initially had a seedy reputation.

➤ It took much effort on the part of a few to get women's competitive rowing off the ground and into the water.

➤ The collapse of communism led to the ascendancy of Canadian rowers.

Part 5

Ride Like the Wind— Riding Sports

For some women, the need for speed is a motivator like no other. It has pushed female car enthusiasts like Janet Guthrie to risk life and limb racing at speeds in excess of 250 miles per hour and has led jockeys like Julie Krone to endure countless bruises and broken bones riding thoroughbred horses. Cyclists like Jeannie Longo move a little bit slower, but no by much. Are these women daring or just plain crazy? The debate could last a long time, but probably not as long as 51-year-old Shirley Muldowney's drag racing career.

Chapter 19

Watching the Wheels: Cycling

In This Chapter

➤ A cycling craze is born

➤ Women embrace cycling, bloomers and freedom

➤ Women start competing, but stop a few decades later

➤ Cycling enjoys a revival in the 1970s

➤ A Frenchwoman pushes women's cycling to new heights

➤ Other European women make their mark on the road, track and dirt path

Italy's Paola Pezzo turned some heads when she crossed the finish line of the mountain bike competition at the 1996 Atlanta Games with her jersey unzipped to her navel. But she didn't cause as much of a stir as the women who discarded their long dresses and mounted bicycles in loose-fitting trousers a hundred years before. Times have changed, of course, but women's enthusiasm for cycling has not. Today, women race on the road, the track and on dirt paths around the world.

A Work in Progress

Decades before women first tried on trousers, German inventor Baron von Drais attached two same-sized wheels to a wooden frame. Straddling the contraption, he moved forward by pushing off the ground with his feet and steering with the front wheel. The motion was more similar to walking than riding. (The Flintstones, the

Let Me Explain

When Pierre Lallement introduced a riding machine with pedals on its front wheel in the 1860s, he could not have foreseen the various forms of cycling that would evolve in the next 140 years. Today, competitive cycling falls into five major categories. Of these, the most popular are road racing, track racing and mountain bike racing. BMX racing and cyclo-cross are less popular. In BMX races, packs of riders zip around turns and jump over hills on dirt tracks. In cyclo-cross—which is often described as the equivalent of cross-country running for cyclists—riders compete on a short loop of varied terrain, including dirt, pavement, steep inclines and turns. Natural and artificial barriers force riders to dismount and remount their bicycles on the go.

modern stone-aged family, used a similar method of travel in prehistoric times, but no one took them seriously because they were cartoon characters.)

In the 1860s, Frenchman Pierre Lallement introduced a riding machine with pedals on its front wheel, which was a little larger than the back wheel. The wooden machine was called a *velocipede* ("fast foot") but was widely known as a boneshaker because its metal tires made riding on cobblestones a jarring experience.

The *velocipede* was soon replaced by the first official bicycle. Its pedals were also attached directly to the front wheel. But the metal vehicle provided a relatively smooth ride because its tires were rubber and its bigger front wheel had long spokes to absorb the shock. It wasn't long before designers made an important discovery: the larger the front wheel, the farther a rider could travel with each rotation of the pedals. As a result, the wheel was enlarged dramatically. Unfortunately, this meant a rider was forced to sit high above the centre of gravity, and ran the risk of plummetting to earth whenever the bike went over a bump in the road.

Jittery cyclists were soon introduced to the safety bike, which had front and rear wheels of equal size and a sprocket-chain drive connecting the pedals with the rear wheel. This vehicle was much safer to ride than the high-wheel model. Unfortunately, it was not as comfortable; the wheels had rubber tires but not the shock-absorbing spokes necessary for a smooth ride. Cycling enthusiasts were forced to choose between the comfort of the high-wheel bike and the security of the safety bike. But not for long.

In the 1890s, an Irishman invented the air-filled tire, which was more springy than the hard rubber version. Manufacturers started producing safety bikes with these new tires, and a cycling craze was born.

Free To Go

When scores of men started riding bicycles here, there and everywhere, women put away the adult-size tricycles they had been riding in circles, shed their corsets and bustles, and mounted bicycles. Riding naked was out of the question—at least until the streaking craze of the 1970s—so women rode in bloomers, which were loose-fitting trousers, sometimes worn with skirts. Their new outfits and newfound mobility contributed to a profound change in the social landscape—women began to assert themselves in all spheres of life. "Let me tell you what I think of bicycling," said American suffragist Susan B. Anthony in 1896. "I think it has done more to emancipate women than anything else in the world. I stand and rejoice every time I see a woman ride by on a wheel. It gives women a feeling of freedom and self-reliance."

The Race Is On

People had no sooner learned to ride bikes than they began to crave competition. They started racing on roads in events such as the Tour de France, and on specially constructed tracks with steeply banked sides. Cycling was included at the first modern Olympics in 1896, the same year the Union Cycliste Internationale (UCI) was established to oversee the sport.

Let Me Explain

The Tour de France is the world's most prestigious bicycle race. Established in 1903, the month-long stage race attracts top riders, thousands of spectators and a huge television audience. Almost 200 men cover some 3600 kilometres, riding over flat and mountainous terrain in France, Belgium, Italy, Germany and Spain. Some of the stages emphasize climbing hills, while others test the riders' skills in sprinting or time trials. A women's race was added in 1984. The Tour de France Féminin (as it is still commonly called, though the official name has changed to "La Grande Boucle") is a 1000km stage race run during the final two weeks of the men's event. The stages are shorter, but do include difficult climbs.

Female cyclists were banned from the Olympics, the Tour de France and other major competitions, but refused to simply sit pretty. In 1868, French women raced in Bordeaux. The following year, four of them competed alongside men in a road race from Paris to Rouen. Amelie Le Gall beat another woman in a 100km race in 1896, and later competed against top male cyclists.

The competitive bug had bitten women in other countries, too. England's Tessie Reynolds rode from Brighton to London and back (about 193km) in under nine hours in 1893. Two years later, American Frankie Nelson won a six-day race in New York, NY.

On the Outs

Such exploits drew a little praise and a lot of criticism. The vision of women pedalling all about rankled conservatives. A woman on a bike could not be supervised, they argued, and she needed to be—just look at her scandalous attire! Conservatives also claimed bike riding jeopardized a woman's virtue. The saddles, or seats, were thought to stimulate their genitals and, therefore, put them at risk of becoming sexually promiscuous.

In response, manufacturers introduced a wide-saddled, high-handlebarred bike. The new model allowed female cyclists to remain virtuous but prevented them from racing, as the design was far from aerodynamic. The change was dramatic but barely noticed by the masses because cycling was waning in popularity. With the arrival of the automobile, bike races no longer satisfied the public's need for speed. By the mid-1900s, cycling seemed old-fashioned and the sport fell off the radar screen. Cycling was out of sight for a while, but not for long.

Everything Old Is New Again

The 1950s ushered in an era of peace and prosperity for much of the Western world. People celebrated the good times by loafing in front of their televisions, gorging on bucket-sized servings of caramel corn. Before long, living room sofas were collapsing under the weight. Something had to be done. In the 1970s, people ventured outside for some sunshine and exercise.

Suddenly, adults were jogging along park trails while their children were zipping through schoolyards on skateboards or roller skates. People of all ages were pedalling around on light, streamlined bikes with gears and low handlebars. Racing was soon back in vogue.

Let Me Explain

Road racing is the oldest type of bicycle competition, and includes many kinds of races:

➤ The stage race often lasts for weeks and covers thousands of kilometres. One stage is a single day's race. The winner is the rider who has the lowest cumulative time after completing all the stages. The most famous stage race is the Tour de France.

➤ The one-day race can last anywhere from two to five hours (women) or four to seven hours (men); distances range from 65km to 200km. This race begins with a mass start, and the winner is the first rider to cross the finish line. The most famous one-day race is the Olympic road race. At the 2000 Olympics in Sydney, Australia, women rode a circuit seven times, covering a distance of 120km.

➤ The time trial is a race in which the object is to ride as fast as possible from one point to another while being timed by a clock. Riders start at 30-second or 1-minute intervals from a starting ramp. The winner is the rider with the fastest time over the entire course, which was 31.2km at the 2000 Sydney Games.

➤ A criterium is similar to a one-day race except that a group of riders races on a short loop course with each lap being a few kilometres in length. Unlike stage racing and time trials, criterium emphasizes speed and bike handling rather than endurance.

Females were not willing to be excluded from major competitions this time around. Women's cycling made its Olympic debut in 1984, the same year a women's race was added to the Tour de France, and some big racing names started to emerge.

French Toast

Frenchwoman Jeannie Longo (b. 1958) became the greatest female cyclist in history, but few would have predicted her success; she spent most of her childhood playing the piano and skiing. However, when Longo missed the cut for the French national ski team in 1979, she changed gears and took up cycling.

Let Me Explain

Track racing is held in a velodrome, a steeply banked oval track made of wood or concrete. There are various kinds of track events. Women don't take part in all of them but do compete in many:

➤ The sprint is a best-of-three competition between two riders. Only the last 200m of the three-lap race is timed. Riders start out slowly in the first lap, jostle for position in the second and go for broke on the third.

➤ The individual pursuit is a race in which two riders start on opposite sides of the track and chase each other around it. A rider wins by catching the other rider or by posting a faster time.

➤ A points race is an event in which riders are awarded points during lap sprints that occur every fifth or sixth lap. The leader gets five points, the runner-up gets three, the third place rider gets two and the fourth place rider gets one. In the final sprint, points are doubled. The world championship distance for a points race is 30km.

➤ The 500m time trial is a race against the clock. The winner is the rider with the fastest time. Riders compete one at a time at the Olympics. There are no qualifying rounds.

Between 1985 and 2000 she won 12 world titles, including 8 on the road and 4 on the track. Longo was also successful at three Olympics, winning a gold (road race) two silver (road race and road time trial) and a bronze (road time trial). She also won the Tour de France Féminin three times.

Despite her success, Longo was not well liked. In fact, most people found her unpleasant at best. "She's selfish and arrogant," sportswriter Samuel Abt told *Outside Online*. "She has antagonized officials and cost some of them their jobs. She has said nasty things about coaches and teammates. When she competed for the French team at the world championships in 1989, the other women on the team were so fed up with her behaviour that they came up with a rule: Anytime someone mentioned her name, that person had to pay a fine. Jeannie Longo is an extremely turbulent person who happens to be a very good cyclist." Longo's compatriot and fellow rider Valerie Simmonet was more succinct: "It's a pity that such a great champion has such a poor character."

Longo didn't let the criticism slow her down, however. A few weeks before her forty-second birthday, she won a bronze (road time trial) at the 2000 Sydney Games. Three months later, she broke her own world record by covering 45.094km in one hour on a track in Mexico.

Sports Shorts

The United States is not a superpower in women's cycling, but it has produced a few world champions, including Rebecca Twigg (b. 1963). More involved with textbooks than pedalling pursuits in her childhood, Twigg was an exceptional student who started university when she was just 14 years old. She took up cycling soon after and began collecting national titles. Twigg went on to win six world titles on the track. She set a world record 11 days after breaking her collarbone in 1993, but is best known for her gritty performance in the road race at the 1984 Olympics in Los Angeles, CA, the first Games to include women's cycling. Twigg had a decisive lead with 100m remaining, but compatriot Connie Carpenter (b. 1957) made a mad dash for the finish line and won by half a wheel. Twigg retired after failing to make the U.S. Olympic team in 1988, but she couldn't adjust to life in the slow lane. She came out of retirement and won a bronze medal in the individual pursuit at the 1992 Olympics in Barcelona, Spain.

Star Babies

While Longo was still a strong contender in 2000, she was no longer the top banana in women's cycling. A bunch of younger women had made their mark, including one from the Netherlands. Leontien Zijlaard (b. 1970) won an incredible three gold medals (3000m individual pursuit, road time trial and road race) and a silver medal (points race) in Sydney. She set a world record (3000m individual pursuit) in the process.

Believe it or not, Zijlaard had been written off five years before. The cyclist showed signs of greatness in the early 1990s, by capturing three world titles—two on the road and another on the track—and by winning the Tour de France Féminin twice. Then, determined to improve her performances, Zijlaard began to diet. She ended up suffering

Sports Shorts

Canada has produced several world-class cyclists in recent years, including two women from Winnipeg, MB, the Gateway to the Canadian West. Road specialist Clara Hughes (b. 1972) distinguished herself in a handful of international events, including the 1996 Olympics in Atlanta, GA, where she won two bronze (road time trial and road race). Hughes was less impressive at the 2000 Olympics in Sydney, Australia; she competed with a bad cold and went home without a medal. Compatriot Tanya Dubnicoff (b. 1969) also had a tough time in Sydney. Having won several international competitions, including the 1993 world sprint championship, Dubnicoff was expected to climb the medal podium in Australia. But she struggled in both her cycling races and left the velodrome without a medal and in tears. "I feel like laughing and crying and throwing up all at the same time," Dubnicoff told reporters. "My gawd, and that's gawd, G-A-W-D, not God, I'm looking for an answer to pop out of the sky."

from anorexia nervosa and left competitive cycling. Observers said her career was kaput, but her husband didn't listen. Under his guidance, Zijlaard returned to good health and to competitive cycling. She won two more world titles, both in the road time trial, and arrived in Sydney on a mission to silence her critics. "With the things that happened, a lot of people talked badly about her and she didn't forget it," Michael Zijlaard told reporters after one of his wife's medal-winning performances. "Even today, she used all those things in her head when she suffered. She thought 'Hey, s—, all those people, [they were] laughing, I'll let them see now they [were] so wrong.'"

Despite her success, Zijlaard didn't have the spotlight to herself in Australia. She shared it with Frenchwoman Felicia Ballanger (b. 1972), who won two gold (1000m match sprint and 500m time trial) to put in her trophy case next to the gold (1000m match sprint) she won at the 1996 Atlanta Games. Unlike Zijlaard, Ballanger's victories didn't surprise anyone—she had already won 10 world titles on the track, and was the world record holder in both her Olympic events.

Ain't No Mountain High Enough

While Ballanger was learning to ride a bike, cyclists in Marin County, CA were hurtling down mountain trails on tough, versatile bikes with a wide-range of gears. The fun and games were infectious; before long people were racing on backwoods trails and roads and on dirt paths around the world. Mountain biking was the fastest growing cycling competition in the 1990s and both men's and women's events were added to the Olympics in 1996.

The women's race at the 1996 Atlanta Games was an eye-popping affair, with Italian Paola Pezzo (b. 1969) competing with her jersey unzipped almost to her navel. Pezzo fell early in the race and scraped her knees, but managed to keep her private parts to herself. She then charged to the front and won gold, just ahead of Canada's Alison Sydor (b. 1966).

Pezzo also won the event at the 2000 Sydney Games, while Sydor finished fifth. The Canadian had been a medal favourite; she had won three world titles, one more than her Italian rival. But she was not too despondent over the results in Australia. She told The Canadian Press she would return the following year "very motivated and ready to do some damage again."

Let Me Explain

In mountain biking, riders race on backwoods trails, on dirt paths and on the road. Mountain biking consists of several events, including downhill, downhill slalom and hill climbs. The most popular event is the cross-country race, which was added to the Olympics in 1996.

Table 19.1: Initiation of Olympic Cycling Competition

Event	Men	Women
Road	1896	1984
Track	1896	1988
Mountain	1996	1996

The Least You Need to Know

➤ The bicycle was developed in fits and starts in the 1800s.

➤ Cycling made early and significant contributions to the women's rights movement.

➤ Women started racing bicycles simultaneously with men—but not at the same events.

➤ Victorian women were told to put down their bikes and uphold their virtue.

➤ Women cyclists couldn't compete in the Olympic Games until eighty years after men did.

➤ European women have dominated international competition.

High on a Horse: Equestrian and Horse Racing

Equestrianism is more than a passion of the privileged, a sport of kings. It's also a source of business for surgeons who regularly treat riders that end up on the wrong sides of their horses. Some of the fallen are women; they compete alongside men, leading their horses over fences and down straightaways, and hit the ground just as hard. Their broken bones attest to their devotion to their sport.

Knight on the Town

Centuries before the fibreglass cast was invented, the Ancient Greeks were taking tumbles in equestrian events at the Olympic Games. Horsemanship was also popular in the Middle Ages, when crowds gathered to watch armoured knights joust. Their equestrian skills were known as *haute école*, the French phrase indicating sophisticated horsemanship. It survives to this day at the famous Spanish Riding School in Vienna, Austria, where riders and Lipizaner horses perform several series of complicated and intricate movements.

Let Me Explain

Strictly speaking, an equestrian sport is one that includes people on horseback. Polo and rodeo fall into this category, as do hunting and horse racing. However, the term equestrian is almost always identified with disciplines recognized by the Fédération Equestre Internationale (FEI). These include the Olympic disciplines of show jumping, dressage and eventing, as well as endurance, driving, vaulting and reining.

In the 1700s, members of North America's upper crust started attending exhibitions where horses executed jumps or manoeuvers in competition. These horse shows also sprang up in Mexico, Brazil, Australia and several European countries, creating the need for an international governing body. The Fédération Equestre Internationale (FEI) was established in 1921.

Equestrianism made its debut at the modern Olympics in 1900. Women weren't allowed to compete at first, even though they had been riding since the Middle Ages when ladies of means rode and hunted alongside the men.

Let Me Explain

Women started riding side-saddle in the 1300s following the lead of prominent women such as the first wife of England's King Richard II. Riding with both feet on one side of the horse wasn't practical but according to *Nike is a Goddess*, it was deemed "appropriate" for ladies for many centuries. Riding astride wasn't socially acceptable for women until the 1900s.

All Dressed Up

Dressage, an event in which the rider guides the horse through a series of intricate movements, was introduced as an individual event at the 1912 Stockholm Games and as a team event at the 1928 Amsterdam Games. Only military officers could compete at first, but competition was opened to civilian men in 1920 and women in 1952.

Four women entered the individual dressage at the Helsinki Games. One of them, Denmark's Lis Hartel (b. 1921), won silver to become dressage's first female medallist. The victory was exceptionally sweet for Hartel because she suffered from polio. Six years before, she had awoken one morning with a headache and stiff neck;

paralysis soon spread through her body. Pregnant at the time, Hartel gave birth to a healthy daughter then began working to regain mobility in her limbs. She made a partial recovery and returned to competition in 1947.

She qualified for the 1952 Helsinki Games though she was still paralyzed below the knees and had to be helped on and off her horse. When she won the medal in Finland, gold medallist Henri Saint Cyr of Sweden helped her onto the podium, sending teary-eyed spectators searching through handbags and breast pockets for handkerchiefs. Hartel also won silver behind Saint Cyr four years later.

Hartel's success notwithstanding, dressage has been dominated by riders from Sweden, France, Switzerland and especially Germany, which produced the first female individual gold medallist in an equestrian event. Liselott Linsenhoff (b. 1927) won a silver (team dressage) and a bronze (individual dressage) at the 1956 Olympics (that year the Olympics were held in Melbourne, Australia, but equestrian events were held in Stockholm, Sweden due to rigid quarantine laws Down Under). She reappeared at the 1968 Mexico City Games, and won gold (team dressage). Linsenhoff completed her medal haul with a gold in individual dressage at the 1972 Munich Games. She also added a silver in the team event.

Women have won at least one medal in individual dressage at every Olympics since then. Indeed, female riders fared especially well at the 1988 Seoul Games, winning all three medals in the discipline.

Jock Talk

"It was the first time women competed equally with men in the equestrian games, and this really brought my name into the limelight worldwide, because not only was I a woman, but a handicapped woman."

—Dressage medallist Lis Hartel, on the 1952 Olympics in Helsinki, Finland, in *Nike is a Goddess.*

Q & A

Q: What equestrian medal winner gave birth to another?

A: Liselott Linsenhoff. Her daughter, Ann-Kathrin, won gold in the dressage team event at the 1988 Olympics in Seoul, South Korea.

Jump Right In

Dressage is popular but often takes a back seat to a more dramatic event. Show jumping, where riders lead their horses through courses dotted with obstacles, spread through Europe in the late 1800s. The individual event made its Olympic debut at the 1900 Paris Games. The team event was introduced at the 1912 Stockholm Games.

As with dressage, jumping competition was closed to all but military riders at the outset, but male civilians started competing in the event at the Olympics in 1948. When women were admitted to competition eight years later, Britain's Patricia Smythe (b. 1928) won a bronze (team jumping). Smythe had been competing for a decade, but had been forced to surrender her horses to men for two Olympic Games when women were banned from competition.

Germany became the dominant show jumping force in the 1950s, but a British rider named Marion Coakes won a silver in the individual event in 1968. Believe it or not, Coakes didn't ride a horse in the competition. And, no, she didn't clear combination jumps on a camel. Coakes rode to victory astride the only pony ever to compete in an Olympic Games. Germany re-emerged as a power in Olympic show jumping in the 1990s, and won gold in the team event at the 2000 Sydney Games.

Q & A

Q: What famous rider fell during the endurance segment of the three-day eventing competition at the 1976 Olympics in Montréal, QC, and suffered a concussion but still completed the course?

A: Britain's Princess Anne.

Main Event

Though demanding, show jumping is as perilous as a walk in the park compared to the three-day competition known as eventing. The most dangerous and challenging equestrian discipline, eventing includes simplified versions of both dressage and jumping with a gruelling endurance test wedged in between.

Eventing made its debut at the 1912 Stockholm Games with individual and team competitions. The discipline in its current form was established at the 1924 Paris Games. Competition was restricted to army officers at the time— the event was called "the military"— but was opened up to male civilians in 1936. Competition was further expanded to include female civilians 28 years later.

Let Me Explain

The endurance segment of the three-day eventing competition includes four phases. The first and third phases involve roads and tracks that combine for a total length of 12.5 miles. The second phase is a 2-mile steeplechase and the fourth phase is a difficult cross-country course. Often in excess of 4 miles, it includes up to 32 obstacles. The horse must compete each phase within a specified time.

At the 1964 Tokyo Games, American Lana Du Pont became the first woman to compete in Olympic eventing and the first to win a medal in it. She and her horse, Mr. Wister, fell in the jumping segment. They stumbled to their feet and carried on, then fell a second time. When the pair finished, Du Pont was in fine form but her horse wasn't—it had broken its jaw in the first fall. Still, the American team won silver. Du Pont wasn't commended for her bravery, but she should have been; just like the long ago chariot races in Ancient Rome, the three-day event pushes horses to their physical limits and riders often suffer the consequences.

For example, the course was so difficult at the 1936 Berlin Games, just over half of the 50 competitors in the individual competition finished. Then, at the 1960 Rome Games, just 35 of 73 entrants finished. Organizers made the competition less treacherous after two horses died of exhaustion at the 1968 Mexico City Games.

Still, eventing remains a dangerous enterprise. When Australian Wendy Schaeffer took a tumble during the team competition at the 1996 Atlanta Games, her attitude was typical of competitors. "It's nothing drastic," she said in all seriousness, "just a broken leg." Are broken bones worth the effort? The answer's a resounding "yes" among women who compete in equestrian events, and even more so among those involved in thoroughbred racing.

All the King's Horses

Ancient Egyptians raced horses and passed on their need for speed to the Greeks. Then, quicker than you can say, "Hail, Caesar!" Romans were flocking to chariot races. Some of these contests took place in the Circus Maximus, which seated over two hundred thousand spectators. When Rome collapsed in the fifth century, horse breeding and racing declined in the West.

However, it made a comeback three hundred years later when Arabs rumbled through Spain on fast horses that were unfamiliar to Europeans. The animals impressed King Henry I and, like the Beatles a thousand odd years later, became the toast of England. The Arabian horses were mated with strong but plodding English mares to produce horses with speed and endurance, making them ideal for military use.

Noblemen started betting on private two-horse races, and the first public racetrack of the modern era was constructed in London in 1174. Horse

Let Me Explain

There are many forms of horse racing. Harness racing features horses pulling a driver in a two-wheeled carriage, while the steeplechase features horses racing over a course that includes hurdles and shallow water jumps. Flat racing, in which mounted horses run across set distances, comes in the form of quarter-horse racing and the more popular thoroughbred racing.

Let Me Explain

Thoroughbred racing is popular in many countries, most of which hold high profile events. In Canada and the United States alone there are more races than you can shake a riding crop at. In the United States, three classic races for three-year-olds garner the most attention: The Triple Crown consists of the Kentucky Derby, the Preakness Stakes and the Belmont Stakes. The annual Breeder's Cup Championship, a one-day event consisting of seven races with differing conditions, is also popular. Canada's Triple Crown consists of the Prince of Wales Stakes, the Breeders' Stakes and the Queen's Plate, which is the oldest annual race in North America.

racing became popular at fairs and in royal circles, earning a reputation as the "sport of kings."

Horse racing went professional in the 1700s, when spectators flocked to race courses to bet on contests featuring several horses. Organizers started offering larger purses to attract top horses, and breeding and owning the animals became a profitable undertaking. English enthusiasts formed the Jockey Club to oversee the sport in 1750.

Similar developments took shape in North America. Settlers began staging ad hoc races on roads in the 1600s. A racetrack was built in Long Island, NY in 1665 and the sport flourished across the continent. Governing bodies were soon established to oversee the proceedings.

Thoroughbred horse racing has been a male-dominated sport from day one, but a few women have made their mark as owners or trainers. Fewer still have captured headlines as jockeys.

Mistress of Deception

Upper crust Englishwoman Alicia Thornton challenged her brother-in-law, William Flint, to a four-mile race in 1804. Thornton was victorious, and later challenged a top jockey to a two-mile race. Thornton won by a neck before a large crowd and became an instant celebrity. But her luck ran out when she was discovered to be the mistress of Thomas Thornton rather than his wife; high-society women turned their powdered noses in the air, making her a pariah.

Let Me Explain

Much to the chagrin of some religious leaders and social reformers, betting has been part and parcel of horse racing from the outset. Betting started out as a private matter, and later included a bookmaker who offered odds against each horse and accepted bets against his predictions. Today racetracks organize "pari-mutuel" betting, a term derived from the French phrase, "to bet among us." Under this system, the money wagered on horses is combined into a pool. The odds are based on the proportion of the money in the pool to the amount that has been placed on each horse. After the race, most of the money in the pool is divided among those who bet on the winning horse. The racetrack, the government, and the owners of the top-finishing horses also receive a certain percentage of the money in the pool.

Change of Pace

American Kathy Kusner (b. 1940) forged a brilliant career in show jumping, competing in three Olympics (1964, 1968 and 1972) and other top international competitions. Mid-career she sought a dramatic change of pace and applied for a jockey's license. When the Maryland Racing Commission turned her down, Kusner took her case to court. A judge found the commission guilty of sexual discrimination and ordered it to reverse its decision. In 1968, Kusner became the first American woman to receive a jockey's license.

Q & A

Q: What is the average weight of a jockey?

A: 110 pounds (50 kilograms).

Kusner competed in races along the U.S. Eastern Seaboard and in Canada. She also became the first licensed female jockey to compete in Mexico, Germany, Columbia, Chile, Peru, Panama and South Africa.

Kentucky Rein

Kusner's success paved the way for compatriot Diane Crump (b. 1949), who burst onto the scene in 1969 when she became the first female jockey to ride in a race on a major American track. The next year she became the first woman to ride in the Kentucky

Jock Talk

"Having a squeaky voice is paying off."

—Julie Krone, to The Associated Press. Krone worked for a television racing show and did voice-overs for *Nickelodeon* after retiring from competitive racing.

Jock Talk

"Now I'm less apt to leap off curbs when I'm rollerblading and I will actually leave my home on time so I don't have to drive fast. I'm a little more balanced and basic. My friends would say I'm more grown up."

—Julie Krone, the most successful female jockey in history, to The Associated Press one year after retiring in 1999.

Derby, the most prestigious thoroughbred race of the year. She finished fifteenth. Other women jockeys, including Mary Bacon and Robyn Smith, soon began to compete. In addition to going down in history as a pioneer for women jockeys, Smith also had an interesting personal life. In 1980 she married Fred Astaire. But the magic was short lived; he died seven years later in her arms due to complications from pneumonia.

Over the Top

Kusner's accomplishments were later surpassed by Julie Krone (b. 1963) who grew up on a horse farm in Michigan and quit high school to focus on riding. Krone became a leading rider at major race tracks when she was in her twenties, and captured international headlines in 1993 by becoming the first woman to win a race in the U.S. Triple Crown; she rode Colonial Affair to victory in the Belmont Stakes.

Two months later, the 4-foot-10 athlete shattered her right ankle, bruised her heart and punctured her elbow in a spill. Her ankle was repaired with two steel plates and 14 screws. She returned to competition in January 1995 and was thrown from her horse two weeks later; she broke both her hands.

Krone returned to the track once more and competed until 1999. She retired with more wins (3545) than any female jockey in history. With purse earnings of $81 million, she was one of the most successful jockeys of all time. Krone later became the first woman inducted into the Thoroughbred Racing Hall of Fame. At the height of her career, Krone was asked what she did when not around horses: "The rest of it," she said, "is wasted time."

Sports Shorts

Julie Krone was the first woman to ride in the prestigious Queen's Plate in Toronto, ON. The second was Canadian Francine Villeneuve (b. 1964). She was the country's most successful female jockey, and perhaps its most accident prone. A rearing horse pinned her against the starting gate door and snapped her thigh bone in 1988. She suffered a fractured pelvis the following year when a spooked horse flipped and fell on her. While preparing to come back in 1990, Villeneuve injured her elbow in another fall. She broke her right leg in another starting gate accident two years later. She considered quitting after becoming a mother, but decided against it. "I have more responsibilities," she told *The Hamilton Spectator*. "But then I have to make a living to support [my son]. And I make a good living at this."

Table 20.1: Initiation of Major Worldwide Equestrian Competitions

Event	Military Personnel	Civilian Men	Civilian Women
Olympic Dressage	1912	1920	1952
Olympic Jumping	1900	1948	1956
Olympic Eventing	1912	1936	1964

The Least You Need to Know

➤ Equestrian events are one of the few in which men and women compete together.

➤ Horse racing has a long history as "the sport of kings."

➤ Women have not been warmly welcomed into the world of horse racing, but a few have managed to make their mark.

Chapter 21

Drive My Car: Auto Racing

In This Chapter

➤ The first auto races are held in the 1890s

➤ Women try their hand on the world's most glamorous auto racing circuit

➤ Women get their own sports car circuit

➤ Several women have success on racing ovals

➤ One woman makes her mark in drag. Racing, that is

Zooming around town in her sports car wasn't enough of a rush for American Janet Guthrie. Her need for speed landed her behind the wheel of an Indycar and, ultimately, in the 1977 Indianapolis 500. Not to be outdone, compatriot Shirley Muldowney fastened the strap of her pink helmet under her chin and took the driving world by storm, winning three national drag-racing championships and giving new meaning to the term, "crazy women drivers."

Gearing Up

No sooner had the gasoline-fuelled, internal-combustion engine been invented than people were racing cars. The first recorded automobile competition was an 80km reliability test held in France in 1894. North Americans got in on the action the following year, when drivers competed in an 87km race in Illinois. Auto racing then took off at breakneck speed on both sides of the Atlantic Ocean. Europeans developed

Sports Shorts

In the decade after World War II, oval tracks in North America sometimes held promotional races featuring wives or girlfriends of car owners and drivers. These were called "Powder Puff Derby" events. Peering over the wheels in seats much too large for them, the women often ended up spinning off the track or crashing into each other at low speeds, much to the amusement of spectators.

Let Me Explain

Professional and amateur automobile races are now held throughout the world on roads and ovals. The most popular involve Formula One cars, Indycars, stock cars, sports cars and dragsters. Local, national and international sanctioning bodies divide racing cars into various classes and subclasses and supervise competitions. The most prominent sanctioning body is the Fédération Internationale de l'Automobile (FIA), the international governing body for almost all professional automobile racing outside the United States.

road racing while North Americans focused on oval racing, where cars race on circular courses requiring only left hand turns.

Men have dominated auto racing from the outset, but women have been making inroads in recent years. Dozens have managed to slip behind the wheels of high-powered race cars and speed toward the checkered flag.

Racy Women

Formula One races—featuring open-wheeled, single-seat cars considered the pinnacle of automobile technology—have been devoid of female drivers, with a few notable exceptions. Italian Maria-Teresa de Filippis (b. 1926) became the first woman to compete in Formula One after the introduction of the World Drivers' Championship in

Let Me Explain

Fédération Internationale de l'Automobile (FIA) has recognized l'Autorit, Sportive Nationale du Canada de la Fédération Internationale de l'Automobile (ASN) as the national governing body for auto racing in Canada. ASN sanctions various professional racing series from time to time.

Let Me Explain

The Automobile Competition Committee for the United States (ACCUS) coordinates activities between FIA and the following eight major sanctioning bodies in the United States:

➤ Championship Auto Racing Teams (CART)

➤ Indy Racing League (IRL)

➤ National Association for Stock Car Auto Racing (NASCAR)

➤ Professional Sports Car Racing (PSCR)

➤ Sports Car Club of America (SCCA)

➤ National Hot Rod Association (NHRA)

➤ Grand American Road Racing Association

➤ United States Auto Club (USAC)

1950. She competed in three races in 1958. Her best result was a tenth place finish in her first outing. She retired the following year.

Compatriot Lella Lombardi (1943–1992) joined the circuit in 1975. She finished sixth in the Spanish Grand Prix, becoming the first—and only—woman to score a world championship point in a Grand Prix. She finished seventh in another race, but left the circuit after a string of poor results in 1976. She took up stock car racing but retired due to poor health. She succumbed to cancer in 1992.

Britain's Divina Galica competed in alpine skiing in four Olympics but her need for speed lingered so she turned to Grand Prix racing. She failed to qualify for three races, one in 1976 and two in 1978, then quit. She later had some success in British truck racing.

South African Desiré Wilson (b. 1953) failed to qualify for the British Grand Prix in 1980 but decided to hang tough and try other forms of racing.

Let Me Explain

The Formula One car, with a design regulated by the Fédération Internationale de l'Automobile (FIA), is sophisticated enough to make Formula One races the world's most glamourous. Formula One cars compete on many road courses called Grand Prix. The Monaco Grand Prix and the British Grand Prix are among the most popular. At the end of each year, the Formula One driver with the best results wins the World Championship of Drivers award. Another award is given to the company whose cars are the most successful in a given year (companies field a team of two cars each). That prize is called the Constructors' Championship. FIA also sanctions competitions for less sophisticated cars. Such races fall into various categories, including Formula Two (F2), Formula Three (F3), Formula Renault, and Formula Ford.

Italian Giovanna Amati (b. 1962), the daughter of a wealthy Italian businessman, was once kidnapped and held for ransom but the ordeal didn't faze her. Quite the opposite. The fearless Amati spent four years competing in a series from which Formula One drivers are recruited. Her best result was a seventh place finish in 1991. The following year, Amati joined the Brabham team. She failed to qualify for the first three races of the season and was replaced by Damon Hill, who later became a world champion with the Williams Formula One Team.

Amati described the circuit as a predominantly male environment: "They want to keep it that way—the drivers, the journalists, everyone," she told a racing magazine. "Only one person came up to me and offered me his hand at my first Grand Prix in South Africa, and that was Brazilian driver Ayrton Senna [who died in a crash in 1994]. He came over and said, 'Welcome Giovanna, I'm glad you're here. My congratulations.' The others ignored me, and when I failed they shrugged and said it was because I was a woman."

Sisters Are Doin' It For Themselves

Women have been more successful on the road in sports car races. In 1998, for instance, entrepreneur Don Panoz—who owns the rights to the American Le Mans Series, sanctioned by Professional Sports Car Racing (PSCR)—decided to launch an all-female series for the 1999 season. He had no trouble attracting interest from intrigued racing fans and female drivers. Some 200 women from around the world attended tryouts. Just 69 were chosen to compete in the inaugural season of the Women's Global GT Series (WGGTS), which included six races on the American Le Mans circuit.

Let Me Explain

A sports car is a low, fast car designed for superior acceleration and performance at high speed. Souped-up sports cars of various classes are raced in series throughout Europe and North America.

One of the Series' first stars moonlighted as a piano teacher. American Audrey Zavodsky was a nurse by trade and spent her leisure time teaching piano, gardening and giving motivational speeches. She also liked to mix it up a bit and strap on a helmet and climb behind the wheel of a race car. In October 2000, *USA Today* described her as "pure hell on wheels" and "one of the best female auto racers in the country." The newspaper noted Zavodsky had beaten top male drivers from Michigan, Ohio and Indiana in amateur races. "I like speed, and I like horsepower," she told the paper. "Give it to me."

The WGGTS folded in December 2000. Some of the drivers joined a new circuit, the Panoz GT Series. "The women's series was a fantastic idea and an outstanding vision but unfortunately, it may have been ahead of its time," said Scott Atherton, president of Panoz Motor Sports Group. "Despite very strong efforts by many people, a title sponsor to help offset the enormous costs of operating the series could not be secured."

Big Wheel

Overall, women have been a bigger presence racing on ovals in Indycars. The MacMillan Ring-Free Oil Company got caught up in the freewheeling spirit of the 1960s and assembled a team called The MacMillan Ring-Free Motor Maids. The team included Smokey Drolet, Suzy Dietrich, Donna Mae Mims and, last but certainly not least, Janet Guthrie (b. 1938).

In 1977, Guthrie became the first woman to compete in the Indianapolis 500, the most prestigious American auto race. Two decades before, however, her life seemed headed in a decidedly different direction. Guthrie got her pilot's licence as a teenager and learned to fly more than 20 kinds of aircraft. After graduating from university with a physics degree, she worked as an aerospace engineer at an aviation company. While there she qualified for NASA's scientist-astronaut program along with three other women. She was

Let Me Explain

An Indycar is an open-wheeled, rear-engine, turbocharged car. Indycar racing in North America split into two different series in 1996. It now includes the Championship Auto Racing Teams (CART), whose top-level series is the FedEx Championship Series, and the Indy Racing League (IRL), whose top-level series is the Northern Lights Indy Racing Series. CART races are held on road and oval courses whereas IRL races are held strictly on ovals.

disqualified when officials made a doctorate a requirement, so Guthrie turned her attention to land-based pursuits.

A long-time sports car enthusiast, Guthrie began racing regularly in 1963. She became a top-notch driver and won several big races on the professional Indycar circuit. She joined the MacMillan Ring-Free Motor Maids in 1966 and stayed with the team for five years.

Guthrie tried out for the Indianapolis 500 in 1976 but failed to qualify. She decided to sharpen her skills driving stock cars, and became the first woman to drive in a National Association for Stock Car Auto Racing (NASCAR) Winston Cup event. Guthrie never lost sight of her goal, however, and tried out for the Indianapolis 500 again in 1977. She succeeded that time, setting a qualifying-lap record in the process. With Guthrie and her opponents lined up at the starting line for the main event, the announcer spoke his

Let Me Explain

A stock car looks like a commercially produced vehicle but beneath its shell, it's a high quality racing machine. Stock car racing is a worldwide event but is most popular in the United States. Races take place on paved ovals, with a few exceptions. NASCAR's major series is the Winston Cup. North of the border, the Canadian Association for Stock Car Racing (CASCAR) sponsors several professional series including the prestigious Super Series.

now-famous words: "In company with the first lady ever to qualify at Indianapolis, gentlemen start your engines." Guthrie took off with the others, but pulled out of the race 27 laps later due to mechanical troubles.

However, she returned a year later, just days after breaking her wrist playing tennis, and drove to a ninth-place finish. Not bad considering she had to drive the entire race with her left arm extended across her body to change gears.

Guthrie also drove in the 1979 Indianapolis 500, but her engine blew on the first lap. "I was dead flat certain that I would be in the hunt all day," she told The Associated Press. "It's still something of a mystery [as to] what happened."

With 11 Indycar races under her belt, Guthrie retired in 1980, frustrated with sponsors' reluctance to finance her. Though disappointed at the end of her career, Guthrie had distinguished herself as a trailblazer; it's amazing to think that just seven years before she drove in the Indianapolis 500, women weren't even allowed in the pits or garage area. "I don't think a woman coming into racing now will find the kind of unrealistic objections to her presence that I encountered," Guthrie told The Associated Press in 1997. "At least in the case of the drivers, once I had gone down into the turns with them or passed them or given them some good competition, almost universally the attitude changed. That was a great pleasure for me."

Jock Talk

"You drive the car; you don't carry it."

—Indycar racer Janet Guthrie, on the importance of strength in auto racing.

Q & A

Q: Years before she became an Indycar driver, Janet Guthrie used her salary as an aerospace engineer to make a big purchase. What was it?

A: She bought a Jaguar sports car.

Keep On Drivin'

Guthrie's accomplishments inspired Desiré Wilson, who had failed to qualify for the British Grand Prix in 1980. Wilson competed in eight Indycar races in 1983 and another three in 1986. Wilson tried, and failed, to qualify for the 1982 Indianapolis 500.

Lyn St. James (b. 1947) was more successful, climbing her way through the ranks of oval racing to make her debut at the Indianapolis 500 in 1992. The 45-year-old American finished eleventh and was named rookie of the year. St. James went on to forge a successful career on the oval, competing in her seventh Indianapolis 500 in 2000. In

Sports Shorts

International professional rally driving presents a test of endurance and speed over great distances, and under difficult conditions. Competitors drive racing cars across deserts and other challenging terrains. One of the most popular international rallies is the Monte Carlo, which starts in a different European city each year and finishes in Monaco. In January 2001, Jutta Kleinschmidt (b. 1962) of Germany became the first woman to win the Dakar Rally, a gruelling 10,7000km race that started in Paris on New Year's Day and ended in the Senegalese capital, Dakar.

that race, St. James—the oldest driver in the field—clipped the wheel of the youngest driver, Sarah Fisher (b. 1981). The 19-year-old wasn't pleased with the outcome of her first Indy 500, but left the speedway aware she had some good years ahead of her.

St. James had never topped her eleventh place finish, but Fisher aimed to do better. "[St. James] helped kick the door open," the teenager told The Associated Press. "I want to blow it open. I want to win and I think that's maybe a different attitude." It was an attitude Fisher developed before she memorized her grade school times tables. Her race-crazy parents entered her in competitions when she was five years old. "At 5 you can't be taking it very serious," Fisher told *People* magazine. "At 8 we got serious."

Let Me Explain

A dragster is a car built or modified to take part in drag races, in which two cars start side by side and drive as fast as possible to the end of a straight-line course, which is usually a quarter-mile (0.4km) long. There are many forms of dragsters, including those that have engines behind the driver and parachutes that fan out at the back when the driver breaks.

Drag Queen

While St. James kept on truckin' well into her 50s, another woman did the same in drag racing. Shirley Muldowney (b. 1940) raced cars in the street when she was a teenager and worked her way through the ranks of drag racing. She started out in souped-up street cars, then moved on to Funny Cars (extremely dangerous vehicles covered with plastic shells painted in wild designs) and finally ended up racing Top Fuelers, the fastest earth-bound machines in the world. They reach 60 miles per hour in less than a second and exceed 250 miles per hour.

Muldowney was not welcomed into the male world of drag racing, and endured some verbal abuse. "I resent her sitting in the cab of that truck filing her nails while those turncoat men flog her car for her," rival Don "Big Daddy" Garlits said, according to *Women in Sports*. Muldowney's response? She donned a pink helmet, got behind the wheel of her pink car and took off on a record-breaking career. Muldowney was the first woman to drive a Top Fuel dragster professionally and to break the five-second barrier in the quarter-mile race. She also won the National Hot Rod Association (NHRA) championship three times, in 1977, 1980 and 1982.

Her career almost ended during a race near Montréal, QC, in 1984. When Muldowney blew a tire, her car flipped and shattered. She landed in a field five hundred feet away and regained consciousness to find her left foot in her lap, all but severed from her leg. Muldowney suffered broken bones in all ten fingers, a broken pelvis and, of course, mangled legs. Five operations and eighteen months of rehabilitation later, she was back behind the wheel—and not for a quick trip to the supermarket. She continued to rack up victories and, unwilling to rest on her laurels as the one of the best drag racers in history, was still going strong in 2000. Indeed, Muldowney has never expressed an interest in easing her foot off the pedal. "Don't count on [me retiring]," she said when she was inducted into the Motorsport Hall of Fame in 1990. "I'm still ready to wax some tails."

Jock Talk

"There's no room for bimboism in drag racing."

—Drag racer Shirley Muldowney, in *Cool Women: The Thinking Girl's Guide to the Hippest Women in History*.

Q & A

Q: What was drag racer Shirley Muldowney's nickname early in her career?

A: "Cha Cha." It's not clear how she got the moniker, but it's certain how she lost it. At first, Muldowney relished the name and her role as drag racing's *femme fatale*. However, according to *Cool Women: The Thinking Girl's Guide to the Hippest Women in History*, after a close call in 1973 she decided the sport was too dangerous for fun and games. She encouraged other female auto racers to focus on their cars, not their gender, and stopped going by name "Cha Cha."

The Least You Need to Know

➤ The very first recorded auto race was held in France.

➤ Women haven't had much success in Formula One, but not for lack of trying.

➤ The Women's Global GT Series made women's racing serious business.

➤ Janet Guthrie is in the history books as a trailblazer on the oval.

➤ Shirley Muldowney made a name as queen of the drag scene.

Part 6

Step Inside—
Indoor Sports

When softball players go indoors, the weather has taken a turn for the worst and the fun is over. For other athletes, however, going inside means the fun is just beginning. In gymnasiums, professional basketball stars like Sheryl Swoopes and Chamique Holdsclaw develop precision passing and superb shooting skills while gymnasts like Svetlana Khorkina practise the twists and turns that made Olga Korbut and Nadia Comaneci household names. Meanwhile, volleyball players practise their sets, spikes and serves while wearing the shortest of shorts. Who said the inside's out?

Chapter 22

I'll Tumble 4 Ya: Gymnastics

In This Chapter

➤ Acrobatic women start out entertaining and end up competing

➤ Eastern Europeans dominate women's gymnastics starting in the 1950s

➤ Olga Korbut wins hearts and a few events, too

➤ Nadia Comaneci lifts women's gymnastics to new heights

➤ Mary Lou Retton and "The Magnificent Seven" make their mark

➤ Debate rages over the size and age of female gymnasts

➤ Rhythmic gymnasts and trampolinists put on a show

Was American Kerri Strug a praiseworthy pixie or a pitiful woman-child? The debate about women's gymnastics and the toll it takes on competitors' health began when Nadia Comaneci catapulted the sport into the limelight at the 1976 Montréal Games and intensified when Strug performed her memorable vault at the 1996 Atlanta Games with a severely injured ankle. Is it healthy for young girls to sacrifice so much in the pursuit of excellence? The debate continues.

That's Entertainment

Centuries before Comaneci did her first flip, talented men and women entertained the rulers of Ancient Egypt and Ancient Rome with dance routines that incorporated acrobatics, starting a tradition that would last for generations. Females were still

Let Me Explain

On the vault, the gymnast begins with an accelerated run, jumps off a springboard and then pushes off the vault apparatus, performing a combination of rotations in the air before landing.

performing with acrobatic troupes in the Middle Ages. These women were respected in the Orient but not in the West, where they were regarded with scorn usually reserved for prostitutes. After all, what respectable woman would stand on her head?

By the early 1900s, men were drooling over high-kicking cancan girls at Le Moulin Rouge, a famous Parisian nightclub, and women were performing at dance halls and in circuses throughout the West. These women were certainly acrobatic, but at the time they weren't considered athletes.

The Glory of Sports

Though men started using gymnastics to prepare for military service in antiquity, women didn't take their first steps toward an apparatus until the sport was deemed healthy for both sexes in the late 1800s.

The International Gymnastics Federation (FIG) was formed in 1881, opening the way for international competition. Male gymnasts first competed at the Olympics in 1896, and female gymnasts made their Olympic debut in 1928. The only women's event that year was the team competition. The gold medal went to the Dutch team, which included four Jewish women, three of whom died with their families in Nazi concentration camps during World War II.

Today both sexes also participate in the world championships and a host of regional competitions. Women compete in five individual events (all-around, vault, uneven parallel bars, balance beam, floor exercise) and the team event.

Let Me Explain

On the uneven parallel bars, the gymnast moves from the low bar to the high bar, executing a series of continuous, swinging movements involving body rotations as well as changes in grip. The dismount involves somersaulting, twisting, or both, and a perfect landing is crucial for a top score.

Let Me Explain

A balance beam routine consists of a combination of jumps and gymnastic and acrobatic elements, performed on a 500cm-long and 10cm-wide surface. Gymnasts are expected to use the entire length of the beam and display elegance, flexibility, balance and self-control. This exercise usually culminates in a series of moves that provide the momentum for a difficult acrobatic dismount.

Communist Cause

A group of social reformers, including playwright Anton Chekhov, formed the Russian Gymnastic Federation in 1883. By the time Gary Cooper was gunning down bad hombres in *High Noon*, Soviet Bloc countries had become a world power in women's gymnastics. They would dominate the sport for four decades.

One of their biggest stars was Larissa Latynina (b. 1934). Between 1956 and 1964 the Ukrainian won countless medals, including 18 from the Olympic Games, more than any athlete in history. She collected nine gold (three in the team event, two in the all-around, two in the floor exercise,

Let Me Explain

In the floor exercise, the competitor displays artistry, coordination, agility and fitness. Her routine consists of a blend of tumbling and dance set to music.

one in the vault and one in the uneven parallel bars), five silver (one in the all-around, one in the vault, one in the uneven parallel bars, one on the balance beam and one in the floor exercise) and four bronze (two in the uneven parallel bars, one in the vault and one on the balance beam). Latynina was a bona fide super hero, but a former skater was soon tugging on her cape.

Vera Caslavska (b. 1942) seemed destined for greatness in figure skating, but the blonde sprite hung up her skates as a teenager and responded to a nationwide search for gymnasts in her native Czechoslovakia. She went on a medal-winning tear and toppled Latynina to capture gold in the all-around event in 1964 at the Tokyo Games. She won two additional gold (vault and balance beam) and a silver (team event) at those Games.

Four years later, Caslavska signed a public declaration opposing Soviet involvement in Czechoslovakia. When Soviet tanks rolled in to Prague (the Czech nation's capital) a few months later, she fled to the mountains and trained in a meadow for the 1968 Mexico City Games. She ended up winning four gold (all-around, vault, uneven parallel bars and floor exercise) and two silver (balance beam and team event).

But Caslavska wasn't done making headlines. Days later, she married compatriot Josef Odlozil, who had finished eighth in the 1500m in Mexico City. But there would be no happy ending; the couple divorced and their son later killed Odlozil during an argument at a pub.

Sports Shorts

Hungary's Agnes Keleti (b. 1921) qualified for the 1940 Olympic Games, but they were cancelled due to World War II. Though she was Jewish, Keleti survived the war living with forged identification papers. When the war ended she returned to training, but was sidelined with torn ligaments in her ankle a few weeks before the 1948 Olympics in London, England. But all was not lost. She made her Olympic debut four years later at the 1952 Olympics in Helsinki, Finland, winning a gold (floor exercise), silver (team event) and bronze (uneven parallel bars). At the 1956 Olympics in Melbourne, Australia, the 35–year-old athlete won three gold (uneven parallel bars, balance beam and floor exercise) and two silver (all-around and team event). While she was competing in Melbourne, Soviet troops were quashing an uprising in her homeland; Keleti received political asylum in Australia and later moved to Israel.

Caslavska was appointed president of the Czech National Olympic Committee following the collapse of the communist regime in 1989. She had been unemployed for the better part of two decades because she had refused to disavow the anti-communist declaration she had signed back in 1968.

Munchkin Land

Despite the success of these athletes, gymnastics had not yet caught on and was not very popular in the West. That changed with the arrival of Russia's Olga Korbut (b. 1955) who took home three gold (balance beam, floor exercise and team event) and one silver (uneven parallel bars) from the 1972 Munich Games.

Korbut thrilled Western audiences with her dazzling skills and then won them over by bursting into tears following a poor performance in the all-around competition. Her public display tugged at the heartstrings of spectators and television viewers, who started rooting for the little girl with the pigtails and the endearing smile. Even hard-bitten U.S. President Richard Nixon praised Korbut, crediting her with helping to ease East-West tensions. Would Nixon have steered clear of trouble with the wholesome "Munchkin of Munich" as a political advisor? The world will never know, as Korbut returned home after the Munich Games. Later, while Nixon languished in forced retirement thanks to Watergate, she soared to great heights, wedding a Russian rock star.

Television exposure made a star out of Korbut and women's gymnastics in general. In the United States alone, sales of balance beams, uneven parallel bars and tumbling mats increased by more than 50 percent during the 1970s, and the number of girls involved in high school gymnastics doubled to 35,000.

Korbut picked up a gold (team event) and a silver (balance beam) at the 1976 Montréal Games, but few noticed. By then, all eyes had turned to another wonderful waif.

Q & A

Q: What top gymnast received over twenty thousand fan letters in one year?

A: Russian Olga Korbut. After her success at the 1972 Olympics in Munich, Germany, the post office in her hometown was deluged with fan mail and had to designate a special clerk to handle all of it.

Teen Queen

Romanian Nadia Comaneci (b. 1961) was less perky than Korbut and rarely smiled during competitions. But she made a monumental contribution to women's gymnastics, setting new standards for routines and for competitor physique and age.

Comaneci was just six years old when an unknown coach named Bela Karolyi discovered her playing in a schoolyard. Within a few years she had become one of the world's top gymnasts and was executing acrobatic moves that women had never tried before. At the 1975 European championships, she beat Russian Ludmilla Tourischeva, who had won there five times. Comaneci went on to stun the world with an historic performance at the 1976 Montréal Games.

Q & A

Q: What Soviet coach was fired because none of her country's gymnasts could defeat Nadia Comaneci?

A: Larissa Latynina, whose truck-load of medals helped her first land the coaching job in 1967.

When she finished her routine on the uneven parallel bars in Montréal, a 1.0 appeared on the scoreboard. Comaneci had scored a perfect 10.0, a mark so unprecedented the scoreboard was incapable of displaying it. She notched up six more perfect scores, and left the Games with three gold medals (all-around, uneven parallel bars and balance beam), one silver (team event) and one bronze (floor exercise). She returned to a hero's welcome in Romania.

Four years later at the 1980 Moscow Games, she won two gold (balance beam and floor exercise) and two silver (team event and all-around). The all-around victory was marked by allegations that Soviet Bloc judges conspired to keep her from winning gold over a Soviet rival; they had debated her score for almost half an hour.

Sports Shorts

Nadia Comaneci's defection was a drama worthy of a Hollywood film, or at least a made-for-television movie. After the 1980 Olympics in Moscow, USSR, she worked as a state-subsidized coach in Romania, where she was rumoured to have had an affair with Nicu Ceausescu, son of the country's dictator. She left home one night in 1989 and walked almost seven hours to the Hungarian border, where she was met by an émigré named Constantin Panait. They went to the United States and moved in together, even though Panait had a wife and four children. The couple separated after a few months. She later married American gymnast Bart Conner, who had won two gold medals at the 1984 Olympics in Los Angeles, CA.

Comaneci was 4-foot-11 and 86 pounds at the 1976 Montréal Games. Her success accelerated a trend in which female gymnasts became smaller and smaller. At the 1992 Barcelona Games, the average height and weight of U.S. team members was 4-foot-9 and 83 pounds. That was seven inches shorter and 41 pounds lighter than the average measurements of U.S. team members at the 1956 Melbourne Games. In addition, Comaneci was 14 years old at the Montréal Games. In the wake of her success, gymnasts not only became smaller, but younger, too.

Great American Heroes

The collapse of communist regimes and their sports machines cleared the way for top Western gymnasts coached by Karolyi. The man who had made Comaneci a champion defected to the United States in the late 1980s and set up a training centre in Texas.

There he moulded several American champions, starting with Mary Lou Retton (b. 1968).

Ronnie and Lois Retton didn't intend for their daughter to become an Olympic champion when they enrolled her in acrobatics class; they just wanted the hyperactive girl to expend some energy and stop running into things.

But the young Retton was indomitable and devoted herself to gymnastics. Just a month after undergoing knee surgery in 1984, she qualified for the national team headed to the Los Angeles Games. There, in her first international competition, she narrowly defeated Romanian Ecaterina Szabo (b. 1966) to become the first American to win the individual all-around competition. Retton captured the gold with a perfect score on the vault. She also won a silver (vault) and two bronze (uneven parallel bars and floor exercise). Her team finished second.

Q & A

Q: What gymnast's father was a shortstop in the New York Yankees' farm system?

A: Mary Lou Retton's.

Sports Shorts

Shannon Miller became the most decorated U.S. gymnast ever by winning two silver (all-around and balance beam) and three bronze (uneven parallel bars, floor exercise and team event) at the 1992 Olympics in Barcelona, Spain, and two gold (balance beam and team event) at the 1996 Olympics in Atlanta, GA.

American women had a greater impact at the 1996 Atlanta Games. The team was so successful it was dubbed "The Magnificent Seven." Shannon Miller (b. 1977) won gold on the balance beam, Amy Chow (b. 1978) took silver on the uneven parallel bars and Dominique Dawes (b. 1976) took home bronze in the floor exercise. But it was the little known Kerri Strug (b. 1977) who stole the show.

Strug tore the ligaments in her ankle on her first vault in the team competition. But she overcame the pain to execute a solid second vault, complete with a two-foot landing, and the Americans won their country's first gold medal in team competition. Little did they know at the time that Strug's second vault was unnecessary because victory had already been sewn up. Nonetheless, the image of Karolyi carrying Strug, with her

Sports Shorts

Dominique Moceanu (b. 1981) was the most popular gymnast on the American team heading into the 1996 Olympics in Atlanta, GA. At 13, she had been the youngest national champion in history. Though the Comaneci look-alike failed to win an individual medal in Atlanta, she remained in the news as her life assumed the dimensions of a Jackie Collins novel. She ran away from home and sued her parents to gain her independence. She also accused her father of conning her out of millions of dollars, and had a restraining order issued against him.

bandaged limb, to the medal podium secured her place in American sports lore. It also fanned the fire under the debate about the perils of competitive gymnastics for young girls.

Questions and Answers

Many observers complain that top gymnasts are too young and too vulnerable physically and emotionally to contend with the sport's extreme standards. They point to the danger of various manoeuvres and to several competitors who have sustained serious injuries. One book, *Little Girls in Glass Houses*, looks at two American gymnasts, one whose death was linked to eating disorders and another who died after breaking her neck on the vault. Critics also cite studies that claim rigorous training delays the onset of puberty. And questions are frequently raised about the often symbiotic relationship between young gymnasts and their coaches.

In response, the FIG has raised the age at which gymnasts can start competing internationally to 16 years old. "Coaches were pushing gymnasts too fast too early," observes Dwight Normile, editor of *International Gymnast*. One outcome of the 1996 ruling is that it has helped shift the emphasis in gymnastics from acrobatics—the so-called "big tricks" favoured by young, unseasoned competitors—to artistry. "Tricks should never be at expense of form," says Normile.

Today, there are several active gymnasts experienced enough to understand the importance of form. With decent prize money offered at various invitational competitions, gymnasts are staying competitive longer, helping to ease the emphasis on extreme youth. Russia's Svetlana Khorkina (b. 1979) is still competitive at the ripe old age of 21. In 2000, she won the European championships for the second consecutive year, stunning observers who had dismissed her as a has-been. The platinum-haired athlete was also in fine form at the 2000 Sydney Games where she won a gold (uneven parallel bars) and two silver (floor exercise and team event).

Two members of the "Magnificent Seven" competed in Sydney as well. Dawes, who once appeared in a Prince video, strutted her stuff in Australia at the age of 23. She was a little older than Chow, who had taken a year off from her studies at Stanford University to train for the Games. Neither won a medal, but they helped the United States to a surprise fourth-place finish in the team competition.

Jock Talk

"When I will retire? You know it's not very polite to ask a girl that."

—Russian gymnast Svetlana Khorkina, to *International Gymnast*.

European Flavour

Despite gains made by Western gymnasts in recent years, Eastern European women are still the dominant force in international competition. Russia alone accounted for three of the six gold medals awarded in women's gymnastics in 2000 at the Sydney Games. One team member, Elena Zamolodtchikova (b. 1982), took two gold (floor exercise and vault) and a silver (team event) home to John, her beloved Yorkshire terrier.

Romanian Andreea Raducan (b. 1983) would have also headed home with two gold and a silver were it not for her team doctor. Raducan won the all-around competition but was then stripped of her gold when she tested positive for pseudoephedrine, a stimulant found in two cold tablets she had taken. The Romanians appealed the IOC ruling, insisting that the gymnast shouldn't be punished for the doctor's mistake. Raducan assured officials she did not benefit from the medication—it had made her dizzy. But rather than give her a citation of bravery for performing on the balance beam with head spins, the court of arbitration upheld the decision, noting that Raducan had committed an offence, whether or not she had intended to. Nonetheless, she returned to Romania with a gold (team event) and a silver (vault) and quickly signed a contract with a Romanian film company with plans to make a movie about her experience.

While Eastern European gymnasts stole the show in Sydney, a Chinese woman managed to sneak onto the medal podium. Liu Xuan (b. 1979) won a gold and a bronze in individual events (balance beam and all-around). She was just one of several strong contenders on the Chinese team, which had done well leading up to the Games and earned a bronze in Sydney.

Table 22.1: Initiation of Major Worldwide Competitions

Event	Men	Women
Olympics (team)	1904	1928
Olympics (individual)	1896	1952
World Championships (team)	1903	1934
World Championships (individual)	1903	1938

Rhythm Nation

Rhythmic gymnastics is a combination of gymnastics and dance derived from classical ballet, German apparatus work and Swedish free exercise. It was developed in the early 1900s and soon became popular in Eastern Europe. The FIG recognized it as an independent sport in 1962, and the first world championships were held in Hungary two years later. The rhythmic all-around competition was introduced at the 1984 Los Angeles Games and the team event was added 12 years later.

Let Me Explain

Rhythmic gymnasts work with five apparatus—rope, ball, hoop, ribbon and clubs—in most competitions, but only with four in international events. A competitor's routines must include at least three leaps with the rope and three with the hoop. She also uses a rubber ball and a satin ribbon. One part of the ribbon is folded and doubled and is attached by a cord to a stick that the gymnast holds. The ribbon must stay in perpetual, fluid motion throughout the routine. The gymnast also works with two clubs shaped like ten pin bowling pins.

At the Los Angeles Games, Canadian Lori Fung (b. 1963) won gold much to everyone's surprise. She had finished just twenty-third at the world championships the year before. Marina Lobach (b. 1970) of the Soviet Union won the gold at the 1988 Seoul Games, but nearly squandered a certain victory. When she came close to exceeding the time limit in her routine, her pianist sped up the tempo but the Soviet gymnast managed to keep up and finish right on the final gong. She received perfect scores.

The sport has yet to produce a big name, but the most likely candidate is a Russian with phenomenal flexibility. Alina Kabayeva (b. 1983) won bronze (all-around) in 2000 at the Sydney Games.

Trampoline Dream

If you believe circus acrobats invented the trampoline, give your head a shake! We have the Inuit to thank for the most recent addition to the Olympic gymnastics program. The Inuit used to toss each other around using walrus skins. They certainly outclassed the English, who had to make due with simple blankets.

Circus entertainers got in on the act in the 1800s, using the trapeze safety net as a form of propulsion as well as a landing device. It wasn't long before the net size was reduced and performers were using it to leap over rows of elephants.

Jock Talk

"We almost stayed in Ukraine. If we had, I would have become a figure skater."

—Russian rhythmic gymnast Alina Kabayeva, explaining to NBC that her family moved around a lot when she was child because her father was a professional soccer player.

An American invented the modern trampoline in the 1930s and quicker than you can say, "Catch me, I'm falling!" the apparatus had popped up in backyards and school gymnasiums everywhere. Some people took it more seriously than others and competitions were soon held at schools and universities throughout North America and Europe. The first world championships were held in 1964, and Europeans have dominated ever since. Russia and Britain have been the most dominant nations in recent years.

Indeed, Russia's Irina Karavaeva won gold when the trampoline made its Olympic debut in 2000 at the Sydney Games (there were two competitions—one for men and another for women).

The Least You Need to Know

➤ The first female gymnasts were lower-class entertainers.

➤ Soviet Bloc countries produced stars whose feats remain unsurpassed.

➤ Olga Korbut confirmed our suspicions that world-class athletes were human, too.

➤ Nadia Comaneci raised the bar for women's gymnastics competition.

➤ Coach Bela Karolyi has worked his magic on both sides of the Atlantic Ocean.

➤ Kerri Strug's heroics impressed us, but also alarmed us about the risk gymnastics poses to girls.

➤ Yes, Virginia, rhythmic gymnastics and trampolining are sports.

Basket Case: Basketball

Women have been hooked on basketball since the first student tripped over her floor-length skirt driving to the basket. Over the years, female enthusiasts have ignored warnings about the sport's purported ill effect on their health and femininity and have pushed basketball forward, creating international competitions and several top-flight leagues. Their efforts have been rewarded with a thriving professional league: the Women's National Basketball Association (WNBA).

The Basketball Diaries

A hundred odd years before the WNBA signed its first player, basketball was invented by a Canadian instructor at the YMCA International Training College in Springfield, MA. In 1891, Dr. James Naismith (1861–1939) was asked to create an indoor activity to occupy his rambunctious students through the winter. He nailed a pair of peach baskets to a balcony in the gymnasium, divided his class in two and threw a soccer ball into the mix. The rest, as they say...

The new sport piqued women's interest but like chugging beer, it was deemed too aggressive and strenuous a pursuit for fair maidens. Senda Berenson (1861–1954), an instructor at Smith College in Northampton, MA, altered the rules and created a more "tame" (i.e. acceptable) version of the game. Her students began to form teams and organize competitions.

The first intercollegiate basketball game for women was held in San Francisco in 1896. Male spectators were barred because the players were dressed immodestly—in bloomers and black stockings—but hundreds of women crammed into the hall and cheered wildly as Stanford beat the University of California Berkeley 2–1. Before long, women were dribbling (on-court) across North America and Europe. An international governing body,

Let Me Explain

Senda Berenson "feminized" basketball in 1892 by dividing the court into three sections and assigning players to designated areas. Players were not allowed to leave these areas (called zones), snatch the ball, hold it for more than three seconds or dribble it more than three times. These restrictions disappeared over the years, however, and according to *The Women's Sports Encyclopedia*, "life gradually crept back into the game." Women were playing Naismith's original game by the 1970s.

Sports Shorts

Senda Berenson went to great lengths to make basketball an acceptable activity for women. She changed the rules of the game and banned loud talking on court, thus delaying the emergence of "trash talk" for a hundred years or so. Berenson also emphasized the "social" aspect of women's basketball by serving refreshments or dinners after games.

the Fédération Internationale de Basketball (FIBA), was founded in 1932 and sanctioned women's basketball.

Naughty Girls

These contests alarmed moral custodians, who feared such competition was unladylike and harmful to the frail female psyche. "Previously well-bred young ladies could be seen running and falling, shrieking in excitement and calling each other by nicknames. Games would end with handkerchiefs and hair pins scattered all over gymnasium floors," wrote Sally Jenkins of *Condé Nast Women's Sports & Fitness*. "This masculine behavior was so scandalous a development that parents forbade their daughters to participate, and medical doctors and physical education instructors wrote long worried studies about the psychological and physical effects of the sport, calling for it to be abolished."

Sports Shorts

Women wore constrictive clothing in the late 1800s, so the first female basketball players took to the court in floor-length dresses. They often tripped over their hems and went home with broken bones, bruises and black eyes. What a relief it was when Clara Gregory Baer, an instructor at Sophie Newcomb College in New Orleans, LA, advised her students to wear bloomers on court in 1896. At that time, these loose fitting trousers were becoming popular with women in all walks of life.

In the face of such opposition, women's basketball beat a retreat. Female students turned to less competitive pursuits or climbed into the bleachers to watch men compete. Some international competitions continued, but drew little attention.

Nice Work If You Can Get It

Though basketball fell out of favour with female students, it gained popularity in amateur and industrial leagues sponsored by local companies in Canada and the United States. In the United States, these leagues were overseen by the AAU. The organization sponsored the first national women's basketball championship in 1926.

Five years later, the Casualty Insurance Company Golden Cyclones won the AAU title thanks to the incomparable Babe Didrikson (1913–1956), who averaged 32 points a

Q & A

Q: Babe Didrikson was the Casualty Insurance Company's star athlete. What was her other role with the firm?

A: She earned $75 a month as a stenographer.

Jock Talk

"These women are as deft at handling the ball as they are lipstick."

—An announcer during a Hazel Walker's Arkansas Travelers game.

game. Didrikson outscored the entire opposing team in her first appearance with the Cyclones. She later became world famous for her exploits on the track and the golf links.

Hazel Walker was an outstanding player in the 1930s and 1940s, and was just getting started when she led the Tulsa Business School Stenos to an AAU title in 1934. She played for several teams throughout her career, including her own professional team, the Hazel Walker Arkansas Travelers.

Walker eventually joined the All-American Red Heads, who barnstormed across the United States playing men's teams. These women were encouraged to wear makeup, look beautiful and play hard. Red hair was also required, so blondes and brunettes resorted to wigs or hair dye. The Red Heads caused a stir and did their best to promote the game. "People loved to watch our team play. School kids would flock to see the Red Heads' cars," said team sponsor Orwell Moore, in *Nike is a Goddess*. "We always tried to sell girls' basketball wherever we went."

Graduation Days

The Red Heads were good, but the Canadian Edmonton Grads were better; they started out as a high school team and ended up a sports dynasty. Between 1915 and 1940 the team played in 522 games across Canada, the United States and Europe. The Grads made quick work of women's and men's squads alike, winning all but 20 of their games (most of their losses were in exhibition games against men's teams).

They won city, provincial and national titles and dominated several championships organized by the FSFI, which also oversaw the short-lived Women's Olympics. By the end of their run, the Grads had become a household name in Canada, catching the attention of James Naismith. The game's creator described the Grads as "the greatest team that ever stepped out on a basketball floor."

Back to School

Three decades later, during the turbulent 1960s, women began pushing for rights in all spheres. While many female students took to the street waving placards, others took to the gymnasium floor practising chest passes and crossover dribbles. Their interest in the sport created a new demand for competition.

In the United States, the CIAW hosted a national women's college basketball invitational in 1969. The organization's successor, the AIAW, took over the event in 1972. Also that year, the U.S. government passed Title IX, a law prohibiting gender discrimination in educational programs. The new legislation prompted American high schools and universities to start adding women's sports to their schedules. The NCAA, the governing body for college sports in the United States, responded to the sea change by holding its first women's basketball championship in 1982. It was the death knell for the AIAW, which lost a big television contract and subsequently folded.

Big Deals

Women's college basketball surged in popularity and attracted fans who followed the exploits of top players such as Anne Meyers (b. 1955) and Nancy Lieberman (b. 1958).

Meyers was the first woman to receive a full athletic scholarship at the University of California Los Angeles (UCLA). She led her team in rebounds, assists, steals and blocks in each of her four seasons at the school, and led the team to an AIAW national title in 1978. Meyers later signed a one-year deal with the Indiana Pacers of the NBA. She attended a tryout but didn't make the cut.

Fans also loved Lieberman, whose incredible ball handling skills earned her the nickname "Lady Magic." Lieberman was a tough customer on the court having spent her childhood competing against boys and men on the asphalt playgrounds of Harlem. Lieberman led Old Dominion University to two national titles in 1979 and 1980. She went on to become the first woman to play in a men's professional basketball league, spending two seasons with the Springfield Flame of the United States Basketball League (USBL). Her stint was short but gave her enough time to bond with teammate Tim Cline, who later became her husband. In 1987, Lieberman joined the Washington Generals, a travelling team that played against the Harlem Globetrotters.

Q & A

Q: What famous athlete did Anne Meyers marry?

A: Major league pitcher Don Drysdale. The couple has three children.

Jock Talk

"Mom, it's okay. I'm going to make history."

—Nancy Lieberman, whose mother once punctured a hole in a basketball to discourage her daughter's hoop dreams.

Around the World

The resurgence of women's basketball led to renewed emphasis on international competition and female hoopsters made their Olympic court debut at the 1976 Montréal Games.

The Soviet Union won gold thanks to Uljana Semjonova (b. 1952), who averaged 19.4 points a game. The Latvian was 7-foot-2, heads and shoulders above her rivals—and just about everyone else. Semjonova never lost an international game in her 18-year career.

The Americans won silver in Montréal, making Lieberman—an 18-year-old high school student at the time—the youngest basketball player ever to win an Olympic medal. Meyers was also a member of that team.

Q & A

Q: In 1985, American Olympian Lynette Woodard became the first woman to play for what team?

A: The Harlem Globetrotters.

The Soviets won gold again at the 1980 Moscow Games. Those Games were boycotted by the United States, Canada and several other countries that opposed the Soviet invasion of Afghanistan. The Soviet Union responded by leading a boycott of the 1984 Los Angeles Games. This cleared the path for University of Southern California (USC) star Cheryl Miller (b. 1964), who averaged 16.5 points a game and led the American women to their first Olympic basketball gold. University of Georgia star Teresa Edwards (b. 1964) was solid in Los Angeles, but she was truly outstanding at the 1988 Seoul Games where she averaged 16.6 points a game in the Americans' successful bid for another gold. Edwards, who spent nine years playing for professional clubs in Europe and Japan, would return for three more Olympic Games.

The Americans were favoured to win gold at the 1992 Barcelona Games, but were upset in the semifinals by the team from the former Soviet Union. The Americans finished third, while their rivals captured gold under the leadership of Lithuanian Natalya Zasulskaya, who averaged 17.4 points a game. The Chinese team won silver.

The Americans regrouped and climbed to the top of the medal podium at the 1996 Atlanta Games, and again at the 2000 Sydney Games. In Sydney, the American "Dream Team" dedicated its win to Edwards, the only American basketball player, male or female, to compete in five Olympic Games. Edwards lingered at centre court after the medal ceremony. "I wanted to sit on the floor and relish the moment," she told the *Minneapolis Star Tribune*. "It was a great moment to have by myself." The newspaper said Edwards knew it was "time to go," to make way for the next generation of stars, most of whom play in the WNBA.

A League of Their Own

The heightened exposure of women's basketball in schools and at the Olympics led an increasing number of girls to embrace the sport and create a demand for a women's professional league. The Women's Professional Basketball League (WBL) was launched in December 1978, but despite the inclusion of big names like Ann Meyers, the eight-team league folded after three seasons.

In 1991, the Liberty Basketball Association was launched. Players competed on smaller courts, shot at lower nets and wore tight, one-piece outfits. But not for long. The league folded after just one exhibition game. Five years later, the American Basketball League (ABL) was founded. It grew from eight to ten teams and included top players such as Teresa Edwards. But it filed for bankruptcy and folded midway through its third season.

Some of its players were absorbed by the WNBA, established in 1996 by the powerful NBA. The proliferation of female talent combined with the NBA's marketing might helped the new women's league thrive. Before signing its first player, the WNBA forged partnerships with three U.S. networks (ESPN, NBC and Lifetime) to ensure its games would be broadcast on a regular basis. WNBA games attracted some 50 million viewers in each of the league's first four seasons. By the end of 2000, the league had expanded from 8 to 16 teams and overall game attendance had more than doubled, from 1.1 million in its first season to 2.5 million in its fourth.

Q & A

Q: Who was the first female athlete to have a basketball shoe named after her?

A: Sheryl Swoopes, who plied her trade wearing Air Swoopes. The athlete helped Nike design the shoe and promoted it in commercials directed by Spike Lee.

Cream of the Crop

The WNBA has made celebrities out of several top players.

Sheryl Swoopes (b. 1971)

Swoopes had a stellar collegiate career at Texas Tech, leading her team to an NCAA national title in 1993. Following graduation, she packed her bags and headed for a professional league in Italy. But the bald eagle, apple pie and drive-through convenience stores were never far from her mind. Swoopes competed on the American national team at the 1994 world championship and at the 1996 Atlanta Games. She left Atlanta with a gold medal and a bright future.

Jock Talk

"Michael Jordan is my role model and my idol. When I found out I was pregnant, I actually talked to Michael and asked him if he would give me the honour of allowing me to name my child after him."

—Sheryl Swoopes, who once played one-on-one with the basketball legend, in *The Daily Telegraph*. She named her son Jordan.

In January 1997, she became the first player to join the WNBA. Swoopes had been hailed as the female Michael Jordan, but soon did something even the living legend could not: she got pregnant. Swoopes went on maternity leave and played very little when she returnd to the game in her first season with the Houston Comets. She soon got her groove back, however, and led the team to three more titles.

Swoopes started the new millennium with a bang. She proved an offensive powerhouse, averaging a league leading 20.7 points a game. She was no less stellar in her own end of the court, winning the league's best defensive player award. She also started in the league's all-star game for the second straight season and was honoured as the WNBA's most valuable player. "It seems like when I think things can't get any better, they get better," she said while accepting the award. A month later, Swoopes went to the 2000 Sydney Games with the U.S. team and came home with another gold medal.

Rebecca Lobo (b. 1973)

Lobo had a brilliant career at the University of Connecticut, leading the team to a 35–0 record in 1995 and the NCAA title. Lobo was the youngest member of the U.S. basketball team at the 1996 Atlanta Games and one of the first women to join the WNBA. She hit her stride with the New York Liberty but tore her anterior cruciate ligament in the first minute of the 1999 season. Following a gruelling six-month rehabilitation, Lobo returned to competition and promptly reinjured herself. She sat out the entire 2000 season.

Lisa Leslie (b. 1972)

Leslie distinguished herself at USC and, later, in an Italian league. She represented the United States at the 1994 world championship and played a pivotal role at the 1996 Atlanta Games, averaging 19.5 points a game and scoring 29 points in the U.S. team's final against Brazil. Leslie was soon signed by the WNBA, assigned to the Los Angeles Sparks. In 1998, she led the American team to a gold medal at the world championship and returned to the WNBA in fine form. She was named the most valuable player in the league's first all-star game in 1999. She started in another all-star game the following year and then joined the American team at the 2000 Sydney Games. Leslie signed a contract with a modelling agency and, on special occasions, slips out of her uniform and into something more comfortable—like a stylish Armani ensemble.

Cynthia Cooper (b. 1963)

Cooper led USC to two national titles and then moved to Europe. There, she learned to speak Italian and Spanish while mastering her bounce pass. She took time out to play for the American team at two world championships (1986 and 1990) and two Olympic Games (1988 and 1992). Then she clicked her heels together, declared "there's no place like home," and returned to the United States. Cooper signed with the WNBA and joined Swoopes on the powerful Houston Comets. She started in two all-star games and was named the league's most valuable player twice. She also led the league in scoring for three seasons. Cooper retired from competition in 2000 and has since become a WNBA coach.

Sports Shorts

American women dominated the basketball tournament at 2000 Olympics in Sydney, Australia, but a player from a rival team made her presence felt. Australian scoring sensation Lauren Jackson (b. 1981) had 15 points in the final game, though the Aussies lost to the United States. Described as "a one-woman band, playing beautiful music," Jackson exchanged elbows with American Lisa Leslie, who accused the Australian of pulling out her hair extensions: "I only had one fabulous moment," Jackson later said, "and that's when the hair came out." Jackson had joined the Australian national team three years before and won a bronze medal at the 1998 world championship. She has twice been named the most valuable player of Australia's Women's National Basketball League (WNBL). Jackson seemed destined for greatness in the more prestigious WNBA, however. The fierce competitor's success hasn't surprised observers. Her mother, Maree, was a top player a couple of decades ago, representing Australia internationally and forging a brilliant career at Louisiana State University. Lauren got a tattoo on her lower back in tribute to her mother. It's a clover accompanied by the word "Mum."

Chamique Holdsclaw (b. 1977)

Holdsclaw was a star at the University of Tennessee, leading the Lady Vols to three straight NCAA national titles and graduating as the school's all-time leading scorer with 3025 points. Holdsclaw competed for the gold medal winning American team at the 1998 world championship and before you can say, "show me the money," signed with the WNBA's Washington Mystics. She was named rookie of the year in 1999 and started in two consecutive all-star games. She also joined the American team at the 2000 Sydney Games and brought home a gold medal. Is it any wonder she has a street named after her in Tennessee?

Odds are more streets will be named after female basketball players in years ahead. "There's a star power to women's basketball now," *The Record* (in Bergen County, NJ) reported in 2000. "Women's basketball has never been so popular, so celebrated."

Table 23.1: Initiation of Major Worldwide Competitions

Event	Men	Women
Olympics	1936	1976
World Championships	1950	1953

The Least You Need to Know

➤ Women took up basketball about the same time as men, but played by their own rules.

➤ Even the watered down version of the game drew criticism for being too aggressive for women.

➤ Working women pushed the game forward in the mid-1900s.

➤ Women's basketball enjoyed a resurgence in North American schools in the 1970s, and has become one of the most popular collegiate sports.

➤ The Soviet Union dominated international competition before giving way to the United States.

➤ The thriving WNBA has made celebrities of its top players.

Chapter 24

Roll with the Punches: Boxing

> ### In This Chapter
>
> ➤ Women start duking it out in the 1700s
>
> ➤ Women's professional boxing is born in the 1950s and gains momentum over the next 30 years
>
> ➤ Women's boxing becomes a legitimate sport in the 1990s
>
> ➤ Famous daughters emerge as the sport's first celebrities

Laila Ali may be the most famous female boxer in history, but she isn't the first woman to have stepped into the ring. The daughter of legendary boxer Muhammad Ali was born more than two hundred years after titillated fans watched a no-holds-barred battle between two women in England. Women have been boxing ever since and, lo and behold, some have managed to gain acceptance as legitimate athletes. With numbers growing in professional and amateur ranks, it seems just a matter of time before women will be exchanging blows in the Olympic ring.

Feeling Punchy

Boxing has been around as long as the sundial. It existed in the Mediterranean in 1500 BC, and the Greeks later included it in their Olympic Games. The sport then collapsed along with the Roman Empire and disappeared altogether as a competitive endeavour. However, it resurfaced in the Middle Ages when it became a staple at local fairs and religious festivals in Europe.

Sports Shorts

In Ancient Greece, boxers used soft leather thongs to bind their hands and forearms. The Romans were less delicate. They used gloves studded with metal and fought to the death. The modern-style boxing glove didn't become fashionable until the late 1800s.

Let Me Explain

A prizefight is any boxing match contested for money.

English boxing, which mixed elements of wrestling and run-of-the-mill street fighting, produced its first recorded champion in 1719. Some women gawked at the brawny James Figg, but others climbed into the ring themselves in pursuit of glory. In the 1700s, crowds gathered at contests in which women scratched, kicked and beat each other senseless. Needless to say, combatants were often seriously injured.

Most women's matches took place in England, but at least one was staged in New York, NY. In 1876, Nell Saunders and Rose Harland battled for a silver butter dish—butter not included.

First in Line

Men's boxing became a little more civilized in the late 1800s with the introduction of rules prohibiting barefisted fighting, wrestling and hitting fallen opponents. Amateur and professional organizations and governing bodies were established for the sport in the early 1900s.

Male boxers competed at the 1904 St. Louis Games. Women's boxing was still unruly and unorganized at the time. Nonetheless, as the century progressed, an increasing number of women were drawn to the ring. The first female boxer to gain prominence was England's Barbara Buttrick. Standing 5 feet tall and weighing 100 pounds, Buttrick was the size of a gymnast. But she wasn't interested in developing her tumbling skills—she was a proud pugilist.

She moved to the United States in the 1950s and fought in prizefights across North America and Central America. In 1954, Buttrick's match in Canada was the first female bout to be broadcast on the radio. She ended a 12-year career in 1960 with 30 wins, 1 loss and 1 draw. At that point, she had also fought in over 1000 exhibition matches, most of them against men.

Fight for Your Rights

As Buttrick's career wound down, women's boxing was gaining momentum. In 1977, Yvonne Barkley defeated Smokey Robinson (*not* the Motown singer) in Pointe-aux-Trembles, QC. In that same year, promoters held a show in Fayetteville, NC. It included the first professional bouts to be held there in almost a hundred years—the county had imposed a ban on boxing in 1880—but didn't generate much interest. Promoters responded by adding a twist to their second installment two months later.

On that occasion, they included a match between two female boxers, Margie Dunson and Cathy "Cat" Davis (b. 1952), who had recorded six wins and no losses. Davis knocked out her opponent 2 minutes and 34 seconds into the first round. Unfortunately for promoters and boxers alike, that match didn't draw crowds either.

American Lady Tyger Trimiar was determined to improve the sad situation. She lobbied for more prize money in women's boxing and more television coverage. Her campaign made headlines in 1987 when she staged a month-long hunger strike outside the New York office of boxing promoter Don King. "Unless women get more recognition, we will be fighting just as a novelty for the rest of our lives. There will be no future," Trimiar explained. Observers feared there would be no future for Trimiar; she lost 30 pounds making her case. She did, however, live to spar another day.

The Real Deal

Trimiar's campaign gained exposure for women's boxing, but it was American Christy Martin (b. 1968) who put the pastime on the map. Following in the footsteps of titans such as Mike Tyson and Evander Holyfield, Martin signed a contract with Don King. In March 1996 he paired her with Diedre Gogarty on the undercard of a title fight between Tyson and Frank Bruno. Some thirty million viewers worldwide watched the battered and bloodied Martin defeat her Irish opponent.

Observers raved about the action-packed bout, claiming it was more interesting than the night's main event. The bout "brought more attention to women's boxing than any other single event before or since," said the *Women's Boxing Page*. "It was the

Let Me Explain

A knockout is recorded when one boxer is knocked down and can't recover sufficiently to continue the bout within a count of 10. The boxer doesn't have to be unconscious or unable to get up for a knockout to be called.

Sports Shorts

Several New York area clubs held boxing matches featuring bikini-clad women in the late 1970s. These women, dubbed the "Foxy Fighting Knockouts," were quite popular with patrons, though not with local communities.

Let Me Explain

An undercard is a bout that gets second billing to the event's main match.

271

sight of a female bleeding like a stuck pig while winning her fight that put [women's boxing] on the world's media radar." Martin survived more bouts and more bloody noses, ending the century with 41 wins, 2 losses and 2 draws.

Jock Talk

"I had just finished the interview and tried to get past her, and I never said anything to her. I tried to step around her because I didn't want trouble. I have a fight on Friday, and that's my main objective. But she took a cheap shot and hit me on my blind side. It didn't faze me, and I guess that's got to have her worried."

—Professional boxer Christy Martin, on exchanging blows with Lucia Rijker at a media event promoting a fight between Martin and another boxer in February 2000, in the *Las Vegas Review-Journal.* Rijker and Martin had yet to face each other in the ring.

Q & A

Q: How did professional boxer Christy Martin meet her husband?

A: It's a romantic tale, though not in the traditional sense. After graduating from college in 1991, the boxer set out to pursue her career in the ring. She approached trainer Jim Martin at a gym in Bristol, TN. He was so skeptical about the idea he planned to have someone crack her ribs to discourage her. In the end, however, Martin became the boxer's trainer, manager, public relations director and...husband.

Prodigal Daughters

Despite her accomplishments, Martin didn't capture as many headlines as one less successful boxer. Journalists and boxing fans from around the world flocked to Verona, NY in October 1999 to watch the professional boxing debut of Muhammad Ali's daughter. The second youngest of the boxing legend's nine children, Laila Ali (b. 1977) dabbled in street fighting and shoplifting while growing up in the hard-bitten 'hood of Malibu, CA. Believe it or not, she didn't rush headlong for the ring. Instead, she attended a community college and then opened a nail salon.

However, her attention turned from cuticles to upper cuts. Over the protests of both her parents, she headed into her professional debut without a single punch thrown as an amateur. No problem. Ali dismissed her opponent, April Fowler, in just 31 seconds with her famous father watching ringside. "I know that because I am [Muhammad Ali's] daughter I naturally have boxing skills most people probably don't have when they start," she told reporters in Verona. Sure enough, the famous daughter went on a roll and ended the twentieth century with eight wins (including seven knockouts) and no losses.

Q & A

Q: Laila Ali and Jacqui Frazier-Lyde weren't the only daughters of famous boxers to step into the ring in 2000. Who was a third?

A: Freeda Foreman (b. 1977). Her father, George, battled Muhammad Ali in the "Rumble in the Jungle" in 1974, three years before Freeda was born. She had recorded three wins and no losses by the end of 2000.

Ali seemed unbeatable, but at least one woman was eager to take her on, and she also had a famous last name. The daughter of Joe Frazier, one of Muhammad Ali's biggest rivals, was also a competitive boxer. Jacqui Frazier-Lyde (b. 1961) had recorded six wins (all knockouts) and no losses by the end of the century and was ready for the much younger Ali.

Their fathers' rivalry was one of the fiercest in boxing history and there seemed to be no love lost between the daughters. "I've never spoken to her. Don't want to," Ali told Knight Ridder in December 2000. "Her father attacked my father in ways that were not appropriate," Frazier-Lyde countered, referring to Muhammad Ali's infamous verbal jabs. Both women agreed to fight in March, 2001 on the thirtieth anniversary of their fathers' first showdown. About the scheduled fight, Frazier-Lyde said: "For me, this is about the rivalry that existed between our fathers. It's about tradition."

Jock Talk

"It would be a great draw. It would establish Laila financially, and then I would establish her horizontally."

—Professional boxer Jacqui Frazier-Lyde, a few months before Laila Ali agreed to fight her, on *Women's Boxing Page* Web site.

Q & A

Q: What are three major differences in rules governing amateur boxing for women and men?

A: Women have to wear breast protectors and must prove they are not pregnant. In addition, women's rounds are two minutes rather than the standard three.

Staying Power

Thanks in part to such drama, women's professional boxing is now thriving. Bouts are sanctioned by a handful of governing bodies, including a few devoted to women's boxing alone, including the International Female Boxing Association (IFBA), the International Women's Boxing Federation (IWBF) and the Women's International Boxing Federation (WIBF). Women's amateur boxing is thriving, too, after a decade-long struggle.

While Trimiar and Martin battled for legitimacy in the professional arena in the late 1980s and early 1990s, other women focused on the amateur arena. At the time, images of women wearing mouth guards and exchanging kidney punches elicited howls of laughter from some officials and gasps of horror from others; they refused to sanction women's boxing. But their opposition ultimately crumbled due to growing interest among women.

The Canadian Amateur Boxing Association (CABA) sanctioned a women's bout in Sydney, NS in 1991, and, after losing a court case in 1993, USA Boxing lifted its ban on women's bouts. It sanctioned a fight between Jennifer McCleary (a.k.a. Dallas Malloy, b. 1978) and Heather Poyner in Lynnwood, WA. The following year, the Amateur International Boxing Association (AIBA)—the sport's international governing body—recognized women's boxing.

Before long, women were boxing in amateur bouts at the national level in Canada, the United States and several countries around the world. As of December 2000, the United States was scheduled to host the first world boxing championships for women in 2001. "The 400 female pros and more than 1400 amateurs worldwide represent a fivefold increase over the numbers three years ago and have brought a corresponding increase in the game's popularity and skill," *Time* magazine reported in May 2000. "Women garner better ratings than men on ESPN and sell out casinos." Former heavyweight champion Evander Holyfield gave the sport a plug in the same article: "[Women's boxing] is here to stay," he said. "The women can fight."

Sports Shorts

In January 2001, newspapers around the world ran photos of a pair of four-year-old girls trading blows in a tournament in Turkey. The match caused an uproar in their homeland, but the women's national team trainer assured critics the girls weren't serious and the event was "purely spectacle."

The Least You Need to Know

➤ Early women's boxing was an unsavoury spectacle.

➤ Barbara Buttrick battled hard in the ring before it was actually fashionable.

➤ Female boxing became a legitimate sport thanks in part to the efforts of Lady Tyger Trimiar and Christy Martin.

➤ Laila Ali and other famous boxing daughters have brought unprecedented exposure to women's boxing.

➤ Female boxing has exploded in popularity as a participation sport.

Chapter 25

We've Come to Serve: Volleyball

In This Chapter

➤ Volleyball is developed for overweight men

➤ World wars turn volleyball into an international pastime

➤ Japanese women rule the courts

➤ American Flo Hyman forges a memorable career

➤ Cuba produces a world power in women's volleyball

➤ Volleyball branches out to the beach

➤ Beach babes lift the game to new heights

When William Morgan designed a game involving an inflated ball and a net strung across a court in 1895, he had his class of stout, middle-aged businessmen at the Massachusetts YMCA in mind. He wasn't thinking of players the likes of Gabrielle Reece. But a hundred odd years later, women worldwide play Morgan's game in gymnasiums and on beaches, where Reece and her partially clad peers impress and titillate fans.

Heavy Duty

A year after Morgan blended elements of basketball, baseball, tennis and handball into a game well-suited for his pudgy pupils, an observer noted players were volleying the ball back and forth over the net and suggested changing the game's name from *"mintonette"* to "volleyball." It turned out to be a smashing idea.

Let Me Explain

In a set-and-spike attack, one player passes (sets) the ball to a teammate who then smashes (spikes) it over the net into the opponents' court. Needless to say, the hitter should be airborne when she makes contact with the ball.

Let Me Explain

When serving, a player puts the ball into play by using her hand to send the ball over the net and into the opposing court. An underhand serve is allowed, but top players prefer an overhand serve, similar to the one used in tennis, or a jump serve, which is a spike from behind the service line.

The YMCA promoted the sport worldwide and in no time it was being played in Asia. Players in the Philippines introduced the set-and-spike style of attack that characterizes the game today. Volleyball also caught on in Canada, where inter-city competitions were staged during the 1920s.

Women were not very involved with the sport at this time. Even the early, tame version of volleyball encouraged jumping and that was a no-no for women, who were assured by doctors such activity would harm their reproductive organs.

War Games

Volleyball was added to the U.S. Armed Forces' recreation program in 1914, so American soldiers packed nets and gym shoes when they left for foreign shores during World War I. As a result, the game spread to many regions. It became especially popular in Eastern Europe, where the harsh winter climate made indoor recreation an appealing prospect. National volleyball associations were soon formed in Japan, Russia and the United States.

American soldiers returned to foreign shores during World War II, making the world safe for democracy and the overhand serve. Two years after the Japanese surrender ended the war in 1945, representatives of 14 countries (including the United States but not Canada) met in Paris and founded the Fédération Internationale de Volleyball (FIVB). The first men's world championship was held in 1949.

Meanwhile, more and more women were taking up the sport, competing on school teams and in leagues formed by the YWCA. International competition was inevitable. The first women's world championship was held in 1952 in Moscow, USSR. The hometown team was triumphant. For the next three decades, countries from the former Soviet Bloc dominated top-level competition along with Japan, which produced an elite women's squad in the 1950s.

Made in Japan

The Japanese team was sponsored by a spinning mill and was coached by Hirofumi Daimatsu, its manager in charge of office supplies procurement. He was an early advocate of tough love, hitting and kicking his players and insulting them during training sessions. There was no respite for the players, most of whom were mill employees. The team trained 6 hours a day, 7 days a week, 51 weeks of the year.

Daimatsu's draconian methods were effective, however. The team won the world championship in 1962, 1966 and 1967. It was at its peak when volleyball made its Olympic debut. The team swept to victory at the 1964 Tokyo Games losing just one set to Poland, when Daimatsu pulled top players because the Soviet coach was taking notes. Some 80 percent of Japanese television viewers watched the event.

Daimatsu retired four years later but the team soldiered on, winning silver at the 1972 Olympics in Munich, Germany, gold at the 1976 Olympics in Montréal, QC and bronze at the 1984 Olympics in Los Angeles, CA.

Go with the Flo

American women won a silver medal at the 1984 Los Angeles Games thanks to the effort of one of the world's top players. Flo Hyman (1954–1986) was a formidable presence on the court in Los Angeles and elsewhere. She was confident, strong and probably capable of leaping over tall buildings in a single bound—she was 6-foot-5.

As a youngster, Hyman towered above her classmates who called her "The Jolly Green Giant" in homage to her height and a popular television advertisement. Hyman slouched in her seat at school but stood tall on the volleyball court, and later won a scholarship to the University of Houston. She joined the national team in 1974 and rose to the top of her

Q & A

Q: What did Japanese coach Hirofumi Daimatsu contribute to women's volleyball, aside from fierce training tactics?

A: He introduced the rolling receive, in which the defending player dives to the ground, digs the ball, rolls over and springs back up on her feet.

Q & A

Q: When Japanese team captain Masae Kasai visited her country's Prime Minister after the 1964 Olympics in Tokyo, Japan, what did she confess to him?

A: She admitted she wanted to get married but her training schedule made it difficult to meet men. The Prime Minister then played matchmaker, introducing her to a man she would later wed.

Jock Talk

"When it all works well, it feels like heaven. That's the best way I can describe it. You feel like you're playing a song."

—Flo Hyman, on the American women's 1984 Olympic volleyball team.

sport, pulling her teammates along with her. She was named the best hitter at the 1981 World Cup in Tokyo and was in fine form three years later in Los Angeles.

There, she and her teammates defeated several teams, generating unprecedented interest. The Americans lost to the powerful Chinese team in the final, but not before drawing some of the highest television ratings of all the Olympic sports. Hyman celebrated by setting her car license plate in frame that read: "1984 Olympian: A Silver Lined with Gold."

Hyman retired from amateur competition the following year. At the time, the only professional women's volleyball leagues were abroad, so Hyman joined a circuit in Japan. In 1986, she came out of a match during a regular substitution and sat down on the bench. A few moments later, she collapsed and died. An autopsy revealed that Hyman had suffered from Marfan's syndrome, a connective tissue disease that weakens the aorta. She died when the weakened artery ruptured. A year later, the Women's Sports Foundation started presenting an annual award to a female athlete "exemplifying dignity, spirit and commitment to excellence." The award is named for Hyman.

The Dominators

The United States continued to perform well internationally, and put in a good effort at the 1992 Barcelona Games. But in the semifinals the Americans lost to the Cubans, who went on to win the gold medal.

Cuba dominated the game for the next eight years, winning every major international competition, including two more Olympic tournaments. At the 1996 Atlanta Games, the Cubans thumped the Brazilians in a semifinal match that ended in a brawl, then rolled up their sleeves and dismissed the Chinese. There was no pushing or shoving on the court at the 2000 Olympics in Sydney, Australia, but the Cubans battled hard. They came from behind to topple their Russian rivals and become the first team ever to win three consecutive gold medals in Olympic volleyball.

Sports Shorts

In the early days, female volleyball players were cautioned not to expose too much (don't let us see your arms or legs!). A hundred years later, they were encouraged to expose more (come on—where are those buttocks?). In 1998, the Fédération Internationale de Volleyball (FIVB) ruled that female players had to wear tight, high-cut lycra shorts. Teams that refused to wear them at that year's world championship were fined. "The perception is the sport needs to be presented attractively for both television and spectators," Volleyball Australia CEO Craig Carracher told the *Daily Telegraph*. "Indoor volleyball is a ticketed event and we need to get bums on seats." The move, which was meant to increase the game's exposure (pun intended), angered many observers. Among the critics was Marg McGregor, head of the Canadian Association for the Advancement of Women and Sport and Physical Activity (CAAWS), who said, "a Neanderthal attitude still pervades sports."

The feat surprised many observers; they had predicted the Cuban team would falter in Sydney because it had kept the bulk of its roster intact over the years rather than develop young players. Indeed, 7 of the 12 players on the Cuban team had also competed at the 1992 Barcelona Games. Among them was Regla Torres (b. 1975), who was 17 years old when she became the youngest woman to win a gold medal in Olympic volleyball in Spain. She starred on the gold medal winning squad at the Atlanta Games four years later, and then led the team to its second straight world championship title in 1998. She was named the most valuable player of that tournament. By the time Torres pulled up her knee pads and strolled onto the court in Sydney, the 25-year-old athlete was considered "the grand old dame" of international volleyball.

Table 25.1: Initiation of Major Worldwide Indoor Volleyball Competitions

Event	Men	Women
Olympics	1964	1964
World Championship	1949	1952
World Cup	1965	1973
World Grand Prix	n/a	1993

Life's a Beach

While indoor volleyball's popularity was spreading through the icy nether regions of Eastern Europe in the 1920s, families in Santa Monica, CA were playing a different version on the beach. Beach volleyball was soon a popular summer pastime in Czechoslovakia, Latvia, Bulgaria and at a nudist colony in France. Before long, beach volleyball was as hip as the hula hoop. At one Los Angeles beach, matches were popular enough to catch the attention of U.S. President John F. Kennedy, who checked out the scene, and the Beatles, who dropped in for a few hits. Sponsors began taking an interest in the sport in the 1970s, turning it into a professional pursuit for men and women.

Sports Shorts

Kuwait scaled back television coverage of beach volleyball at the 2000 Olympics in Sydney, Australia, after an Islamic parliamentarian complained about the competitors' scant attire. Ultra-conservative Deputy Waleed al-Tabtabai said the sport, along with diving and swimming, were unacceptable and inappropriate for television. "Some of the competitions offer more sex than sports," he said.

Sports Shorts

Beach volleyball goes hand-in-hand with loud music, which is played during breaks in competition. The top tunes at Bondi Beach during the 2000 Olympics in Sydney, Australia included "Sex Bomb" by Tom Jones, the theme song from *Hawaii Five-0* and "Bad to the Bone" by George Thorogood.

The Women's Professional Volleyball Association (WPVA) was formed in 1986 and lasted for a dozen years, staging competitions throughout the United States, Puerto Rico and Japan. Only professional tennis, golf and bowling offered bigger purses for women by 1995. The FIVB sanctioned beach volleyball in 1986 and launched a professional tour for men. The tour expanded to include women's events in 1992.

Thanks in part to aggressive lobbying by the FIVB, beach volleyball made its Olympic debut in 1996 at the Atlanta Games and was the third fastest sport to sell out. Brazilian teams won gold and silver in the women's competition, becoming the first females from their country to win Olympic medals. Brazilian women were favoured to win at the 2000 Sydney Games, but were upset by the hometown favourites in the final match.

Flesh for Fantasy

The sport's meteoric rise was fuelled in part by its sex appeal, or "jiggle appeal" in the case of female competitors, who played in (surprise!) beachwear. Exposure of the women's bronzed, lithe bodies generated enough excitement to spark a debate. Was beach volleyball a sport or a glorified peep show?

The fuss upset some female players, but most were unfazed. "If people want to come check us out because they're scoping our bodies, I don't have a problem with that, because I guarantee they'll go home talking about our athleticism," American Holly McPeak (b. 1969) told *Sports Illustrated*. "It's not such a bizarre notion. The sex appeal is unavoidable, but it's not the basis of the sport."

"We've been fighting the [belief] that the only reason our sport is selling is because we're wearing the skimpiest possible uniforms," American Linda Hanley (b. 1960) told the magazine. "But think about it, if you're at the beach, you wear a bathing suit. This is my office, and it's a little tough for me to play in pumps and panty hose."

Jock Talk

"[On] Bondi Beach are the most lean, toned, long-legged women baring thighs, midriffs and cleaved buttocks that you'll ever witness [outside] the catwalks in Milan. They are the bikini-clad Olympic beach volleyball competitors, and there aren't many more popular events here than theirs. They get a packed house of 10,000 every time out."

—*The Dallas Morning News* on the beach volleyball event at the 2000 Olympics in Sydney, Australia.

Officials downplayed the game's sexual allure at first, emphasizing the women's athleticism and competitive spirit. But they later decided to capitalize on the game's biggest selling point. In 1999, the FIVB ruled that female beach volleyball players had to wear (very) brief bikinis. The bottom of the bikini, where it sits on the hips, was not to be wider than 2.4 inches. However, competitors were allowed to wear one-piece suits at the Sydney Games.

Gab Fest

Among all the tanned competitors on the beach in the 1990s, one caused quite a stir. American Gabrielle Reece (b. 1970) was good in the sand and great in front of the camera. The statuesque athlete started modelling while playing indoor volleyball at Florida State University and went on to become as popular for her cover girl looks as for her athletic accomplishments on the pro beach circuit, where

Let Me Explain

A kill is a spiked ball that ends play in favour of one's own team and wins a point or regains the serve.

Let Me Explain

A block occurs when one or more players stop the ball before it crosses over the net into their court.

she was a leader in kills and blocks. Her face appeared on the covers of many magazines, including *Women's Sports & Fitness, Harper's Bazaar* and *Life*. She also graced the cover of *Elle* magazine, which named her one of the five most beautiful women in the world.

She proved she was more than a gorgeous athlete by writing a column for *Women's Sports & Fitness* and co-writing a book about her life as a professional athlete. *Big Girl in the Middle* was released in 1997. And whom did Reece pick as a husband? Who else but Laird Hamilton, one of the world's top big-wave surfers.

Golden Opportunities

While stars such as Reece and Torres captivate audiences, another generation of players has been waiting in the wings. And these women are being presented with more career options than their predecessors. Beach Volleyball of America (BVA), a U.S.-based professional league, held is first season in 2000. Also, a new indoor league, United States Professional Volleyball (USPV), is scheduled to start competition in 2002.

The USPV is a risky venture considering several professional women's indoor leagues have already failed in the United States while those in Brazil, Italy and Japan have thrived. But organizers are enthusiastic. Their words echo those of Reece: "You have to keep attacking, putting yourself in situations where you could possibly fail," she said in *You Go Girl! Winning the Woman's Way.* "You have to stick your neck out where you could take a fall."

Table 25.2: Initiation of Major Worldwide Beach Volleyball Competitions

Event	Men	Women
Olympics	1996	1996
World Championships	1997	1997

The Least You Need to Know

➤ Volleyball was born in the United States but early on, it was more popular overseas.

➤ The Japanese women were more or less abused by their driven coach.

➤ American Flo Hyman rose to the top of her game and then died tragically.

➤ Cuba produced a dynasty in women's volleyball.

➤ Sex sells beach volleyball, and sells it well.

List of Abbreviations

AAGPBL	All-American Girls Professional Baseball League
AAU	Amateur Athletic Union
ABL	American Basketball League
ACCUS	Automobile Competition Committee for the United States
AIAW	Association for Intercollegiate Athletics for Women
AIBA	Amateur International Boxing Association
ASN	l'Autorit, Sportive Nationale du Canada de la Fédération Internationale de l'Automobile
ATA	All-Black American Tennis Association
BVA	Beach Volleyball of America
CAAO	Canadian Association of Amateur Oarsmen
CAAWS	Canadian Association for Advancement of Women in Sport and Physical Activity
CABA	Canadian Amateur Boxing Association
CART	Championship Auto Racing Teams
CASCAR	Canadian Association for Stock Car Auto Racing
CCA	Canadian Curling Association
CFSA	Canadian Figure Skating Association
CIAU	Canadian Interuniversity Athletic Union
CIAW	Commission on Intercollegiate Athletics for Women
CSA	Canadian Soccer Association
FA	English Football Association
FEI	Fédération Equestre Internationale
FIBA	Fédération Internationale de Basketball
FIFA	Fédération Internationale de Football Association
FIG	International Gymnastics Federation

FINA	Fédération Internationale de Nation Amateur
FIS	International Ski Federation
FISA	Fédération Internationale des Sociétés d'Aviron
FIVB	Fédération Internationale de Volleyball
FSFI	Fédération Sportive Féminine Internationale
GDR	German Democratic Republic
IAAF	International Amateur Athletic Federation
IFBA	International Female Boxing Association
IHL	International Hockey League
IIHF	International Ice Hockey Federation
IOC	International Olympic Committee
IRL	Indy Racing League
ISU	International Skating Union
ITA	International Tennis Association
ITU	International Triathlon Union
IWBF	International Women's Boxing Federation
IWPSA	International Women's Professional Softball Association
LGA	Ladies' Golf Union
LPGA	Ladies' Professional Golf Association
LOHA	Ladies Ontario Hockey Association
NAAF	National Amateur Athletic Federation
NAAO	National Association of Amateur Oarsmen
NASCAR	National Association for Stock Car Auto Racing
NBA	National Basketball Association
NCAA	National Collegiate Athletic Association
NFL	National Football League
NHL	National Hockey League
NHRA	National Hot Rod Association
NWRA	National Women's Rowing Association
OHA	Ontario Hockey Association
OWHA	Ontario Women's Hockey Association
PGA	Professional Golf Association
PGRC	Philadelphia Girls Rowing Club
PSCR	Professional Sports Car Racing

Rowing Canada Aviron	Canadian Amateur Rowing Association
SCCA	Sports Car Club of America
SOCOG	Sydney Organizing Committee for the Olympic Games
UCI	Union Cycliste Internationale
UIPMB	Union Internationale de Pentathlon Moderne et Biathlon
UNC	University of North Carolina
UCLA	University of California Los Angeles
USAC	Untied States Auto Club
USBL	United States Basketball League
USC	University of Southern California
USCA	United States Curling Association
USFSA	United States Figure Skating Association
USGA	United States Golf Association
USLTA	United States Lawn Tennis Association
USPV	United States Professional Volleyball
USRowing	United States Rowing Association
WAAA	Women's Amateur Athletic Assocition
WAAF	Women's Amateur Athletic Federation
WBL	Women's Basketball League
WCF	World Curling Federation
WGGTS	Women's Global GT Series
WIAU	Women's Intercollegiate Athletic Union
WIBF	Women's International Boxing Federation
WNBA	Women's National Basketball Association
WNBL	Women's National Basketball League
WPSL	Women's Professional Softball League
WPVA	Women's Professional Volleyball Association
WTA	Women's Tennis Association
WUSA	Women's United Soccer Association
YMCA	Young Men's Christian Association
YWCA	Young Women's Christian Association
YWHA	Young Women's Hebrew Association

Summer and Winter Olympics

The Summer Olympic Games

Olympics	Year	Location
I	1896	Athens, Greece
II	1900	Paris, France
III	1904	St. Louis, United States
IV	1908	London, Great Britain
V	1912	Stockholm, Sweden
VI	1916	Berlin, Germany
VII	1920	Antwerp, Belgium
VIII	1924	Paris, France
IX	1928	Amsterdam, Holland
X	1932	Los Angeles, United States
XI	1936	Berlin, Germany
XII	1940	Tokyo, Japan; Helsinki, Finland*
XIII	1944	London, Great Britain*
XIV	1948	London, Great Britain
XV	1952	Helsinki, Finland
XVI	1956	Melbourne, Australia
XVII	1960	Rome, Italy
XVIII	1964	Tokyo, Japan
XIX	1968	Mexico City, Mexico
XX	1972	Munich, Germany
XXI	1976	Montréal, Canada
XXII	1980	Moscow, U.S.S.R.
XXIII	1984	Los Angeles, United States
XXIV	1988	Seoul, South Korea
XXV	1992	Barcelona, Spain
XXVI	1996	Atlanta, United States
XXVII	2000	Sydney, Australia

*Games not held because of war

Source: *The Complete Book of the Summer Olympics*

The Winter Olympic Games

Olympics	Year	Location
I	1924	Chamonix, France
II	1928	St. Moritz, Switzerland
III	1932	Lake Placed, United States
IV	1936	Garmisch-Partenkirchen, Germany
–	1940	Sapporo, Japan; St. Moritz, Switzerland; Garmisch-Partenkirchen, Germany*
-	1944	Cortina d'Ampezzo, Italy*
V	1948	St. Moritz, Switzerland
VI	1952	Oslo, Norway
VII	1956	Cortina d'Ampezzo, Italy
VIII	1960	Squaw Valley, United States
IX	1964	Innsbruck, Austria
X	1968	Grenoble, France
XI	1972	Sapporo, Japan
XII	1976	Innsbruck, Austria
XIII	1980	Lake Placid, United States
XIV	1984	Sarajevo, Yugoslavia
XV	1988	Calgary, Canada
XVI	1992	Albertville, France
XVII	1994	Lillehammer, Norway
XVIII	1998	Nagano, Japan
XIX	2002	Salt Lake City, United States

*Games not held because of war

Source: *The Complete Book of the Winter Olympics*

Governing Bodies

Here is a list of the Canadian and American organizations that oversee and organize sport in North America.

Tennis

Tennis Canada
3111 Steeles Avenue W.
Downsview, ON, Canada
M3J 3H2
(416) 665-9777
www.tenniscanada.com

U.S. Tennis Association (USTA)
70 West Red Oak Lane
White Plains, NY, USA
10604
(914) 696-7000
www.usta.com

WTA Tour
1266 East Main Street, 4th Floor
Stamford, CT, USA
06902-3546
(203) 978-1740
www.wtatour.com

Golf

Canadian Ladies Golf Association
Golf House, Glen Abbey
1333 Dorval Drive
Oakville, ON, Canada
L6J 4Z3
(905) 849-2542
1-800-455-2542
www.clga.org

The United States Golf Association
PO Box 708
Far Hills, NJ, USA
07931
(908) 234-2300
www.usga.com/

Ladies Professional Golf Association (LPGA)
100 International Golf Drive
Daytona Beach, FL, USA
(904) 274-6200
32124
www.lpga.com

Track and Field

Athletics Canada
Suite 606–1185 Eglinton Avenue E.
Toronto, ON, Canada
M3C 3C6
(416) 426-7181
www.canoe.com/athcan/home.html

USA Track & Field
Suite 140–1 RCA Dome
Indianapolis, IN, USA
46225
(317) 261-0500
www.usatf.org/

Distance Running and Triathlon

Triathlon Canada
4050 Wheelwright Crescent
Mississauga, ON, Canada
L5L 2X5
(90) 820-1678
www.triathloncanada.com

USA Triathlon
Suite F-1–3595 E Fountain Boulevard
Colorado Springs, CO
80910
(719) 597-9090
www.usatriathlon.org/fs_home.htm

Baseball and Softball

Softball Canada
Suite 704
2197 Riverside Drive
Ottawa, ON, Canada
K1H 7X3
(613) 523-3386
www.softball.ca

Amateur Softball Association of America
2801 Northeast 50th Street
Oklahoma City, OK,USA
7311
(405) 425-3463
www.softball.org

Soccer

Canadian Soccer Association
Place Soccer Canada
237 Metcalfe Street
Ottawa, ON, Canada
K2P 1R2
(613) 237-7678
www.canadasoccer.com

U.S. Soccer
1801–1811 South Prairie Avenue
Chicago, IL, USA
60616
(312) 808-1300
www.us-soccer.com

Alpine, Freestyle and Cross-Country Skiing, plus Biathlon

Alpine Canada
Suite 405, Palliser Square
Calgary, AB, Canada
T2G OP6
(403) 777-3200
www.canski.org

U.S. Ski and Snowboard Association
P.O. Box 100
Park City, UT, USA
84060
(435) 649-9090
www.usskiteam.com

Freestyle Skiing
Canadian Freestyle Ski Association
Box 33
Priddis, AB, Canada
T0L 1W0
(604) 729-9214
www.fresstyleski.com

Figure Skating

Canadian Figure Skating Association
508–1600 James Naismith Drive
Gloucester, ON, Canada
K1B 5N4
(613) 748-5635
www.cfsa.ca

U.S. Figure Skating Association
20 First Street
Colorado Springs, CO, USA
80909
(719) 635-5200
www.usfsa.org

Speed Skating

Speed Skating Canada
Suite 402–2781 Lancaster Road
Ottawa, ON, Canada
K1B 1A7
(613) 260-3669
www.speedskating.ca

U.S. Speed Skating
P.O. Box 450639
Westlake, OH, USA
44145
(440) 899-0128
www.usspeedskating.org

Hockey

Canadian Hockey Association
Suite N204–801 King Edward Avenue
Ottawa, ON, Canada
K1N 6N5
(613) 562-5677
www.canadianhockey.ca/index2.html

USA Hockey, Inc.
1775 Bob Johnson Drive
Colorado Springs, CO, USA
80906-4090
(719) 576-USAH (8724)
www.usahockey.com/

Curling

Canadian Curling Association
Suite 511–1600 James Naismith Drive
Gloucester, ON, Canada
K1B 5N4
1-800-550-CURL
(613) 748-5628
www.curling.ca

United States Curling Association
1100 Center Point Drive
P.O. Box 866
Stevens Point, WI, USA
54481
(715) 344-1199
www.usacurl.org

Swimming

Swimming Canada
2197 Riverside Drive
Ottawa, ON, Canada
(613) 260 1348
www.swimming.ca

USA Swimming Inc.
One Olympic Plaza
Colorado Springs, CO, USA
80909
(719) 578-4578
www.usa-swimming.org

Diving and Synchronized Swimming

Canadian Amateur Diving Federation
703–2197 Riverside Drive
Ottawa, ON, Canada
K1H 7X3
(613) 736-5238
www.diving.ca

U.S. Diving Inc.
Suite 430–201 South Capitol Avenue
Indianapolis, IN, USA
46225
(317) 237-5252
www.usadiving.org

Synchro Canada
Unit 14/Suite 200–1010 Polytek Street
Gloucester, ON, Canada
K1J 9H9
(613) 748-5674
www.synchrocanada.com/

Synchro Swimming USA
Suite 901–201 S. Capitol Avenue
Indianapolis, IN, USA
46225
(317) 237-5700
www.usasynchro.org/

Rowing

Rowing Canada
NOTC Venture
Box 17,000 STN Forces
Victoria, BC, Canada
V9A 7N2
(250) 361-4222
(877) RCA-GROW
www.rowingcanada.org

United States Rowing Association (USRowing)
Suite 400–201 S. Capitol Avenue
Indianapolis, IN, USA
46225-1068
(800) 314-4ROW
www.usrowing.org/

Cycling

Canadian Cycling Association
702–2197 Riverside Drive
Ottawa, ON, Canada
K1H 7X3
(613) 248-1353
www.canadian-cycling.com/

USA Cycling
One Olympic Plaza
Colorado Springs, CO, USA
80909
(719) 578-4581
www.usacycling.org

Equestrian and Horse Racing

Canadian Equestrian Federation
2460 Lancaster Road
Ottawa, ON, Canada
K1B 4S5
(613) 248-3433
www.equestrian.ca

U.S. National Governing Body/National
Equestrian Federation
American Horse Shows Association
4047 Iron Works Parkway
Lexington, KY, USA
40511
(859) 225-6923
www.ahsa.org

293

Auto Racing

ASN Canada FIA (l'Autorit, Sportive
Nationale du Canada de la Fédération
Internationale de l'Automobile)
Unit 115–2155 Leanne Boulevard
Mississauga, ON, Canada
L5K 2K8
(905) 403-9000
www.fia.com/tourisme/infoclub/
canada.htm

Automobile Competition Committee for the
United States (ACCUS)
Suite 101–1500 Skokie Boulevard
Northbrook, IL, USA
60062
(847) 272-0090

Gymnastics

Gymnastics Canada
Suite 203–5510 Canotek Road
Gloucester, ON, Canada
K1J 9J4
(613) 748-5637
www.gymcan.org

USA Gymnastics
Suite 300–201 South Capitol Avenue
Indianapolis, IN, USA
46225
(317) 237-5050
www.usa-gymnatics.org

Basketball

Canada Basketball
Suite 102–557 Dixon Road
Etobicoke, ON, Canada
M9W 1H7
(416) 614-8037
www.basketball.ca/

USA Basketball
5465 Mark Dabling Boulevard
Colorado Springs, CO, USA
80918-3842
(719) 590-4800
www.usabasketball.com/

WNBA
Olympic Tower, 645 Fifth Avenue
New York, NY, USA
10022
(212) 688-9622
www.wnba.com

Boxing

Boxing Canada
Canadian Amateur Boxing Association
888 Belfast Road
Ottawa, ON, Canada
K1G 0X6
(613) 238-7700
www.boxing.ca/

USA Boxing
One Olympic Plaza
Colorado Springs, CO, USA
80909
(719) 578-4506
www.usaboxing.org

International Female Boxers Association
#223–22700 Crenshaw Boulevard
Torrance, CA, USA
90505
(310) 539-4127
www.ifba.com/

Volleyball

Volleyball Canada
5510–2 Canotek Road
Gloucester, ON, Canada
K1J 9J5
(613) 748-5681
www.volleyball.ca

USA Volleyball
715 S. Circle Drive
Colorado Springs, C0, USA
80910
(719) 228-6800
www.usavolleyball.org

Bibliography and Web Sites

Bibliography

Bernhardt, Gale. *The Female Cyclist: Gearing up a Level.* Boulder: Velo Press, 1999.

Chipman, Dawn, Mari Florence, and Naomi Wax. *Cool Women: The Thinking Girl's Guide to the Hippest Women in History.* Chicago: Girl Press, 1998.

Christensen, Karen and David Levinson, eds. *Encyclopedia of World Sport: From Ancient Times to the Present.* New York: Oxford University Press, 1996.

Cox, Gerry. *The Dictionary of Sport.* London: Carlton Books Ltd., 1999.

Doren, Kim and Charlie Jones. *You Go Girl! Winning the Woman's Way.* Kansas City: Andrews McMeel Publishing, 2000.

Dowling, Colette. *The Frailty Myth: Women Approaching Physical Equality.* New York: Random House, 2000.

Greenberg, Judith E. *Getting into the Game.* New York: Franklin Watts, 1997.

Guttman, Allen. *Women's Sports: A History.* New York: Columbia University Press, 1991.

Herzog, Brad. *The Sports 100: The One Hundred Most Important People in American Sports History.* New York: Macmillan, 1995.

Johnson, Anne Janette. *Great Women in Sports.* Detroit: Visible Ink Press, 1996.

Jones, Constance. *1001 Things Everyone Should Know About Women's History.* New York: Doubleday, 1998.

Kidd, Bruce. *The Struggle for Canadian Sport.* Toronto: University of Toronto Press, 1996.

Layden, Joe. *Women in Sports: The Complete Book on the World's Greatest Female Athletes.* Santa Monica: General Publishing Group Inc., 1997.

Leder, Jane. *Grace & Glory: A Century of Women in the Olympics.* Chicago: Triumph Books, 1996.

Leslie, Mary E., Zina R. Rose, Ruth M. Sparhawk, and Phyllis Y. Turbow. *American Women in Sport, 1887–1987: A 100-Year Chronology.* Metuchen: The Scarecrow Press Inc., 1989.

Lessa, Christina. *Women Who Win: Stories of Triumph in Sport and Life.* New York: Universe Publishing, 1998.

Liebman, Glenn. *Women's Sports Shorts: 1,001 Slam-Dunk One-Liners by and about Women in Sports.* Chicago: Contemporary Books, 2000.

Long, Wendy. *Celebrating Canadian Excellence: Canadian Women Athletes.* Vancouver: Polestar Book Publishers, 1995.

Lopez, Sue. *Women on the Ball: A Guide to Women's Football.* London: Scarlet Press, 1997.

Lovett, Charlie. *Olympic Marathon: A Centennial History of the Games' Most Stories Race.* Praeger Publishers, 1997.

Markel, Robert, Susan Waggoner, and Marcella Smith, eds. *The Women's Sports Encyclopedia.* New York: Henry Holt and Company Inc., 1997.

McComb, David G. *Sports: An Illustrated History.* New Yor: Oxford University Press, 1998.

McFarlane, Brian. *Proud Past, Bright Future: One Hundred Years of Canadian Women's Hockey.* Toronto: Stoddart Publishing Co. Limited, 1994.

Newsham, Gail J. *In a League of Their Own! The Story of the Dick, Kerr Ladies Football Team.* Scarlet Press, 1997.

Oglesby, Carole A., with Doreen L. Greenberg, Ruth Louise Hall, Karen L. Hill, Frances Johnston, and Sheila Easterby Ridley. *Encyclopedia of Women and Sport in America.* Phoenix: The Oryx Press, 1998.

Rappoport, Ken and Barry Wilner. *Girls Rule! The Glory and Spirit of Women in Sports.* Kansas City: Andrews McMeel Publishing, 2000.

Sherrow, Victoria. *Encyclopedia of Women and Sports.* Santa Barbara: ABC-CLIO Inc., 1996.

Smith, Lissa, ed. *Nike is a Goddess: The History of Women in Sports.* New York: Atlantic Monthly Press, 1998.

Sports Illustrated editors. *Sports Illustrated 2000 Sports Almanac.* New York: Time Inc., 1999.

Wallechinsky, David. *The Complete Book of the Summer Olympics.* New York: The Overlook Press, 2000.

Wallechinsky, David. *The Complete Book of the Winter Olympics.* New York: The Overlook Press, 1998.

Woolum, Janet. *Outstanding Women Athletes: Who They Are and How They Influenced Sports in America.* 2nd ed. Phoenix: The Oryx Press, 1998.

Web Sites

Historical Overview

www.caaws.ca/Milestones/Kidd_Olym.htm (*The Women's Olympic Games: Important Breakthrough Obscured By Time*, by Bruce Kidd, in CAAWS Action Bulletin Spring 1994)

www.library.csi.cuny.edu/dept/history/lavender/386/truewoman.html (*The Cult of Domesticity and True Womanhood*, by Dr. Catherine Lavender, Director of American Studies Program, Department of History, College of Staten Island/CUNY)

Tennis

38.144.33.166/home (National Organization for Women)

www.monica-seles.com (Monica Seles Web Site)

www.wtatour.com (Sanex WTA Tour)

www.about-tennis.com (About Tennis Online)

216.199.22.140/index.html (United States Tennis Association)

www.britannica.com (Encyclopedia Britannica Online)

www.stefanie-graf.com (Stefanie Graf Personal Web Site)

Golf

www.lpga.com (The Ladies Professional Golf Association)

www.clga.org (Canadian Ladies Golf Association)

Track and Field

sportsillustrated.cnn.com/siforwomen/top_100/1/ (Sports Illustrated for Women, "Top 100 female athletes of the 20th century")

www.iaaf.org (International Amateur Athletic Federation)

Distance Running and Triathlon

www.realrunner.com (Real Runner Online)

www.hickoksports.com

www.marathonguide.com (Marathons, Running Directory and Community)

sportsillustrated.cnn.com (CNNSI from CNN and *Sports Illustrated*)

www.nbcolympics.com (NBC Olympics)

Softball and Baseball

www.acusd.edu/~jsartan/womenbaseball.htm (University of San Diego student Joel Sartan)

archive.www.worldsport.com/worldsport/sports/softball/home.html (International Softball Federation)

www.dlcwest.com/~smudge/viewmode.html (All-American Girls Professional Baseball League)

baseballhalloffame.org/index.htm (National Baseball Hall of Fame)

www.prosoftball.com/ (Women's Pro Softball League)

www.softball.ca/ (Softball Canada)

www.softball.org/ (Amateur Softball Association of America)

Soccer

www.nbcolympics.com (NBC Olympics)

www.soccergirls.com (Soccer Girls Web Site)

www.soccertimes.com (Soccer Times Online)

tarheelblue.fansonly.com (Official Athletic Site of the University of North Carolina)

www.canadasoccer.com/eng/nationals/w_wc/schedule.asp (Canada Soccer/National Teams/Women's World Cup Teams)

wwc99.fifa.com (1999 FIFA Women's World Cup)

www.sportsforwomen.com/contents/index.html (Sports For Women)

Alpine, Freestyle and Cross-Country Skiing, plus Biathlon

www.complete-skier.com (Complete Skier Online)

www.britannica.com (Encyclopedia Britannica Online)

www.solsnowboarding.com (Snowboarding Online)

www.ibu.at/biathlon (International Biathlon Union)

www.usbiathlon.org (United States Biathlon Association)

Figure Skating

www.isu.org (International Skating Union)

users.aol.com/tanddfanp/ (Torville & Dean Web Site)

www.cfsa.ca (Canadian Figure Skating Association)

www.britannica.com (Encyclopedia Britannica Online)

Speed Skating

www.usspeedskating.org (Official Web Site for U.S. Speedskating)

www.98skate.org/isu.htm (International Skating Union)

www.speedskating.ca/ (Speed Skating Canada)

Hockey

www.cbs.sportsline.com (CBS SportsLine)

sportsillustrated.cnn.com (CNNSI from CNN and *Sports Illustrated*)

www.jwa.org/main.htm (Jewish Women's Archive)

www.nlc-bnc.ca

www.city.cambridge.on.ca (Official Web Site for the Municipality of the City of Cambridge)

www.nsccalgary.ab.ca (National Sports Centre—Calgary)

www.whockey.com/ (The Women's Hockey Web)

Curling

www.icing.org/ (International Curling Information Network Group)

www.sweepmag.com (Sweep! Curling's Portal)

www.canoe.ca (CANOE—Canada news, sports, entertainment)

Swimming

www.nbcolympics.com (NBC Olympics)

Diving and Synchronized Swimming

www.usadiving.org (US Diving Online)

www.cnn.com/ASIANOW/time/ (Asia Now—Time Asia Home)

www.times-olympics.co.uk/ (The Times, latest news and sports stories from Sydney)

www.synchrocanada.com/ (Synchro Canada Official Web Site)

www.usasynchro.org/ (U.S. Synchro)

www.esther-williams.com/ (Official Esther Williams Web Site)

Rowing

www.rowingcanada.org (Rowing Canada)

www.fisa.org (Fédération Internationale des Sociétés d'Aviron)

www.aviron.org (National Rowing Foundation)

www.usrowing.org (US Rowing)

www.wellesley.edu (Wellesley College)

Cycling

www.ibike.org (International Bicycle Fund)

www.pedalinghistory.com (Pedaling History Bicycle Museum)

www.nbcolympics.com (NBC Olympics)

Equestrian and Horse Racing

www.horsesport.org (Fédération Equestre Internationale)

www.olympic-usa.org/usoc/sports_az/eq/az_over.html

www.floridahorse.com/HOPE.html (HOPE—Horses Helping People of North Florida, Inc.)

dressagedaily.com (Dressage Daily)

www.chronofhorse.com (Chronicle of the Horse Online)

www.about.com (About—The Human Internet)

www.showjumpinghalloffame.com (Show Jumping Hall of Fame)

Auto Racing

www1.newsmedia.com/index.shtml (Seventh Gear.com: CART Racing Web Site)

cascaronline.com (Cascar Online)

www.racerchicks.com/ (Racer Chicks Online)

www.lynstjames.com (Lyn St James Web Site)

www.sarahfisher.com (Sarah Fisher Web Site)

www.muldowney.com/shirley_home.htm (Shirley Muldowney Web Site)

www.mshf.com/ (Motorsports Hall of Fame)

www.indyracing.com (The Official Web Site of the Indy Racing League)

www.nascar.com/ (Nascar Online)

www.professionalsportscar.com (Professional Sports Car Racing Online)

www.nhra.com (Official Web site of the National Hot Rod Association)

www.usacracing.com (United States Auto Club)

Gymnastics

usa-gymnastics.org (USA Gymnastics)

www.intlgymnastics.com (International Gymnast Online)

www.gymnastics.worldsport.com (International Gymnastics Federation)

www.ighof.com (International Gymnastics Hall of Fame)

www.olympics.com/eng/sports/GA/about/home.html (Official Site of the 2000 Sydney Olympic Games)

Basketball

www.wnba.com (WNBA)

library.usask.ca (University of Saskatchewan Library)

www.nlc-bnc.ca (National Library of Canada)

www.ncaa.org (Official Web Site of the NCAA)

www.hoophall.com (Official Web Site of the Naismith Memorial Basketball Hall of Fame)

www.foxsports.com/ (Fox Sports)

www.nba.com (NBA)

Boxing

www.geocities.com/Colosseum/Field/6251/index.htm (Women's Boxing Page)

www.rgtboxing.com/ (Rgtboxing Online)

www.girlbox.com/ (Boxing for Everyone: Women's Boxing on the Web)

www.womenboxing.com/(Women's Boxing Archive Network)

Volleyball

www.volleyhall.org/fivb.htm (Volleyball Hall of Fame)

www.volleyball.org (U.S. Volleyball Association)

www.volleyballone.com (Volleyball One)

www.olympics.com (Official Site of the 2000 Sydney Olympic Games)

www.fivb.ch (Fédération Internationale de Volleyball)

www.nbcolympics.com (NBC Olympics)

Index